# WATCHERS

## FROM THE SHADOWS AND THE LIGHT

The Red Path Spirit Adventure Series

## *Other Works by the Author*

❈

When Spirits Touch the Red Path
Book 1 in The Red Path Messenger Series
ISBN: 0-9786664-0-2


The Message
Book 2 in The Red Path Messenger Series
ISBN: 0-9786664-1-0


The Season of the Long Shadow
Book 3 in The Red Path Messenger Series
ISBN: 0-9786664-2-9


Watchers From The Shadows and The Light
Book 1 in The Red Path Spirit Adventure Series
ISBN: 0-9786664-4-5


More information on Speaking Wind may be found at:
www.dolphinmedia.com

# WATCHERS
## FROM THE SHADOWS AND THE LIGHT

a Red Path spirit adventure

"Speaking Wind"
Patrick Quirk

Dolphin Media, LLC
Huntsville, Alabama

# WATCHERS
## from The Shadows and The Light
a Red Path spirit adventure

Dolphin Media, LLC

For information address:
Dolphin Media, LLC
6275 University Drive, Suite 37
Huntsville, AL 35806

www.dolphinmedia.com

Cover layout and design by Cliff Collier and Jim King.

Photo on back cover by Bryan Rohbock.

Edited by the author, David and Sharon Dooling, and Jim King.

ISBN: 0-9786664-4-5

Printed in the United States of America

This book is dedicated to: Patrick, Tim, Gene, Cindy, Steve, Butch, Sharon, Dave, and Holly.

# CONTENTS

▼

# Preface

## Watchers From The Shadows and The Light
### Book One in the Red Path Spirit Adventure Series

Cheeway stood at the top of Machu Picchu looking into the valley below. He had been given an ancient stone map that showed the location of a village said to be older than time itself. On the back of the map, a warning had been inscribed, one that neither Cheeway nor his colleagues could decipher. But he knew it was meant for whoever would discover the Ancient City of Prophecy...the city he heard of long ago that revealed the secrets of mankind.

He stood in the center of Machu Picchu and saw a vision. He saw he would be the one to discover the Ancient City of Prophecy, and saw three possibilities for the coming earth changes. He saw his life, and four others close to him, would never be the same.

In his vision, he was given a warning...one that would decide what course the world would take resting in the hands of each person alive today. He was shown that only by individual choice could the impending earth changes be altered in a way that would not be devastating to all mankind. But, if these earth changes were not altered, they would destroy life on this planet, as we know it.

His vision also showed him a group of people coming out of the shadows to find him...a powerful group of people who had unlimited control of peoples lives, but kept their identities secret. They controlled everyone from the shadows, so no one could know them. He saw them come into the light to stop him from telling what he found. For the information he was about to uncover would bring an end to their power and influence, worldwide.

The information contained in this book is presented to you as it was presented to me. However, the names and actual locations have been changed, but the events, have not.

My brother presented his story to me about a year before his death. A death that could not be explained, and told me to keep this information safe until it was time to be released. He said when the volcanic ring of fire in the Pacific Ocean began to wake itself; this information could be shared. For then, it would be accepted, and then, it would be understood.

The ring of fire began to wake from its sleep in 1997, and hearing of this, I began this book. This then is my brother's story. It not only changed his life, but I believe it caused his death as well.

# I N T R O D U C T I O N

▼

My son and I were living in Europe when I received a letter with curious markings on it. While the letter did not have a return address, it looked like there had been an attempt to open it before it was delivered.

Looking at the post markings, I could tell it had come through a place somewhere in Yucatan, Mexico, and then via the U.S. Postal Service. But I didn't recall anyone I knew that lived in the Yucatan.

I set the letter with my other mail and returned to the car to drive home, thinking how strange it was to receive a letter such as this. Then, I began seeing pictures of my brother Cheeway standing in an overgrown jungle, calling to me.

Suddenly, my eyes went from the road to the letter. I knew the letter had to be connected to my brother, and pulled the car off the road and parked.

I reached across and picked it up, and when I did, pictures of my brother came to me even stronger. That's it, I thought. This is from Cheeway and he is in some kind of trouble.

I hadn't heard anything from him in over a year. I opened the letter and recognized his handwriting, but it appeared to be hurried and written with a shaky hand. I knew this was not like Cheeway to put his name on anything that was less than perfect, and for him to send a letter, or even a note that was not typewritten and in perfect format, was not his way of doing things.

So, with great anticipation, I began reading:

Speaking Wind, my brother. I am in great danger. I have found the Ancient City of Prophecy, but the government and the church do not want me to leave with what I have discovered.

I was gifted with a map from a man I met near Machu Picchu named Nauti. It gave me the clue I needed to find what I have been searching for all my life: the ancient village where the three signs warning of the coming earth changes are recorded, what they are, and when they will take place, the time they can be changed, or in some cases stopped, and when they cannot. But there is more, much more, and when you hear what it is, you will be shocked.

The Hallway of Records Grandfather and Two Bears told us about does exist. I have proof of it, but cannot release it until the time is right.

I do not feel I will live much longer. There have been two attempts on my life already. I must meet you, alone. Leave your son at your mom's house because it is too dangerous to involve anyone else in this, but I must pass this information to you for safekeeping. That way, if I do not live to share what I have found, you can. Please, my brother, do not turn away from me. This is more important than I can go into at present. When we meet, I will explain everything; I know you will understand.

I will meet you at Sadie's Restaurant, just north of Coyote, NM. If anyone asks where you are going, tell them you are going to Chaco Canyon. Do not give more information. The safety of our meeting rests on this secrecy.

I will be at Sadie's on the 21st of December. Do not look, or ask, for me. I will find you.

Your brother,

Cheeway

# CHAPTER 1

▼

# VOICES FROM THE STONE

My brother, Cheeway, and his wife Mary, discovered an ancient seaport just below Machu Picchu. This was a big find and they wired their investors.

It wasn't more than a couple of days before they were informed their dig would be fully funded. Anxious to begin, they knew the impact this dig would have and were willing to do whatever they needed to bring it to a successful completion.

Cheeway and Mary were on site when they received a message from town. It said the money from their investors had arrived and had been deposited in a local bank.

They drove to Cuzco to hire some diggers and began making queries about local labor that would be available for the next few months. They introduced themselves to the city officials and showed them their authorization papers denoting the place and length of time they had been given to excavate near Machu Picchu. When they said they were a fully funded expedition and would pay top dollar for labor, the city officials seemed to bend over backwards to help. One official assigned himself to accompany them…said he wanted to make sure the quality of workers would be up to professional standards…and that his name was Paulo.

\*     \*     \*     \*

"Can't be too careful which people you work with these days, señor," Paulo said, as they drove from the city hall to the town plaza. "Don't know if you heard, but there have been some very strange things happen here."

"You mean in town, Paulo?" Cheeway returned.

"No, señor, I mean with some of the excavations near Machu Picchu. Two times I remember there were others who had come to excavate near the old city. They didn't want to use our services, you know, the way I am offering to help you choose your workers. They said they could tell the good from the not so good workers and would make their own choices. I think that was what brought them trouble. Not all of our people are the honest kind. Some have police records for stealing things, you know."

"So tell me, Paulo, what happened to the digs in this area? From what you've seen, that is."

"Well, Señor Cheeway, there were things stolen…things that would not have brought a great price to anyone, but things that were collectable none-the-less. I don't think the thieves knew what they were taking and that's why the really valuable stuff was left. But anyway, that's why I am glad you decided to let me accompany you. My services will be invaluable, as you will see. I know almost everyone here and can tell you who is reliable and who is not."

"I appreciate your concern, Paulo, but tell me, were any of the things stolen ever recovered? Or were the thieves ever caught?"

"No, Señor Cheeway, neither the articles nor the robbers were ever seen again. Our government made many inquiries, but didn't find anything. All they found were trails and rumors that led no place, no place at all!"

Paulo remained with Cheeway and Mary throughout the interviews. Some, he would say were dependable and others he would openly say were not worth hiring. It was a little frustrating, but Cheeway believed in going along with the customs of the country he worked in.

With the exception of embarrassing outcries to some of the locals, Paulo remained silent for the most part when it came to choosing workers. That is, except for one.

They had been interviewing people most of the morning then broke for lunch at one of the outdoor cafes. Mary and Cheeway were discussing the people they had chosen to work on the dig with Paulo, when an old man walked up to the table and asked for a job as one of the diggers…said he was a hard worker and needed money.

When Cheeway looked at him, he was reminded of Grandfather and Two Bears. This must be what they would have looked like had they not found the path they chose to travel.

While the old man walked without a stoop, he didn't have much meat on his bones and it made him look like a worn out shell whose belly hadn't been full in many a year.

He said his name was Nauti and he had eighty-three years on him, but he was a good worker.

"I know you, Nauti, or whatever name you go by now!' Paulo said, rising from the table and pointing his finger at the old man. "You were with the other two digs, weren't you? The ones that had things stolen from them! Go away, old man! You're kind isn't wanted here! You just bring trouble with you, nothing else!"

"I no bring trouble, señor. I good man. Work very hard for you," Nauti returned, as he focused his eyes on Cheeway, then Mary. "I work for almost nothing, señor. No have money to buy food, I am hungry!"

Cheeway looked at Nauti as he stood over the table clutching his walking stick, then at Paulo who was glaring at the old man. My brother felt sorry for Nauti, not having anything to eat and reminding him of Grandfather and Two Bears. But he weighed Paulo's words of caution with importance as well, knowing that Paulo had been among these people longer than he had.

However, when he looked at Mary and saw she was feeling the same about Nauti, he decided to let caution fall to the winds and told Nauti he would hire him and pay him what he would pay everyone else. But he would not have to work with a pick and shovel; he would tell stories to the workers, that is, if he knew any.

"Nauti know many stories, señor, more than enough for this work," he returned, showing an almost toothless smile behind his face.

"Señor Cheeway," Paulo said, still standing. "Before you make an offer to this old man, let me tell you something of him. At least be fully informed before you make your decision."

Cheeway told Paulo he would listen but asked him to sit back down, then pulled up another chair and asked Nauti to join them.

"This old man is a traitor to his own kind," Paulo began. "He says he is a descendant of the old Inca Shaman from these parts and tells everyone he knows many of their secrets. But that is not true, at least not by any standards I know. The last two digs he was on were the ones that were robbed. He wormed his way into their hearts by telling them he was an old man who had nothing to eat. Then he gave them some worthless stones and told them they were very old."

"Stones are old, señor!" Nauti broke in. "Stones older than time itself. Come from a time when all people knew everything. No secrets then, nothing hidden. Not like today."

"Listen to me, Señor Cheeway!" Paulo returned, tapping the table top with his fingers. "This old man is lying to you. He doesn't know any secrets of the old Inca. He doesn't even have a house to live in. He's been living in caves and under rocks most of his life. People here call him the 'crazy one', the one who has nothing and never will. If you listen to him, I'm afraid he will rob your site as well! Tell him to go; it is the best thing you can do for yourself…and him. I tell you, Señor Cheeway, it's not safe to have this old man around."

"What makes you say that, Paulo?" Cheeway asked.

"I can't say too much about it, other than everyone who has taken one of his stones has had terrible things happen to them."

"Like the two previous archeological expeditions?"

"Yes! Just like them. And, I believe this old man was responsible for that."

"Thought you said they were only robbed?"

"There was more, Señor Cheeway, much more. But before this old man showed up, I didn't see a need to burden you with it."

"Perhaps now would be a good time to tell me."

Paulo looked at the old man for a minute…like he was sizing up the situation with him, and us, and then began.

"The old man wormed his way into the hearts of the last two expeditions by giving them some stones with funny writing on them. He told them they were so old, no one knew who made them. But I believe he made those etchings in the stones himself. Not any ancient civilization. But all that aside, Señor Cheeway, this old man was at each of the expeditions that were robbed. We have been keeping our eyes on him though, not much we miss…especially in a small town like this."

"What was it the thieves took, Paulo? Was there a correlation to what each expedition lost?"

"They took fake stones I give them, señor," Nauti responded. "You know, the ones this man tells you are not real. They all that was taken. They keep eyes on me to find where I get stones. Not any other reason for them acting the way they do. Think it is they who rob other people. But I tell you with truth, it not Nauti."

Cheeway looked at Mary after each side had presented their story. He didn't feel they were told everything behind those events and the look Mary had told him she felt the same way.

"You know, Paulo, when I look at this man you say is dangerous, I only see a man in his eighties who doesn't have enough money to eat on a regular basis. You tell me he is dangerous to my dig, but I can't believe that. Tell you what, you can accompany the party if you like. That way, you and he can keep an eye on each other. And I won't accept any of his stones. After all, it seems like they're the central point of the robberies, ya know."

Paulo gave Cheeway a funny look, and then thumped his fingers on his water glass. He looked at Mary, then Cheeway.

"I don't believe I can say anything to change your mind, Señor Cheeway, can I?"

Paulo saw a broad smile cover Nauti's face and that seemed to flare his anger for the old man. "All right then, I will accept your offer to visit the site. Can't remain with you all through your dig, señor, but I will drop by without warning. You hear what I said, old man?"

"Nauti hear what you say, law man. Not mind if you come when you wish. You know where Nauti be. Can come and speak to me if you want to."

"When I come, it won't be to visit with you, old man," Paulo said, with eyes beading a growing anger. "If I come to see you, it will be to put you in jail."

"I think we have discussed this matter long enough, gentlemen," Cheeway said, as he rose from the table. "We leave tomorrow morning around six. Can both of you be here?"

Paulo and Nauti agreed and left. Mary and Cheeway returned to the hotel and discussed what had taken place. They both came to the conclusion that what they witnessed between Paulo and Nauti was something that went back a long time…something like when a family would feud with another family, and when it lasted for generations, both sides had forgotten what the feud was all about. They only believed they were supposed to hate each other.

That was their initial conclusion, but all that was about to change. Within a couple of weeks, they would discover why these two men disliked each other. And when they discovered what it was, everything would change.

✳     ✳     ✳     ✳

Nauti knew Paulo was keeping an eye on him to find where he was getting those stones. And that made Nauti angry. But the reason for Nauti's anger was he knew Paulo had been paid off by a very powerful, but very secret, group of people. They wanted the stones for themselves, according to Nauti. But Nauti didn't give into them and told Cheeway they had tried to do many bad things to him. Even though he didn't explain what they had done, Cheeway could feel the hurt and humiliation behind his eyes.

Nauti revealed the hiding place of the speaking stones to Cheeway and gave him directions on how to get there. He said there was more than the speaking stones there; there were complete maps showing the location of other prophecy sites and more…much more. He called this hiding place The Cave of The Winds…saying it was home to the Spirit Wind that crosses all lands over the earth.

On the second week of his dig, Cheeway asked Nauti why he had chosen to share this information with him. He had been successful in uncovering not only the remains of a port near Machu Picchu, but also found parts of a great boat…one that could have easily traveled across the ocean.

✳     ✳     ✳     ✳

"Mary!" Cheeway began. "Do you know the ancient stories our people speak about trading with other cultures long before the arrival of the Europeans?"

"You mean the ones that say we traded with the Egyptians and Asians long before the Europeans knew about us?" she returned.

"Yes, but it wasn't till the recent discovery of cocaine from the cocoa leaf, and tobacco resins were found in Egyptian mummies, that this old story was looked at for anything more than a myth…just an old story thought up by a bunch of crazy Indians."

"Perhaps that's why they didn't want Nauti to speak to anyone. Maybe that was the secret they wanted to keep hidden and had nothing to do with his old stones. Ever think of that?"

"It did cross my mind, Mary. But when Nauti approached me today, I let those thoughts go. From what he told me, I realized what he was in possession of. He had something that would shake up the entire world. It would change people's way of thinking so much, nothing would ever be the same again.

"When Nauti approached me, I was taking a break by the water trough. The day had really been hot and the sun was beating brighter than usual. I had been told when the sun was bright like it was, it signaled a time for being aware of the movement of animals. Kind of like a prelude to having an earthquake or storm, either of which can catch you unaware. I was washing the back of my neck when

Nauti approached me. I was used to hearing him speak to us in a soft voice. But this time when he spoke, everything about him seemed to change. He no longer sounded like the soft old man I had become used to listening to."

"*Señor Jefe!*" *Nauti said, standing directly behind me.* "*Did you know there was a mark on the back of your neck?*"

"Nauti's remark caught me off guard, Mary. I had forgotten all about the mark on the back of my neck and no one had noticed it since my brother and I were with Grandfather and Two Bears. They told us we each had been born with a map on the back of our necks…a map that outlines the path of our destiny! Nauti told me of the significance of this mark on the back of my neck. He shared a prophecy with me as well. He said I would be the one to open the long closed doorway to our spiritual history and when I did, there would be three other people tie their path to mine. And they would each have the map mark on the back of their neck, but one of them would not have known about it from birth."

"*You know what that mark mean, Señor Jefe?*" *Nauti asked, touching the back of my neck with his finger.* "*It mean something very special. I can tell you 'bout this part of all peoples prophecy, if you wish.*"

"*If you wish, Nauti.*"

"There was something in his eyes that seemed familiar. A look I had seen before."

"*Mark mean you be allowed to bring back something very special, Señor Jefe. It mean you been marked by Creator long before you born to your mother. What you about to find gonna change whole world. Make all peoples look at themselves different too. Mark mean you one who fulfill ancient prophecy for all people of Earth.*"

"*Nauti, please have a seat. There is something I would like to know about you…about what Paulo said.*"

"*Okay, Señor Jefe, I sit. Here okay?*"

"*You want some water or something to eat?*"

"*No, Nauti fine. You not make me work hard for money you pay me. So not have as much need to eat. Save food for men who work hard for you. They need more than I do.*"

"*Very well, Nauti. When Paulo said you gave old stones to the two expeditions who were robbed, did he speak truth?*"

"*Yes, Señor Jefe, Paulo speak truth to that point.*"

"*Were those stones made by you, Nauti? Did you do this in order to make a place for yourself in their expedition? Before you answer, I want you to know I will understand if you did. I know what it is like to have an empty belly and how it feels to go to sleep hungry, and wake up even more so. I will understand if you tell me you did this so you could eat and won't hold it against you. But I ask that you speak the truth to me, I need to know before we go any further."*

*"Nauti no make markings on old stones, señor. Not from this journey anyway. Stones very old though, older than time can count. Markings made by those who no longer come here to visit the people. They the Old Ones from star nation, but they not return for long time now. They leave stones, and more, for us to remember them by. They show many things people can do to help themselves. Things like open doorway to spirit within them. They called speaking stones. When you hold them, they speak to you if you willing to hear. They told me they want to go with the men I give them to."*

*"What was on them, Nauti? There seems to be significance to them. What makes them valuable to the ones who stole them?"*

*"Give one stone that show how to open up head and fix diseased brain, señor. This I give to first man who come here. After he go away, I hear next stone tell me he want to go to next who come to dig. It show how to cut eye open and fix it so it can see again. Not know why stones want to have new home. They only tell me they want to leave place they been resting and need to walk with these men so they can speak to them. They say it time for this now. Say they no longer need to stay in silence where no one can know their medicine. Say soon, it be time to open doorway to Ancient City too. When that happen, everything gonna change, but for the better."*

*"And when the two excavation teams were robbed, Nauti, what did they take?"*

*"Only take ancient talking stones I give them, Señor Jefe. Nothing more."*

*"But you had no part in the robbery, did you, Nauti?"*

*"No, señor, but Paulo did. He and four other men, one of them was a black robe. Same one I saw at town the day you came there."*

*"I don't remember seeing any black robe there, Nauti, and I was attentive to everyone near me."*

*"He very sneaky, Señor Jefe, you gotta watch your back whenever he come around."*

*"Why would he and Paulo only take the stones you gave these men, Nauti? What's so important about them?"*

*"Paulo tell me ancient stones not belong to earth anymore. Say they belong to Father Sanchez and people like him. Tell me they want all stones for their collection and keep it safe from ever being found by someone who might do bad medicine with stone. Paulo also say, if I tell him where speaking stones live he give me big money. They pay me well for all stones, but I not believe him. Not believe he speak truth to me!"*

*"So they want all the stones with the pictures? Only because they show something that might, or might not, be true, Nauti?"*

*"They want stones because they speak, señor. That make them important!"*

*"Among the people I come from, Nauti, we hear everything speak to us. The wind, the clouds, the rocks, the water and so on. Just because these stones speak to you, and perhaps someone else, that can't be anything that would make them so important. Either you aren't telling me everything, or I missed something."*

*"When Nauti say stones speak, he not mean stones only say where they want go. They tell anyone holding them how to do what they show. Stone I give first man show how to make hole in head and fix brain disease inside. Then how to close back up after healing head sickness. When stone held under chest, stone speak telling whoever hold it how to do this. Not need school to know how to do this, señor, stone best teacher there is. Stone talk you through everything you need to do so all people can heal."*

*"You mean like doing what the picture on them shows, Nauti?"*

*"Yes, jefe, but more than that. When you hold stone to chest, you get warm feeling from it. Right after that, stone make air picture in front of you. But that just before it go into person who be sick, then into one who holding stone."*

*"Wait a minute, Nauti! Go back to the air picture. I'm not sure I'm following you."*

*"Air picture same as you see me and I see you. Only there no body to it. You can reach out and touch air picture but you not feel anything, only air. That what air picture all about, jefe."*

*"Sounds like a hologram, Nauti."*

*"Not know what that word mean, but if you do, then that what we call it, okay?"*

*"Yeah, sure, Nauti. Go on then with how these stones talk to you."*

*"Okay, just after stone make air picture—I mean hol-o-gram—it show you everything you going to be doing to one who sick. It form itself in the air, just in front of your face. But only reason is to let you know what gonna happen next. Right after hol-o-gram get so strong you almost believe it real, it go from air and enter sick person. But each stone enter from special place only. If picture on them show head, that where they enter this person. If they have picture that show heart, that where they go into them. Stones only go into people through places they know about. They no go into places they not know about. Hol-o-gram stay in sick person for few minutes, then come back out into air and show itself again. Stone show you what wrong with sick person, then show you steps you gonna do to make them better. Soon as stone finish showing you everything it going to do to make person get better, it go inside you and make you feel strong and filled with energy. You feel presence of stone knowledge fill all of you, then you just know what needs to be done. No guessing, just direction."*

*"So when the hologram fills you with its knowledge, that's when you know what needs to be done, Nauti?"*

*"Yes, Señor Jefe, that when Nauti know what to do."*

*"How do you make your incision in them? Do you have a knife or something sharp?"*

*"Only use fingers on hand, jefe, stone tell me how to touch skin to make it open. And not much bleeding either. When I do what stone say, there maybe only one drop that lost from them. Even when I make hole in them to work on heart."*

*"And if you need to remove something from them, you only use your hands as well?"*

*"That all that needed, jefe. Body not break that easily, it tougher than you think. If something need to come out of them, stone tell me where to grab and pull it from. Then tell me what to touch to make a new part grow. New one, better than the old sick one too. Have used speaking stones many times among the people. Have used on little babies and old people too. Heal them of many things. Nauti make holes in heads, chest, all over body and stones tell me what to do. I do what stones say, then person get well quick. Most time, people not feel hole I make in body. Stones tell me how to make cut so they not feel anything. When I inside their body, stones tell me what to touch so body can heal itself. Sometimes, stones tell me to take something out. But it not hurt them. Stones say this part is bad and can no longer live in balance inside them. Stones then tell me what to touch inside and tell me when I touch this place, it make new part grow so they not miss old one I take out. Sometimes, new part begin to grow before I can close hole. And, other times, takes longer for new part to grow inside them. But always, whenever stones tell me to take something out, it tell me what to touch to make new part grow in them again. Always, people who been treated with speaking stones get better. Even when stones tell me I must open up chest to make heart get better, they get up and walk home same day. Stones share only good medicine with me, Señor Jefe. They not bad and they not make believe. I think that why stones stolen from men I give them to. Think Paulo and Father Sanchez want stones for themselves so they be only ones to hold their medicine. Not believe they want to share with anyone, otherwise stones would tell me they good men and want to go with them. But stones not say this, say they bad men and not want to go with them. So I not tell them where their home is, but I tell you. I tell you home to speaking stones is home of wind spirit, and how to get there, remember?"*

*"If this were true, Nauti, it would truly make these stones valuable. Not only to Paulo and Father Sanchez, but to anyone who heard about them. That is, if what you have shared with me is truth."*

*"Nauti say he only share truth with you. If you not believe what I speak, I can show you result of two men who come to me for healing. They here in work camp. Want to speak to them, señor?"*

*"Yes, Nauti, I would!"*

"Nauti left, then returned with two men who were digging for us. From their size and appearance, I didn't believe there could have ever been anything wrong with them. But Nauti told me he had performed surgery on them both and not more than one month ago. I asked them if what Nauti told me was true. They smiled and said it was. One of them said he had been getting great headaches. The kind that made him throw up and his body bend in pain. He said Nauti came to his house and made a hole inside his head. He said he removed something, then closed the hole. He said there were no more pains in his head, nor jerking movements his body used to make from his sickness. And he told me when Nauti opened and closed his head, he felt nothing.

"The next man told me Nauti made medicine in his chest. He said he had a great pain in his left arm and it caused him to lose all feeling in the left side of his body. He said Nauti made a hole in his chest and fixed his heart. He said he did not feel pain when Nauti opened his body to work on it. But after Nauti closed him up, it only took him an hour to get up and continue his work. He said he worked his fields for the rest of the day and hasn't had numbness in his body since then.

"I asked if they would show me where Nauti had made his holes in them. Without hesitation, they agreed. I looked at the head of the man who said his brain was fixed and saw there had been an incision made in the left side of his skull. But there was only a dull red line where he said the hole had been made. No scar or stitch marks, nothing that showed an incision had been made. It just looked like he had scratched himself. That's all there was.

"When I looked at the man who said Nauti opened his chest to fix his heart, I found the same thing: a reddening in the skin outlining where an incision had been made, but no scar or markings from stitches.

"I have seen enough operations to know the difference between a scratch and an incision. And I tell you, Mary, there had been an incision made in both of these men. I could feel it was a deep one too, but there were none of the markings our conventional medicine makes when they operate. I thanked the men and they returned to their work. Then I continued speaking with Nauti about the voices from the stones."

*"It's not that I didn't believe what you told me, Nauti. It's just that it's so incredible, I had to see for myself."*

*"Señor Jefe believe Nauti now?"*

*"Yes, Nauti, I do. I would like to know more about the speaking stones. There are many people who could benefit from what they have to share."*

*"This not for you, Cheeway!"* Nauti said, as his voice and facial features markedly changed. *"This is the stone we brought for you. All others will be used when time is right, but for now, there is a great journey you must make. One that will allow the rest of the stones to come back into the light and serve humanity without falling victim to the greed of those who do not understand. We bring this stone for you. It is a map to the Ancient City of Prophecy. You have been chosen for this quest, our brother. You were chosen long before you drew your first breath on this earth."*

"Nauti then handed me this stone, Mary," Cheeway said, holding it out for her to see. "And when he did, there was a sudden rush of energy flood into me. Made me feel as if I was being washed clean with an unconditional love for all life, and for a moment…I thought I was about to pass out. But, just before I thought my eyes would slam shut, I felt Nauti's hand touch my head. Suddenly, the feeling was gone and I could see clearly again."

*"Hear us, our brother, we return! We come to show you where you may find us and bring us back into the light. The light we helped to create, the light we love. You will not fear us, for we share understanding with you. It is time to walk with us again. You will not be alone. There will soon come an event that will cause you to feel this way, but it is short in passing. Soon, three others will assist you on the last part of your journey."*

"At first, Mary, I thought it was Nauti speaking. But as the voice continued, I looked at the old man but could not see his mouth move. I knew it had to be the stone speaking to me!"

*"Señor Jefe okay with stone now?"*

*"Yes, Nauti, I'm okay with the stone. But what does it mean? I feel so much from it. It's like I don't ever want to let it go."*

*"Stone speak to you then, señor?"*

*"Yes, Nauti, stone speak to me."*

*"Then you must do what stone tell you. Stone not lead you with false truth. Follow stone; it know what it saying!"*

*"What if Paulo and this Father Sanchez discover I have this stone, Nauti? What if they come into camp and steal it, what then?"*

*"Stone always find way back to you, señor. That what speaking stones all about. They always come back to where they need to be, no one can keep them from path."*

*"What about the other two stones that were stolen, Nauti? Aren't they being held in a place they do not wish to be?"*

*"They back home now. Back in cave of wind spirit. That what make Paulo and Father Sanchez so mad at me. They think I stole them and they want them back. But that not what happen to those two speaking stones. They come back by themselves.*

*Paulo and Father Sanchez get real angry because they cannot hold onto them. But stones tell me they all return to light when Ancient City of Prophecy discovered and its truth is known. That why I speak to you of mark on back of neck, Señor Jefe, stone tell me you chosen to find sacred place. You be one to bring back all ancient truth so everybody can remember again. But you need to leave this place now, señor. If you not leave today, something bad gonna happen to you and wife!"*

"I can't leave now, Nauti. I have commitments to my investors. They have given me a great amount of money to complete this project! They wouldn't understand if I were to just pack up and leave. Not them—and I need to keep them happy. If I am to search for this Ancient City of Prophecy, I will need their financial assistance."

*"You no gonna have choice, señor. If you not leave on your own, you gonna be made to leave. Time for you to start journey now, stones tell me! Hope you listen, señor. Not say this to bring you fear, only tell you so you know what ahead of you."*

"Nauti looked at me with eyes that saw much more than I could. He rested his hand on my shoulder and continued."

*"Stones tell me of great importance for what you about to do, señor. Not waste time here on things that not so important. Will be another who can do this thing you do now. Begin your journey now; not wait!"*

"After he said that, he got up and walked down one of the trails leading back to town. I thought he was going to visit someone, but that wasn't it. He was leaving like he had completed what he came to do and his time with us was over.

"I looked at the stone Nauti gave me and felt it draw me closer. It was becoming a part of me very quickly and I thought about what the old man said...that I should leave today and not wait. But my mind told me we can't leave now, Mary. We can't just pack up and forget about our financial backers. If we were to discover the place this stone map would lead us; we will need their help. And in order for them to trust me with another site dig, we'll have to complete this one.

"I watched the sun setting. I knew the night was not far off and saw the workers heading for their tents. And I thought about what Nauti told me as I drifted off to sleep. When I woke the next morning, I could not find him. I thought he had other business, but wondered why he left without saying anything.

"And, these last few days, Mary, more and more of the workers have been leaving. And just as Nauti had done, without saying why or where they were going."

*    *    *    *

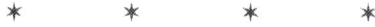

The day after Nauti disappeared, a man came to their camp. He said his name was Father Sanchez. He was traveling with three huge men he called his bodyguards.

He asked Cheeway and Mary if they knew anything about one of the men who had been in the excavation party…an old man who went by the name of Nauti. He said if they could help him find that man, he would be more than happy to donate a little something to their dig.

They didn't think much about his request and told him Nauti had been working there, but had left and they didn't know where he went. That's when they knew something was terribly wrong. Father Sanchez looked at them with eyes that must have been holding back a great hate for something each of them reminded him of. They could feel a cold emptiness of rage surround them. He said they were lying to him and anything the old man had given them was not for them to keep, but had to be returned to its rightful owner.

Cheeway had forgotten about the old stone map Nauti had given him and said nothing about it. When Cheeway failed to give anything to Father Sanchez, he scowled and said he and Mary would pay for their treasonous act. Then he stormed out of the camp with the three giant bodyguards.

They began their dig with more than thirty men, but each day after Father Sanchez's visit, there were between three to four men per day that did not return. Soon, there was only Cheeway and Mary at the site. They knew they couldn't do this excavation by themselves and returned to town to see about hiring more diggers.

When they arrived in Cuzco, they were met by police and taken in for questioning. They said Cheeway was a prime suspect in the murder of an old man at his dig. They said his name was Nauti. He wasn't allowed to make any phone calls and neither was Mary. They left Mary alone. Cheeway didn't know why then, but he found out later.

She took their truck intending to go to the American Embassy to help get Cheeway out of this mess, but that was not to be either.

The police escorted Mary to the outskirts of town to make sure she didn't make any phone calls or visit friends. When she reached the edge of town on the main road, the escort pulled over to the side waving her past. The police then moved to the middle of the road as she drove away and waited there to ensure she did not return.

Mary had driven only a few hundred yards or so when a 'runaway' cement truck ran into her. But the truck hitting her was no accident. There were no other drivers on the road and later Cheeway was told the police had been blocking all traffic for several minutes about a half mile on either side of where she was hit. When the cement mixer hit her, she was crushed inside their pick-up truck. She didn't die right away though, but remained alive for almost half an hour. Once she died, the police let the traffic resume. They made sure whoever passed Mary's crushed truck would see it. They told the passersby this was not an accident, but was associated with the dig on the side of the mountain…a dig that was being worked, without permission, by the greedy American and his wife.

The police kept Cheeway in custody for two days asking him questions that were not related to the dig or to Nauti or his association with him. On the third day, they told him about the accident Mary was in and that she was dead. But, they would not tell him anything further about it. They only said they were driving him to the airport and escorting him out of their country. They emphasized he was not welcome in their lands anymore and would never be allowed to return. They took everything, even his clothes. It seemed like they were looking for something, but didn't find it, otherwise they wouldn't have acted as they did.

After hearing about Mary's fate, Cheeway didn't want to take anything with him. Not much mattered to my brother anymore. All he wanted to do was to claim her body and bring it home. But that wasn't to be either, they said the body had been too badly damaged and they had to burn it.

At the same time they told Cheeway of his wife's fate, they handed him an urn filled with ashes. He didn't know if it had the remains of Mary, or someone else. It really didn't matter though; he knew he would see her again, real soon.

When he got back home and opened it, he spread the ashes to the four winds asking for their acceptance by Creator. But when he opened the urn, he not only found Mary's ashes inside, but the ancient stone map that had been placed inside as well. With it was a hastily scribbled note from someone who hadn't sign it. It said he should not give up on locating the ancient city, that it held great significance for all mankind. And, it said, he had been given the map because of the mark on the back of his neck. This mark was significant and was said to be placed on the one who was meant to discover what has been called The Ancient City of Prophecy.

# CHAPTER 2

▼

# THE LEGACY OF MANKIND

Cheeway arrived at his home in New Mexico, but waited a week before telling his investors about the events that had taken place in Peru. He knew they were waiting for his report, and were expecting it around that time anyway. He wanted that time to be alone with his thoughts. Not only about the dig, and what Nauti had given him, but he had to find balance in life from the loss of his wife, Mary.

Finally, Cheeway set up a meeting up with his three backers, asking to meet them in Colorado Springs the following Monday. They were curious as why he wanted to meet them so far away from his home, and he told them he couldn't go into it over the phone, but would explain when they met. They agreed and he hung up the phone to be alone with his thoughts once again.

His backers—Stevens, Roberts, and Jade—had known Cheeway and Mary for years. They had not only helped Cheeway and Mary get together, but had graduated with their Ph.Ds at the same time.

Roberts and Jade were brother and sister, and Stevens, a good friend to all of them, had become very successful in a business he had started.

Jade's Ph.D was focused on ancient writings while her brother's was in ancient civilizations. But Stevens' was a little different; his doctorate was in international politics. And Cheeway and Mary had received their Ph.Ds in archeology. All of them knew each other well. They attended the same university and made many plans together…the kind one makes when you think nothing can stop you.

Mary and Cheeway worked at various digs, not really doing anything for their careers, but it was something they could put on their list of accomplishments. You know, the kind of things you need to show someone so they know you've done something in the field.

After completing their doctorates, they made a promise to each other. They each agreed the ones who would make it first, financially, would help the others. Mary and Cheeway weren't exactly rolling in success, or money, but knew there was potential if they could work a large site of their own.

Stevens, on the other hand, became successful right out of school. He was offered a consultant job with a foreign government that paid very well. He made a lot of good contacts that helped him start a business. The business required him to travel extensively between Europe and South America. His work became so successful, he needed extra help. That's when he made contact with Jade, her brother Roberts, then with Mary and Cheeway. He offered if they wanted to pitch in with him, he would make all of them equal partners. Jade and Roberts did just that, but Mary and Cheeway decided to continue doing what they always wanted to do…uncover pieces of the past, looking for the one piece missing in archeological history that would tie all races together…something that would prove a commonality among all people. Mary and Cheeway knew how much the world needed this, and told them of their plans. The rest of the group agreed with their decision and wished them well on their journey.

Several years passed as they stayed in contact with each other. Cheeway could see their business was getting more successful with each of their accomplishments. And knew they would soon be so successful that none of them would have to work anymore. He thought that would upset Mary, seeing their friends succeed while they were still scraping the bottom of the barrel, looking for any opportunity of getting a dig of their own. Anyway, their friends had always supported Cheeway and Mary's efforts. And when they met at a reunion, they offered to fund their first expedition…something like a late wedding present from them.

It was really difficult to find money for these kinds of things. Most of their colleagues had to sell their lives in order to be funded, or work under someone who takes all the credit. Roberts, Jade, and Stevens said they didn't want their work to be like that. They wanted Mary and Cheeway to have the credit for whatever they would uncover and made an offer. They would fully fund each of their excavations if they were convinced there was a possibility of something being discovered. They said they didn't want to throw their money down the drain by funding things they only thought had a chance for success, but would support both Cheeway and Mary's theories, that is, if they truly believed something would be found. For years, that had been a good working relationship among them. But now, Cheeway had to tell them of a failure. Not a complete one, but one that did not produce the results they expected.

They met in Colorado Springs and Cheeway told them what had taken place in Peru. Mary and Jade had been best friends since childhood. They had grown up as young girls and graduated with their doctorates at the same time. He told them about the events that led to Mary's death and his expulsion from Peru. He knew they understood the situation, and Mary's death weighed as heavy on their hearts, as it did on my brother's. When he finished with the accounts of the failed expedition, they asked to see the map stone, and the note, that was placed in Mary's urn.

"Odd sort of stone, isn't it, Jade?" Roberts asked, as he held the stone map out. "Ever see writing like this? Here, look what's on the back of it."

When Jade held the stone in her hands, he expected her, of all people to hear it speak, but she did not. Instead, she placed a puzzled look on her face and looked at the etched writings more closely.

"Looks familiar, Cheeway. Is this the stone Nauti said he brought from the cave?"

"Same one, nothing seems to affect it either. I've tried to make scratches in it, but couldn't. Even tried to heat it up to see if that would affect it, but it didn't. All I know about the markings on the back is they are some kind of a warning. Any of it make sense to you, Jade?"

"Some of it does, Cheeway. Seems to be some sort of combination of most of the ancient writings.—But that can't be!"

"What do ya mean?"

"Well these writings are in pictograph form all right, just as most of the ancients used in theirs. But the way these etchings are formed…there's something different about them. Something I haven't seen before. You see the small circles used near the seven points of the body? None of the ancient writings use all of them. Only some. And the way the circles meet, they seem to express tenses. Something the ancient writings didn't do either. What I believe is on the back of this map stone is a recording of the first writing of all people. It seems to have the qualities of all the ancient writings tied together."

"Think it could be something like the Rosetta Stone, Jade?" Roberts asked.

"Yeah, something like that," Jade returned, as she rubbed the etchings with her fingers. "If we could interpret this, it might lead us to discover the clues we need to decipher all the old writings. Especially the old ones from South America."

"That would really be a kick in the face to the old Spaniards, wouldn't it?" Roberts said. "After spending so much of their time destroying all the Aztec records, it would really be an accomplishment to break their writing code and decipher what they left behind."

"Looks like Cheeway's map stone has greater impact than we first thought!" Stevens picked up. "But there's something else you told us, Cheeway. It has to do with the man called Father Sanchez. Sounds like he's someone from the past, the very painful past."

"What do ya mean, Stevens? I'm not sure I'm following."

"Just this, Cheeway, all through history, there have been stories of men who, like this Father Sanchez, wandered the known lands looking for things you mentioned."

"You mean like the ancient city Nauti said existed?"

"Yes, but more importantly, what jarred my memory of these kinds of people was what he told you the name of the city was. I believe he called it the Ancient City of Prophecy, didn't he?"

"Yes, that's what he said. I know it is significant to me because I was told of its existence when I was very young, but that was from the old history of our people. You heard of this place too?"

"Yes, Cheeway, I have," Stevens said, with a look of determination. "I thought all of this was a myth, but some of the things in your story would have me believe otherwise. Listen to me, everyone! What I am about to tell you will make the hair on your neck stand up."

Stevens paused for a moment to ensure he had their complete attention. Satisfied he did, he leaned forward in his chair, lit a cigarette, and began an incredible story.

"Any of you hear of a group call The Illuminati?"

Everyone sat with a blank look on their face, but didn't respond. Then, Stevens smiled, and continued.

"Not many people have, and those who have, don't believe they really exist. But from the description of events that surround this ancient map stone, and what Cheeway's friend Nauti told him, I'm not so sure they are a myth. I'm beginning to believe they are real."

"Well, Stevens, just who are these Illuminati? Care to share what you know about them?" Jade asked, still holding the stone and looking at it every now and then.

"Ever heard of the conspiracy theory?" Stevens asked. "One that was designed to keep people from knowing anything about the truth of their origins?"

"Of course, I don't know of any college freshman who hasn't, Stevens," Roberts returned. "It's a theory that says we didn't begin as amoeba or bacterial growth from the oceans taking millions of years to develop, but we began as we are now. That all the technology we have today was developed by us, long before. Then a great catastrophe took place and wiped everything out. I remember someone saying the conspiracy theory was developed to make all of us live in fear, rather than with knowledge. But the reasons why weren't clear."

"Well, you are kind of correct about what you know of this theory, Roberts. But it goes deeper than that. The people who are allegedly involved in this conspiracy theory are said to have killed all the great thinkers of their time. You know, the ones who would not agree to do as others wanted them to. Anyone, who came up with findings that were contrary to what this group wanted known was killed. Remember what happened to da Vinci when he agreed with Copernicus that the sun did not revolve around the Earth? He was excommunicated and almost killed. And Michelangelo, the same thing. Throughout history, there have been reports of evidence being found that support the theory none of us originated on this planet, but were brought here. Evidence of advanced technology being discovered that was used by ancient civilizations but shouldn't have been known. And all that information was mysteriously lost, and the people who discovered it were either found dead, or ended up missing. Any of this ringing a bell with you?"

"Yeah, some of it does. Keep going."

"Just prior to the dark ages, The Illuminati were said to have come out of their secret places, but only for awhile. It seemed like they were losing their grip on the politics of the known world, and were attempting to reassert their control. They were said to be responsible for drawing the curtain of ignorance and superstition around mankind, keeping society in the dark about their true identity ever since. From their efforts, the writings, records, and ancient histories of mankind were burned and termed seditious to be read. Anyone having knowledge of them would be killed immediately, and all of this was done in the name of God so humanity could be purged of its evil thoughts born from these unholy lies. They considered Aristotle and Plato to be dissidents who only wanted to incite the masses to revolt against established governments…that their sole purpose in spreading those lies was to topple the governments of the world and start over. For The Illuminati, this would not do. For it was from their controlling of world governments that they held their power base. And if the governments fell, so would they. They were said to have purged not only Europe, Africa, and Asia, but the Americas as well. It was they who were said to be responsible for the Inquisition and the deaths of millions of people worldwide. But, there is another mystery. While the Illuminati were said to wield unlimited power over governments, they too answered to a higher organization. One that is so secret, they have no name. They are only known by a symbol they wear on a ring, or under a crucifix. They are the control behind The Illuminati, and they climbed to even greater power just after the Crucifixion. They were founded by the Roman Empire but outlived them, and continue to wield their power throughout the world today. They are said to have power or dominant influence over every country in the world, and from everyone I have spoken to, the story doesn't change. I have heard this from many different countries, but they believe it is something from someone's wild imagination. They, like I, didn't believe anything like that could be real."

"And now you do, Stevens?" Cheeway asked. "What changed your mind?"

"Because what this Father Sanchez is doing, is exactly what The Illuminati and their higher ups would be doing. You see, just before the crucifixion, Christ told his disciples of other locations where ancient teachings were contained, and went on to say that when their knowledge would be shared with the world, there would be no place for secrets to live. And those who sought to control others would find nothing to control them with. When it was time for these teachings to be opened, there would be a great doorway of light that would flood into everyone's life. And this light would dispel all fear. He said where there is no fear, there can be no control. And where there is no control, there is no need for authority. What he shared, he told them to write down then hide it in a secret place. Since then, The Illuminati and their higher ups have been searching for their locations. And when Nauti spoke of them, I knew there was something behind this conspiracy theory...something more than an imaginary creation. From everything I have either read, or heard, about The Illuminati, they have spared no expense in locating these missing places. And what they have found so far, they have kept hidden from everyone. As far as I know, the majority of their own members don't know everything they have discovered. But whatever it is, it has to be something really powerful. Otherwise, why would they make such great effort in keeping it so secret?"

"Perhaps what they have uncovered would take away their power?" Jade asked.

"Maybe, Jade, but I can only speculate on that," Stevens returned. "But I think we are closer right now to finding that answer than anyone throughout history has been. The map stone Nauti gave Cheeway makes me believe we are.

And, when I heard you speak of Father Sanchez, Cheeway, I remembered something more about the theory. It was said, just before the end of time, there would be one last chance to change things…one last chance before all life would be destroyed. Within these writings are said to be three warnings. Before time ends, they must be known by all people, but there is a chance they might not understand what they are looking at. So, in these hidden places, they wrote the warnings, their implications, and what was needed to stop certain disaster. They are said to be mankind's last chance. If they are ignored, the legacy of mankind will not be realized, and everything will be lost. These writings were said to have been compiled by a mysterious group called The Watchers From The Shadows and The Light. They left us everything that has ever been known, and can explain mankind's true purpose and identity. But, according to the theory, something went terribly wrong. According to the story, the Watchers From The Shadows decided this information should not be known by everyone, only by them. They did not want mankind to understand its legacy, and wanted to destroy where this information was stored. But it was said The Watchers From The Light would not allow this. And so, they hid all of it in places The Watchers From The Shadows could not find. When Christ spoke these mystery teachings to his disciples, the Roman Empire heard about it from members of The Illuminati, then employed them to seek out their records and destroy them…all of them. And anyone found to be in possession of the knowledge they contained was to be killed. Only one thing I need to be convinced this conspiracy theory isn't some fantasy. When Father Sanchez spoke to you, Cheeway, did you notice him wearing anything unusual? Something you might not see on some other priest?"

"Yeah, there was something I thought was out of place. He wore a silver plate at the end of his crucifix! Had a strange symbol on it, it looked like…"

"Don't say anything more, Cheeway!" Stevens said, as he almost put his hand over Cheeway's mouth. "Let me see if I know what it was. Was it a symbol of a hooded man holding a curved sword?"

"Yeah…it was! How did you know, Stevens?"

"I've seen it before, Cheeway. It was shown to me by a man in Cairo. He said he found it on the record chambers of a dead pharaoh. He told me there was another symbol drawn as well, one that meant everyone inside, and anyone who knew about it, was to be executed immediately! Cheeway, do you remember seeing another symbol? Did Father Sanchez give you anything with something drawn on it?"

"Not with anything drawn on it, Stevens. He just gave Mary and I his business card, that's all. Didn't think too much about it though."

"Think for a moment, Cheeway, what's a priest doing handing out business cards? Do you think he needs more work? Do you still have it?"

"Yeah, I put it in my wallet. Wanna see it?"

"Please," Stevens said, as he stood up then turned his back to us.

Cheeway looked at Jade and Roberts to see their reaction to Stevens' strange behavior. He saw they, too, were puzzled and were waiting to see if he could find the card.

"Here it is. I found it," Cheeway said, holding it out to Stevens. But he didn't turn around.

"Turn it over, Cheeway! Is there a symbol drawn on the back?"

"Yes!" he said, feeling the shock of this information run throughout my body. "What does it mean? Do you know?"

"It's a drawing of a cross in the middle of a triangle, isn't it?"

"That's it, Stevens!" Jade returned. "Have you been developing your psychic powers behind our backs or something?"

"You were marked, Cheeway. Both you and Mary were marked for death. That's what the symbol on the back of his card means," Stevens said, pausing. "…I have heard enough! I believe we should fund Cheeway and send him to look for the Ancient City of Prophecy, the one shown on the stone map Nauti gave him. I believe if he is successful in finding this ancient site, it will be monumental in explaining what mankind's legacy truly is. What about you two? Do you agree?"

Jade made a groaning sound. Like she was trying to say something, but didn't know how. Then, her face changed, and the voice she spoke with was not hers. It was like someone else was speaking through her.

"Wait!" Jade commanded, standing up as she held the stone out for us to see. "I think I have what this warning on the back means. You need to hear what it says, Cheeway, before you make your decision about locating this ancient city."

A rush of silence filled three rooms, then all eyes focused on Jade.

"I don't have all of it, but here's what I can make out. We were right, it is a warning. An old one too, because it makes reference to land that isn't there anymore, and stars pointing in directions that are almost the direct opposite of where they point now. It explains what we think this place is! It says it is the central point for locating other places where secret information is stored. And that it holds something like the complete history of all of us, and explains what we can do to keep from destroying ourselves."

Jade paused, running her fingers back and forth over the symbols of the map stone.

"But, here is the important part, Cheeway! It gives a warning to the one that is chosen to discover this ancient city. It says he will not be allowed to share this information with others, but must find the one like him to pass this knowledge to. It must be the one who is like him who will ensure this information is shared, because the one who discovers this place, will soon die! If we fund you, Cheeway, and knowing what I said is on the back of the map stone, are you still willing to search for the Ancient City of Prophecy? Even if it might mean your death?"

Cheeway only needed a short time to think of what had been asked. He knew from a place deep within, this was what Mary and he had prepared their lives to do. This was the path of his destiny, and he could not turn away from it now…not now that he knew a little more what the implications were.

"Yes!" he responded. "I will do this quest that has been asked of me. Not because it has been asked of me by you, my friends. I believe this was asked of me long before I was born. This is my destiny, and if you will fund me, I will discover the Ancient City of Prophecy."

"What about the other part of the warning, Cheeway?" Roberts asked. "The part that says you must pass the information to the one who is like you? Is there someone like that?"

"Yes, my friend, there is. He is my brother, Speaking Wind. We were born at the same time and with the same map mark on the back of our necks."

"Will he do such a thing?" Jade asked, with a voice that sounded more like hers. "I mean, after he discovers what dangers could lie in such a venture?"

"I know my brother well enough to answer for him. I know he will do such a thing. We have been raised to know what is, and is not, our path to travel. Our paths have been tied together since birth. I know he will understand. In fact, I will write to him asking that he meet me somewhere on the lands of our birth."

"All right then," Stevens said. "Lets get the paperwork started!"

"We still have to figure out where we are going, Stevens!" Jade returned. "Did you forget that?"

Believing they still had more work ahead of them, there was a loud sigh followed by all of them searching for a clue that would lead them to discover The Ancient City of Prophecy.

The map stone seemed to be naming reference points using animal totems and asking that the one deciphering it use them in a way that would lead them to the ancient city's location.

At least, that's what they thought it was doing. But each lead they followed, lead to another dead end, one that left them no better off than they were before.

Then, Jade came up with a theory, one that finally made sense to the reference points the map stone was using.

"Look at this, will you!" Jade said, holding the map stone near a map of South America. "I think I have something here! Come see what I found!"

Everyone dropped what they were doing and joined Jade near the table. She had a large map opened showing the South American continent, and held the stone map over it.

"This is beginning to make sense to me. Tell me what you think," Jade said, brimming with excitement. "The map stone makes references to this city being built on one of the highest places known. Now, we know it has to have been built near Central or South America because that is where all of the other artifacts have been showing up. You know, the ones making reference to the ancient city. Now, as I look at our conventional map, there are only a few mountains that would be high enough to have such a city on them. That is, if one were to take the map literally."

"Jade, we can't just put a city where it seems to fit," Roberts said, looking at Jade as if she had lost her mind.

"That's not what I'm doing. Listen to me for a minute, will you! Let me finish what I have come up with, okay? When we look at the map stone, it tells us there should be tall mountains all around it. And, should be located on the highest point of the tallest of them. So far, I believe we agree with that, right?"

Jade looked at us when she said this, and we nodded our agreement. While they had not come up with much from their attempts to interpret the stone map, this was one of the few things they did agree on.

"Okay, there have been ancient records from other civilizations tell us about major earthquakes in this area. What if some of them were so severe, it caused some land masses to sink? Couldn't that be a possibility?"

"Well, there have been accounts of land rising and sinking throughout history, Jade," Stevens returned. "But what makes you think a place that is said to be the highest known land on Earth could sink?"

"Think of what Cheeway and Mary found near Machu Picchu. What was a boat dock doing over eight thousand feet above sea level with no signs of water near it? Do you think the old ones would have built such a place just for the fun of it?"

"What are you driving at, Jade?" Roberts asked, as he looked her in the eyes. "Are you saying the place identified on the map might be completely different than we thought? Because if this is what you're getting at, we might as well look anywhere for it. Why not try looking at the maps of Egypt for what it's worth?!"

"Okay, let's pull out the map of Egypt, Roberts!"

"Jade, I was kidding. We're all getting tired now, and really short on patience."

"I'm not kidding, Roberts!" Jade returned, as she pushed the map of South America aside. "Here! I've made room for you to put the map of Egypt here. Come on, Roberts! We still have a lot of things to do before I can finish presenting this."

Roberts unfolded the map of Egypt, and we gathered around to see what Jade would say next.

"Look here!" Jade said, pointing to a small drawing of the three pyramids and the Sphinx. "This is what I am speaking about, right here on this map!"

They looked at the map and saw where Jade had pointed. Even though they saw the three pyramids and the Sphinx, no one had a clue where Jade was going with it, and looked at her with bewilderment.

"Good! I'm glad I have all of you so lost you don't know what to say. Perhaps that will get me the quiet I need so I can continue without interruption. Look how these three pyramids were made. You see, two of them are in direct line with each other, but the third one is just off center from the other two. Now, keep this in mind and look at the map of the Yucatan. Do you see anything similar?"

They looked at the map of the Yucatan Peninsula, but could not see what Jade made reference to with the three pyramids.

"Is it just me, or am I the only one who sees this? Look near the tip of the Yucatan. Don't you see three ancient sites there aligned in the same way the pyramids are? I'll give you, there is not the same distance between them, but the alignment is the same."

"Come on, give just a little more on this, will you?"

"Yes!" Stevens said abruptly. "I see what you mean, Jade. Right here, they have the same alignment as the pyramids of Egypt."

Stevens looked at the rest and they could see he was not pretending, but believed he too had seen what Jade discovered, and was waiting for the rest of us to see it as well.

"Here?" Cheeway said, pointing to three of the old Mayan cities. "Is this what you're looking at?"

"Yes, Cheeway! That's it. Look how they are aligned. If you look at Sayil and Lebna, they are in direct alignment with each other, but when you go down just a little and see Chacmultun, it appears to be off just a little. I bet if we were to measure the degrees of difference between the one off center, and the difference the pyramids are off to each other, we will have a measurement that is so close it won't be funny. What do you think? Is it worth taking the time to do that?"

"You really think there is a relationship here, Jade?" Stevens asked. "I don't know about the rest of you, but I'm getting really tired and don't have much steam left in me. I mean, Jade, if you really believe you have something here, I will go along with you. But, if you're only guessing, then I think we all better call it a night and get some rest."

"I don't think we have the time to not follow up on this," Jade returned, looking just as tired as the rest of them. "Remember what Cheeway said about Father Sanchez and how persistent he was? Do you think he's resting now? I doubt it. I think he's still looking for Cheeway, and I believe he knows we have the map stone. Now, what would you do if you were in his place? Would you take time out to rest, or would you continue the hunt, especially if you thought your prey had something that could reveal something you didn't want to be known!"

"I see what you mean, " Stevens said, with a look of embarrassment. "Let's follow your lead and see where it takes us. But tell me, what makes you so certain this is the place? After all, the Yucatan hasn't ever been very high above sea level."

"The map stone, and the writing on it are what make me think that, Stevens," Jade returned, holding the back of the stone for him to see. "Look at the writings, they come from a time we know nothing about. They might even be older than anything we could dream up. If that's the case, perhaps the topography of their time was so different there wouldn't be anything remotely similar about it. Maybe what we need to look for is something that has transcended what we were looking for. You know, less changeable than the high mountains."

"Now, you're saying we shouldn't even be looking for mountains, Jade?" Cheeway asked.

"No! We should be looking for something that would remain long after a mountain would disappear. Something the old ones knew would be built again and again, regardless of the number of catastrophes that would befall it."

"Like what, Jade?" Stevens asked. "I didn't know there was anything more permanent than a mountain!"

"Energy, my dear Stevens. Energy from a place that could channel it so strong that later civilizations would feel it and honor it by building something sacred there!"

"And the Maya did just that!" Roberts began. "All of their temples and sacred sites were built in the exact locations their priests told them…places the priests felt something very powerful coming from the Earth.

"They believed the places where they felt powerful energy points were open-ings to the underworld…the place they believed they stole their bodies from. And by honoring the underworld, they would ensure a safe life for themselves up here.

"Yes, Jade, I see where you are going now!" Roberts proclaimed. "But why these three? Why not others who might have a similar alignment?"

"Because these three are mentioned, by name, on the map stone, Roberts."

"You found that?"

"Yes! Look at the drawings directly under the landmarks on the map stone.

"But first, think about this. You know what energy does, all of us do. It is the moving element that creates something all of us can feel. Now, what if you knew so much technology that you understood the kind of energy needed to draw cer-tain things to it. Things like small insects…And why insects you ask? Because if anything living would survive the most severe of catastrophes, they would. And if they remained in those energy places, someone who could build would feel that energy and construct a monument. And, not wanting to isolate themselves from the rest of the universe, or their gods, they would name whatever they built after the insects that lived there in such abundance. Also, if one was highly evolved enough to understand the nature of energy, they could focus it so there could be nothing other than a very permanent structure built there. In a way that would cause all other buildings to decay, or not last long, that is, if they were built in a conventional way such as a house or some smaller structure. And, if one under-stood the concept of channeling energy from under the Earth, they could also cause great mounds of Earth to form itself over that spot. So what I am saying, gentlemen, is the Old Ones, the ones who made this stone map that even now cannot be scratched or marred, possessed this higher knowledge that allowed them to create energy vortexes such as the ones I just described. Here, look at the symbol referring to the first landmark. This symbol is similar to an ant biting on a leaf. Do you see it?"

"A leaf cutter ant. That's right, Jade! A leaf cutter ant fits right in, doesn't it? I mean, you can't be more specific than that, can you?!"

"What are you two talking about?" Stevens asked, as he looked at Cheeway for support.

"I'm not sure what you are getting at either. Could you explain it so we could understand too?"

"Sorry," Jade said, as she pushed the hair out of her face. "The leaf cutter ant is very significant to one of the temples made by the Maya. They named it after the ant. They called it Sayil, and it means the place of the leaf-cutter ants!"

"And the second one, Jade, I see the correlation here, too!" Roberts said. "It's a picture of what appears to be an old house. Look at it, it even has places that are broken or missing. Some of the walls are gone and the roof seems to be in need of repair."

"And that identifies the second landmark, gentlemen!" Jade said, with a look of great accomplishment. "That is the name of the second site, Labna. It translates to the old houses.

"Now, the third site was a little more difficult," Jade said, as she rubbed the back of her neck. "Took a little more on that one. I think the reason was if this old stone map had been in color at one time, it has long since vanished. But the drawing on it shows a picture of mounds, lots of them. And the third Mayan site that fits is called Chacmultun, or the place of mounds made of red stone. And, if you look at Sayil and Labna, they are in line with each other. But Chacmultun is not and I bet the difference in their alignment is equal to that of the three pyramids in Egypt."

"But there are four reference points mentioned, Jade, what about the fourth one?" Stevens asked.

"Yes, I was coming to that. The map stone makes reference to something like a sitting cat and its distance from the one that is not in line with its other two brothers. The directions seem very specific in saying from where the cat is sitting, one must walk around the three aligned points, then put the circle in a straight line, and extended it straight as an arrow from the second and over the first point. Where the line ends, is the location of the Ancient City of Prophecy! That's where it is, gentlemen! That's where we will find the Ancient City of Prophecy! I'll bet my bottom dollar on it. As a matter of fact, I am so sure, I am willing to accompany Cheeway to the site myself."

"What about the sitting cat, Jade?" Cheeway asked. "I don't see any mention or sign of it on the map!"

"You have to remember their technology, Cheeway. If they were advanced enough to construct a stone map such as this, and make the speaking stones Nauti has told you of, they had to have known we would eventually be advanced enough to make a correlation between the pyramids of Egypt with the Sphinx and these three ancient cites of the Mayan. And, they must have known if we could make this correlation, we would be able to interpret the rest on our own."

"You mean like the sitting cat that is no longer there?"

"Exactly, if there was something like the Sphinx near these ancient cities, it must have been destroyed, either by natural forces or by people who believed it was something evil. All we have to do is figure the layout of the Sphinx to the three pyramids, then substitute their positions for the three ancient Mayan sites. That's what will give us the location of the sitting cat the map stone makes reference to."

"You know, Jade," Roberts said, as he rubbed his face with his hands. "If you're right, this could change almost everything we thought we knew about the past. History will have to be rewritten."

"If I'm right about this, Roberts, we'll know for certain the Egyptians did not build the pyramids like we've been told. We'll know they actually spent all those years, and generations of slave labor, uncovering them. We'll know who built them when we discover who built the city on this map stone!

"What about it?" Jade asked anxiously. "I'm all for going with Cheeway. What about the rest of you?"

For a moment, there was a heavy silence in the room. No one spoke, only looked at each other…each looking for a kind of supportive direction to Jade's invitation.

Then, Roberts and Stevens gave their reply at the same time. It sounded like they were singing in harmony as they said, " Count us in, Jade! Cheeway can't have all the fun!"

"Do you mind our enthusiasm, Cheeway?" Jade said, as she held his hand. "You didn't really want to go alone, did you?"

"No, not at all, Jade. I would consider it a great honor to have my friends accompany me. But there is something each of you must understand. And, that is the danger involved in this. It won't be like we are the only ones searching for this city."

"You mean Father Sanchez?" Roberts said.

"Yeah, he's going to be great trouble. And for whoever is associated with me."

"Don't worry, Cheeway," Roberts offered. "I have a good friend in the government where we are going. I'll contact him, and he can provide us with reliable escorts. We won't have to worry about Father Sanchez, not as long as they're with us."

"I hope they will serve as a buffer," Cheeway said, as he crossed his arms and looked at the two maps on the table.

"I'm sure they will, Cheeway. Come on! Let's get packing and make our flight reservations for Merida! Everybody got their passports?"

That began the second part of my brother's journey.

# CHAPTER 3

▼

# THE CLOAK OF SECRECY

My son and I arrived in New Mexico in early December. I had placed my brother's letter in my briefcase and had been thinking about it all through the flight from Europe. I felt the urgency in his request to meet him at Sadie's Restaurant just outside Coyote, New Mexico, but I was wondering how I would explain my absence to my mom.

For her, Christmas was a very special time, and she looked forward to all of us being together. But this Christmas, there would be one less member in attendance—me.

I told my son I had to attend a meeting with a special friend and would attempt to return before Christmas Eve. He didn't like this, but I knew he understood, and the look on his face told me he would be all right with this.

The taxi turned into the driveway of my parents' house, and as usual, they, and some of our other relations were waiting on the porch. We exchanged greetings and went inside to talk of who would be doing what this holiday season.

When I told mom I would be gone for a few days, just before Christmas, she nodded her head silently. I knew she did not like it, but understood there was something I had to do.

I stood outside our house thinking of the time I had spent there, and the wonderful memories that had been lived. Then, I thanked the spirits who held this energy for us, got into the rented car and began my drive to meet with my brother, Cheeway.

It was 5 a.m. when I left, and I knew I should arrive at Sadie's Restaurant sometime around noon. The thought of Cheeway being in trouble made me drive faster than usual, and as I did, I reflected on what could have happened to him.

I knew he had always been respectful of the laws that governed his digs, and would not steal anything from another culture or country. I knew this because of how he had spoken to me of the outsiders who came to our peoples' lands and taken whatever they wanted. For Cheeway, this made such a great impact on him, and his work, there were times he left things behind that were not considered important to the country he was digging in.

So, this could not have been the reason for his trouble. I was certain he wouldn't have deceived his backers with stories that weren't true. His backers had been with him for many years, and had always been satisfied with his work. They knew if Cheeway told them he was sure something would be found on one of his sites, it would be found. And if he were not sure, he would tell them in the beginning. That allowed them to know what risks were involved before they invested their time, and money.

As I drove north on Highway 23 toward Santa Fe, I could see the Sandia Mountains setting into the horizon behind me. Looking at them for the last time, I remembered where Cheeway and I were first told about the Ancient Ones' Hallway of Records. I saw Bear Canyon in the mirror, but it was almost at the mountains end.

As it disappeared from sight, I reflected on what had been shared with me many years before—the ancient history that began a life long search for my brother, Cheeway.

Grandfather and Two Bears told us the Hallway of Records was a place where the oldest of the sacred writings were recorded…that it was hidden and would only be revealed to one who had the ability of understanding what the Old Ones left for us as a race of people. Grandfather and Two Bears were very attentive to explain that any reference to a race of people did not just mean the red race, but it meant all mankind. And the one chosen to receive this information must be willing to see all humans as one, not as separate races of people. For this was the intent of their prophecy.

It was said, within the Hallway of Records, are the mirrors of The Ancient Ones' Prophecies. While they appear to be identical to what had been left with us to remember, they would take one additional step. They would explain how these ancient prophecies could be changed, altered, or even stopped. As I thought of these events, my thoughts were clouded by my worries for Cheeway. I was no longer willing to search my past to find more clues to what had been told to us before.

Now, all my thoughts were on my brother, and what could possibly be his trouble, and how I could help him.

I stopped the car in Santa Fe to get gas and a bite to eat, intending to continue my drive through Pojoaque, Espanola, Abiquiu, and then into Coyote. However, when I stopped at the restaurant, I was met with a very unusual event, one that told me I was already tied to my brother's destiny.

I walked into the restaurant, found a table and looked at the menu. After ordering, I lit a cigarette and sipped my coffee. I felt someone looking at me from behind. It was the kind of feeling you get when someone is studying you so closely, it makes the hair on the back of your neck stand up.

I rubbed my neck, then turned around to see who was causing me to feel this way. I saw three men sitting in a booth behind me, looking at me as if they could see right through me. I noticed they were wearing the same kind of clothes, the kind I had seen Native Americans near Mexico City wear. But there was one article that wasn't usual; it was a crucifix with a small silver plate attached to it. On it appeared to be an etching of a hooded man holding a curved sword.

I looked into their eyes and acknowledged their presence, then the one sitting closest to me stood up, walked to my table, and spoke to me in very good, but strongly accented English.

"Pardon us for staring at you, my friend. But we were admiring the mark on the back of your neck. Have you had it long?"

I had to think for a moment about what mark he was referring to. Then, I remembered. When Cheeway and I were born, we each had a mark on the back of our necks. It was red, and located just under the hairline. Grandfather and Two Bears told us we each carried this mark because it was a map of things we were going to do, and showed us where we would travel in order to accomplish our destiny. They told us we carried this birth map in a place neither of us could see alone, but would need the other to read it. However, this mark is not easily seen as the hair usually covered it up. Then I realized I had my hair cut just before leaving Europe. I knew my parents did not like to see it long, so I had it cut especially short for my visit.

"Did you not know a mark was there, my friend?" the stranger asked again, sensing my lack of attention to his question.

"Oh, I was just surprised you noticed it. That's all."

"Well, have you had it long?" he asked again, sounding a little more impatient for my answer than before.

I smiled then shrugged my shoulders. Then I remembered Cheeway's letter and how he said he was being followed and there was great danger. I knew each of us had the same mark on our neck, but what significance it held to this man, and my brother's danger, I did not know. So I decided to play dumb and see if anything would be offered by the stranger.

"I had a barber call my attention to it some years back. But that's the only time I remember anyone noticing it. Why do you ask?"

"It has a great significance, that mark does," the man said, looking deep into my eyes for something only he knew might be found.

"I would love to hear about it," I said, taking a sip of coffee, still looking at him. "Would you care to tell me about it?"

"Only this, my friend," the man said, reaching into his shirt pocket. "There is one other man we know of that has that mark. We have been looking for him for a long time. When you see him, give him this card and tell him it would be in his best interest to contact us immediately. Tell him if he doesn't, there could be great danger for him…and you."

The man reached inside his walking blanket for his shirt pocket and I noticed he was wearing a gun at his waist. Then, he pulled out a card and handed it to me. It had the name of the Hotel Alvarado in Santa Fe. On the back he wrote his room number, and name; then he drew the symbol of a cross within a triangle below them. He handed me the card and I could tell he wanted to make sure I saw the mark he made. Satisfied I had, he continued.

"Give this to him when you see him. It is important."

Looking at the card and thinking about the gun, I asked, "What makes you think I will see this man, whoever he is?"

"Don't be stupid, my friend, we know all about you…and your brother."

My first reaction was to ask this man who he was and what he meant by saying he knew all about me and my brother. I was about to tell him I was going to report this incident to the police because of what he was implying and the gun he was wearing. But, I decided not to and let the matter drop until I could speak to Cheeway.

The man looked at the other two and spoke to them in a language I had not heard before. The two behind me silently rose from the booth and followed him out the door to the parking lot.

I wanted to see what kind of car they were driving, in case I needed this information later. And I was glad I did. They were driving a black Ford Bronco with New Mexico plates. They entered the vehicle and drove out of the parking lot.

As I watched them drive away, the waitress surprised me by setting my ham sandwich on the table with a loud thump. That caused me to jump and so did she, dropping my sandwich on the floor.

"I am sorry, sir, please excuse me. But you startled me, you know. I'll get you another sandwich if you don't mind waiting a few minutes," she said apologetically.

"It's all right," I said, not knowing if I should look at her or follow the black car driving away. "I was going to ask you to make this order to go anyway."

She half smiled at me, and I could tell she was relieved to know I wouldn't be staying at her table much longer. Then, she turned and walked into the kitchen to replace my order. I heard her speak to the cook telling him to put all other orders aside and make my sandwich as quickly as possible.

I really couldn't blame her. If I were in her place, I would have wanted me to leave quickly as well. I paid my bill, and then walked outside to look at the mountains nearest me. The wind was blowing gently across my face as I wondered what Cheeway had gotten himself into. I knew this was no accident, meeting the three men in the restaurant. They knew too much about Cheeway and me, and I knew they must have been following me for quite some time to be here. But what did they want? And, why were they so concerned that Cheeway contact them as soon as possible. The only thing I could think of was they had not located him yet, or if they had, they lost him. Perhaps that's why they followed me today. But if their only purpose was to find Cheeway, why did they make their presence known to me? None of this made sense; not here, not now. And the more I thought about it, the more confusing it got.

I looked at the card the man gave me. I was strangely drawn to the symbol drawing he made on the back. I knew I had seen this before, and there was a great importance behind it, but I couldn't recall what I had heard. All I knew was it looked familiar, and there was significance to it. One that had a direct impact on me, and I was sure, on Cheeway.

I saw the time and knew I stayed here longer than I anticipated. I wanted to arrive at Sadie's Restaurant before noon. I wanted to arrive at least two hours before Cheeway said he would find me. For there were certain precautions I wanted to take.

Halfway between Espanola and Abiquiu I saw another old friend disappear in the rear view mirror, the Sangre De Cristos Mountains. There were many seasons spent there with Grandfather, Two Bears, and my brother, Cheeway, as we learned the ways of the Old Ones...those who left so much of spiritual history with us.

Then I saw the Jemez Mountains on the horizon ahead of me. And these too had been good companions for the four of us. I knew the turn off to Coyote wasn't much further and didn't want to miss it. The exit to Highway 96 was just beyond Abiquiu and was marked with a small signpost, up ahead.

I made the turn for the last part of my drive. From the exit, there was only thirty or so miles left to drive, and still, I didn't have a plan. I didn't want to enter Coyote announced like I did in Santa Fe, for I knew there was much more at risk now. From what Cheeway told me in his letter, there had already been two attempts on his life, and I didn't want to have the three men in the black Ford Bronco follow me to him. For all I knew, they were the ones who wanted to kill him.

I entered Coyote without a plan...one that would allow me to meet with Cheeway without being followed. I was searching my mind for something I could do...something that would allow me to be as unseen as the wind. Just as I was about to give up, my attention was interrupted by the sound of someone blaring their horn behind me.

When I looked in the rear view mirror, I saw the black Ford Bronco and the three men signaling me to stop. But something inside me forced my foot to press the gas pedal down to the floorboard. I was pushed back against the seat as the car lurched forward gaining incredible speed. Then, I looked back and what I thought was there, in truth, was not. Rather than the Bronco, I saw an old truck that looked black, but was covered with so much mud and straw, I couldn't tell what color it was for sure. However, when I saw it wasn't the vehicle I thought it was, I slowed the car down.

The truck pulled up behind me and honked its horn while the driver motioned for me to stop. Not feeling any immediate threat, I pulled off the road and waited for whomever it was that wanted to speak.

"Hey, brother, what's your hurry? Wan' a get yourself killed?" came a familiar voice from behind the car.

First, I recognized the voice, and then turned my head to confirm what I thought. It was Nahe, one who had grown up with Cheeway and me. I felt a surge of relief fill me.

"Gee, Speaking Wind, look at you. You been gone from us all these years and you come back here driving like you're in New York City, or someplace like that. What's driving you anyway? You know I could give you a ticket for this."

"Nahe, I don't have time to explain! Just get back in your truck and follow me, okay?

"You in some kind of trouble or something, brother?"

"Not me, Nahe, its Cheeway! I can't talk to you out here in the open! Hurry, get into your truck and follow me before we're seen!"

The moment I finished my last word, I started the car and drove to one of the side dirt roads. I hoped he understood my urgency and followed. But I couldn't tell, for as I looked in the rear view mirror, the dust behind me was too thick to see anything. All I could do was hope Nahe had followed.

I saw what I thought would be a safe place to stop. It was an old abandoned barn, just off the road. I saw the grass was short enough to keep my tire tracks from being seen, and I hoped the earth was as hard as it looked. For on the hard earth, there are fewer tracks left by something as heavy as a car, or truck.

The doors of the barn were open, and I knew there was enough room to drive the car inside without having to stop. I pulled into the barn, got out and waited for Nahe, but not in the open, not where I could be seen if the three men were following. Rather, I waited behind a large bush, in a crouched position.

It didn't take long before I heard the sounds of a tired engine coming down the dirt road. And from the appearances of Nahe's truck, I knew it must be him. So I stood up and waived. When I knew he had seen me, I returned to the barn and waited inside.

He sensed my urgency and followed me into the barn, pulling in behind my car and waited, shaking his head.

"Kill the engine, Nahe!" I shouted, as I quickly closed both doors behind us. "Did anyone follow you?"

Nahe climbed out of his truck and shook his head again.

"What'd you do, turn into some kind of James Bond since you've been gone? You could get a ticket for what you've been doing, and I'm just the one who can give it to you. After all, I'm the Sheriff in this town now, Speaking Wind."

"Nahe, you've got to listen to me! I don't know how much time we have before we're seen, but I need a favor from you!"

"You mean more than I've given you already?"

"Nahe, I'm serious!"

"So am I, Speaking Wind. Brother or not, if you don't tell me what this is all about, I'm going to take you in and impound your car. You act like you're on drugs or something."

"It's Cheeway, Nahe! I'm afraid he's in big trouble and he's asked for my help. But now, I've got to ask you for yours, before I can help him."

"Man, you're still speaking in circles, Speaking Wind. I can't follow a word you're saying. Slow down a little will ya?"

"What'd Cheeway do this time, walk into a bar full of red necks and ask for one of their white women? Remember when he did that down in Waco? Boy, that was an adventure I won't forget. They must've chased us for three hundred miles before stopping! Remember?"

"Nahe, please…!"

"Okay, but let me guess a little, will ya? After all, I'm the Sheriff here, and I'm supposed to know how to sort through these kinds of things, ya know. Let me see, it's because of some white guys, isn't it?"

"No, Nahe, it's none of the above! Now, will you let me explain what I do know?"

"All right, just don't let it get out I couldn't guess, Speaking Wind. After all, I have a reputation to keep up with, ya know."

"It began when I received a letter from Cheeway. He told me he was in trouble and wanted me to meet him at Sadie's, just outside town. But when I got to Santa Fe, there were three men waiting for me. I wasn't aware of being followed. So they caught me off guard. They said things about me and Cheeway that are only known by a few other people.

"However, before leaving, the man who spoke to me gave me something. He gave me a business card from the Alvarado Hotel with a room number on it. He told me I should give it to Cheeway when I saw him, and if I didn't, he would be in more trouble.

"One other thing, Nahe, when he reached into his walking blanket for his pocket, I saw a gun strapped to his waist, and a crucifix around his neck with a silver medallion attached to it. I didn't see anything peculiar about the crucifix, but the medallion had an engraving on it. It was of a hooded man holding a curved sword of some kind. Perhaps you have seen such a picture?……Anyway, Nahe, I don't feel good about just driving to Sadie's and walking in. Cheeway told me I shouldn't look for him, but he would find me. And, if those three men are still following, as I am sure they are, they will see Cheeway when he finds me. So, I need your help, my brother. I need your help to get to Cheeway without being seen. Will you help?"

Nahe stood in silence. I could tell he was thinking about what I said. Not to determine if I was telling him truth, but to associate what he already knew about something else that was related to what I told him.

Without speaking, Nahe turned, opened the truck door, and pulled out a folded paper. It looked like it had been crumpled, but had been straightened out later.

"Look at this drawing, Speaking Wind, then read the note under it. Does it come close to what you told me, or doesn't it?"

I looked at the paper and saw a drawing of the same crucifix and medallion I had seen on the three men. Below the drawing was a note:

*Nahe, three men were looking for Cheeway this morning. They asked many questions about Grandfather, Two Bears, and Speaking Wind as well. I don't like the looks of them, so I did not give them information. But they asked for directions to Coyote, and I knew they were headed to your neck of the woods. They say they are Spanish, but they dress like Native Americans from the Mexico lands. Be careful if they want to meet with you. Hope this helps out.*

*Bending Water*

"I thought she was teaching at the university in Denver. Is she back on the lands now, Nahe?"

"She returned about two years ago, and works as a drug and alcohol counselor for the northern villages."

Nahe reached for the paper and looked more closely at it.

"Is this what you saw, Speaking Wind? Sounds like it is."

"Yes, Nahe, it's the same thing. But there's one thing missing. When the man gave me the card from his hotel, he drew a symbol on the back. It was a cross with a triangle around it. I don't remember its importance, but I know I've seen it before…somewhere.

Nahe looked at the symbol I drew under Bending Water's note, and said he had seen it before as well, but couldn't remember what it meant. And, he too, remembered something very important about it, but at present, he couldn't recall.

"Guess these guys have really been getting around, haven't they. Will you help me?"

"Of course, my brother. If Cheeway can be helped by my helping you, then I'm all for it. What you wanna do?"

Nahe and I made a plan we both felt good about. I would lie in the back of the truck, covered with a tarp and keep a lookout through a small opening for anyone who might be following. He would drive to Sadie's and circle the block two times. That would allow us to see if the three men were waiting for me to appear. Then, he would pull the truck to the back of Sadie's and let me out.

There are two back doors to the restaurant, but only one was used. He would go inside and open the unused back door to let me in. Then, I could look for any sign of Cheeway, while he waited in the truck behind the restaurant.

This plan gave us a good feeling because it felt right. There would be no sign of my rental car in the parking lot, or even near the restaurant and I could enter without being seen. I got into the truck and signaled I was ready, then pulled the tarp over myself as we started out.

▼

# CHAPTER 4

# FATHER SANCHEZ

We drove around the block two times, and I didn't see anything of the three men, or their truck. Then, Nahe entered a small alley behind the restaurant and I got out and waited. It wasn't long before I heard sounds behind the unused door. I hoped it was Nahe carrying out the rest of our plan. It was, and for that, I was grateful.

"Come on, Speaking Wind, you don't have much time. I told Sadie I was checking her security in the back. And you know her; she won't leave me alone very long. She's very protective about her place, ya know."

"Sounds like there's still some fire between the two of you, Nahe. Maybe it's not security she's interested in."

"Nah, that's been too long ago. Anyway, there are lots of people in the restaurant now, but I know a place we can be unobserved. Come on, we're wastin' time."

Nahe walked past the kitchen and into a private dining room. He walked to a wall and took a framed picture down. "Come on, Speaking Wind, you can see the whole place from here. This was used when Sadie's family sold beer on Sundays—when it was illegal, that is."

I looked out the small opening into the restaurant, but didn't see Cheeway, or the three men who approached me earlier. I thought the coast was clear and told Nahe I would go in and wait for a sign from him. He agreed, and said he would wait by the back door. That way, if I needed to make a quick escape, I could leave the way we came in.

When I walked into the restaurant, it brought back many memories. This was where Grandfather and Two Bears would stop to eat with us. But that was when we were about to begin a great adventure with them. How strange, I thought to myself, how strange the time doesn't seem to change events, or places. Because here I am, waiting to meet my brother, and when I do, it will mark the beginning of another great adventure for us…but without Grandfather and Two Bears, and for this, I felt a passing heaviness visit my heart.

I sat in one of the booths next to the wall. That way, I could see everyone who came in and if the three men entered, I could make a quick exit. From what they said in Santa Fe, I didn't want to speak to them again, not if I could help it. I didn't want to give them information about anything. They seemed very clever about sorting things out, and I didn't want to take a chance in letting anything slip out they might use against Cheeway.

I ordered a cup of coffee and kept my eyes glued to the entrance. I wasn't sure if I would see Cheeway, or the three men enter. But in either case, I wouldn't let either possibility arrive unannounced.

I watched each person enter and leave the restaurant. Everything else slipped into another place…one that was not only out of my thoughts, but out of my sight as well.

Then I felt a hand grab my shoulder, and heard a voice speak to me I wished I didn't remember.

"There is a man who wishes to speak to you! Will you come with me, please?"

I turned my head to confirm whom I thought it might be, and I was right. It was the same man who spoke to me at the restaurant in Santa Fe. Without calling attention to my actions, I lowered my eyes to see if there was still a gun strapped around his waist, and noticed a bulge under his blanket, one that could have hidden the gun I saw him wearing at out first meeting.

He looked at me with eyes that seemed to penetrate past anything I could place in front of him. Then reached for his walking blanket and pulled it up slightly…enough for me to see his gun.

"He wants to speak to you now, Speaking Wind. Will you come with me, or must I convince you further?"

Silently, I rose from my seat and waited for him to signal our direction. He wasted no time and motioned to a table in the far back of the restaurant. I saw the two who were with him earlier, and another man…one who seemed to be in a position of authority over the other three.

When I got to the table, I noticed he was wearing the same crucifix with the silver medallion attached to the end. He made a hand gesture for me to sit. The man who brought me pulled out a chair, then took a standing position against the wall. A very good advantage if one wanted to make sure he could react to any trouble I might cause, or to check my effort of leaving too early.

"How are you today, Speaking Wind? I hope your trip was not too tiring, was it?"

"Who are you? And what do you want with me?"

"Oh yes, please excuse me, my friend. I am Father Sanchez, and these are my bodyguards," he said, motioning to the three men.

"How did you get in? I didn't see you enter, and I've been watching the door ever since I got here."

"How easy it is to overlook the obvious," he said, smiling slightly. "We came in through the front door, and after you had been here for quite some time. But that doesn't matter now. What does matter is the reason I have come to your country."

"What do you mean, my country? Where are you from?"

"That is unimportant for the time being, my friend. Just let me say all four of us are traveling on diplomatic passports, and because of that, we are protected by diplomatic law. But that is not the purpose to our being here. We have come to your country to take back what was stolen from us."

Father Sanchez looked at me for any expressions I might give him. I felt this, more than knew it. But in either case, I decided not to openly show him any reaction from what he said, and felt his frustration grow.

"What do you think about stealing, my son? Do you believe it is something that should be accepted, and ignored?"

"Father Sanchez, I have respected the name you have taken for yourself. It would further our conversation if you would respect mine. Wouldn't you agree?"

"Yes, I apologize, Speaking Wind. This is the name you wish to be called by?"

"It will do. And, in answer to your question, I don't believe stealing is something that should be ignored. But, I have been raised to understand why stealing affects others. While one lives with the illusion they are in control of life, they believe they own it. But this is just another deception the illusion places over everyone. You see, the only things we truly own are what we take with us when we die. Everything else is only borrowed. And when someone believes they have been robbed, they are only feeling the effects of a broken ego...one that tells them they had no control, or ownership over anything in the first place."

Father Sanchez looked at me. There was a perplexed look on his face, one I could not associate with anything.

"But while this thing, as you call it, is with someone, don't you believe they have the right to do with it as they wish? I mean, for the time being, wouldn't you say it is theirs?" the strange priest asked.

"If my spirit was tied down by believing what everyone told me, I would," I replied. "If my eyes were blinded because I would rather see what someone told me to see, I would. And, if my ears could not hear the voice of my spirit, I would believe what you said was truth."

"But you are not in such a place, are you Speaking Wind?"

"I believe this conversation is over, Father Sanchez," I said, starting to get up. But as I did, the man standing next to the wall moved toward me quicker than I anticipated, because of his size. And, the other two men rose and stood to either side of me, then placed their hands on my shoulders and looked to Father Sanchez for additional instructions.

"This conversation is over, when I say it is! Sit down! Now!" Father Sanchez said angrily, motioning to the three men to remain where they were.

When I sat down, the three men resumed their original places. When I looked at Father Sanchez, I noticed he was breathing very hard…the way one does when they are attempting to control their emotions.

"Please excuse me, and my outburst. But your kind are very difficult to reason with."

"My kind?"

"Yes…" he said, covering his face with his hands. "The only way you Indians will listen to reason, is if it hits you in the head with a two-by-four."

When Father Sanchez said that, I looked at the man standing next to the wall. I knew he heard what was said because he lowered his head slightly. I knew he, and the other two, were of Native American blood and felt the same way I did about Father Sanchez's statement.

Next, he raised his head from his hands, and picked up a napkin to draw something on it. When he finished, he looked at me, then continued.

"Have you ever seen this symbol before, Speaking Wind?" he said, holding the napkin for me to see.

He had drawn a symbol of a cross enclosed by a triangle, and under it was the design on the silver medallion each of them wore under their crucifix.

Once again, this symbol was shown to me, first by the man standing next to the wall, and now, by Father Sanchez. While I knew this had a meaning, one of importance, I was not willing to let him know what I felt.

"No, I haven't. Does it mean something?"

Father Sanchez looked at me with eyes that were beginning to burn with a flame within.

"This is the Brotherhood I represent! We are the chosen ones who are to ensure nothing gets out that is not supposed to. Our Brotherhood is not limited to my country, but is influential in all countries, everywhere in the world!

"We are a very old order, one that is known all over the world. We have been involved in things from the beginning of time, and we are just as strong now as we have ever been!"

I looked at Father Sanchez and could see he was filling himself with a pride for what he represented…a society that, according to him, was older than time.

"You know, time has a different meaning for each of us. If you represent an order older than time, for me, that would only be forty or so years."

"Are you playing with me, or are you really that dumb? Because if you are playing with me, let me warn you I have power enough to take care of you too!"

When Father Sanchez said that, he caught himself.

"I don't mean that the way it sounded. I mean, I would take care of things that also concerned you, but only as it pertains to what was stolen from us."

"I understood your meaning the first time. But tell me, Father Sanchez, what is it your brotherhood does? You haven't been too clear on that."

"We make sure things run according to order. We make sure lies are not spread, especially when they pertain to the laws of religion. After all, we all have a responsibility to take care of the flock, don't we? There are those who are chosen to lead, and those who must follow. And our duty is to ensure that balance is not upset."

"So, why are you here? Surely there can't be anything important enough to have one such as you tend to."

"My mission is to find your brother and stop him before he infects thousands…no, millions, of people all over the world."

Father Sanchez drew himself over the table, reminding me of a vulture waiting for its prey to die. I knew he was waiting for me to respond to his statement out of fear, but if I did, he would have the upper hand and my meeting with him would only serve his needs, not mine. And mine were to find out anything about the trouble Cheeway was in.

"Is my brother sick with a contagious disease?" I asked, sitting back in my chair to give the impression of not being affected by his position.

"My God," he said, clinching his fists tightly. "Won't you people ever do what you are told? What's it going to take to get you to do what you are supposed to?"

His actions caused the three men standing next to me to react, and I could feel them filling with a tension that was about to be released, on me. Father Sanchez raised his hand, and they backed off, for the present. But I knew we would have a physical encounter before this meeting was over, and I prepared myself by looking at my surroundings…looking for places I could quickly get to, and things to throw while I made my getaway.

"I can understand your frustration, and for that I apologize. But before we part ways, let me explain a little about my Brotherhood. Then you can make up your mind about helping us, or not. Will you listen?"

Silently, I nodded that I would. That set him a little easier as far as looking like a waiting vulture. And seeing him relax, the three men backed away from me as well.

"Our Brotherhood began in the year 60 A.D. Even though we had been organized long before that, we didn't come into real power until then. Many rumors were being spread by non-believers and those who professed to be Christian, but were not. They were causing many innocent people to suffer for what they were saying about the Christ…the one we believe is the only Son of God. You see, after the crucifixion, many believers lived in fear…fear from the Roman Empire, who considered them rebels, and fear from the various Jewish sects who considered them treasonous to the faith. And then, there were the religions to the south that saw Christianity as something that could take away their holy places. Throughout that time, there was no place a Christian could go to feel safe. So they went underground, and lived a life of secrecy, away from the world that said they didn't want anything to do with them but needed to know what they were up to. However, as Christianity spread to more lands, the empire saw a potential threat to their authority. They believed if these people were meeting in secret, they had the potential of rebelling. For by their secrecy, they believed there was too much freedom for them to speak out against the authority of the Roman Empire.

"Before the end of the year 80 A.D., treasonous rumors were being spread about the Christ. Rumors telling of many wondrous things that waited for the true believers after death. Rumors of writings by the Apostles that said this Earth was not their home, and all their pain and illness could be taken away if they would learn the secrets they had been given to share. Other rumors were spread telling of the return of the Son of God, and how he would retake his thrown here on Earth. But he could not return until the way had been prepared, and what needed to be done, was to be found in secret places where ancient records were kept. In each of those places, records showing the time, and conditions for his return, were recorded. Within these writings, which were said to be located in lands not known of at the time, were three warnings. They told what was needed before his return could manifest. And, what would happen if it were not. I have seen these writings, and I can say without doubt, while they appear to be valid, they are not. They were written to break down the authority of governments, and our established way of life…balances all of us need in order to continue as we have. These writings were recorded long before the Christ shared them with his Apostles. But they did not create panic among the governments of the world until the apostles began speaking of them, and then sealed them away in a secret place. They didn't tell anyone where their secret place was, they only spoke of what was contained in the writings. And, because of these secret documents, many vicious lies began around 80 A.D. What had been written, then hidden by the apostles, was being added to by anyone wanting to gain notoriety. And the best way for them to do that was to change or alter what was written to reflect their own personal needs, and not any heavenly truth that might have been shared.

"Our order was begun by the Roman Empire. We were called in to find their records, then destroy them. However, we conceived a plan that would allow us to gain popular standing with the Roman government. It was a plan that would allow us to remain in power long after they would fall. And stay in power we have. We offered to discover the Apostles hidden records, then review them to determine if they had validity, or were just a bunch of lies. We assured the Roman Empire we would not release anything that could undermine their authority. But in order to do that, we would have to be funded and given a charter, one that would allow us to work independently from all their officials, and report only to the highest authority in Rome. For almost a generation, we searched for the missing records of the Apostles. As our search expanded, and our numbers increased, so did our funding. For in the process of our search, we discovered other ancient records that spoke of the same things the Apostles were said to have written. And at each site we discovered, we removed all writing and references, recorded them, then burned and destroyed the originals along with their temples. We determined these prophecies were written by people who were not satisfied with the government that had authority over them at the time, and they wrote these lies to get the masses to revolt, and overthrow those they accused of having control over them.

"In the year 97 A.D., we discovered the hiding place of the Apostles records. When we informed Rome of our finding they were elated, and gave us a new status, one that would remain with us throughout the Christian World. We were given the title of Examiners with complete freedom to determine what writings, of any kind, would be acceptable, and which would not. And, we were given the right to administer whatever punishment we deemed necessary to anyone spreading unholy beliefs. However, our Brotherhood changed again, and Rome decided to send us undercover so we might be more effective. More than one hundred years after the Crucifixion, Christians were becoming more open. They maintained small pockets of their secret society, but for the most part, many knew who they were, and their numbers were growing. This was becoming a drain on Roman society, and they called on our order to infiltrate their meetings and determine if they were speaking seditiously about Roman rule. We convinced Rome to allow the Christians to gather openly while we became a trusted order within their church. That allowed the government to keep them in check, and offered us an opportunity of reviewing everything written and spoken from the church. The writings we considered seditious, we would stop, and deal swiftly with everyone involved. But more importantly, we could keep an ever constant vigil for other locations where records citing the Ancient Prophecies were hidden. When information concerning them would surface, we would be the first ones there, and stop it before it could spread to the population. By citing the dangers shrouding these Ancient Prophecies, which are nothing more than religious lies written by malcontents, we have successfully placed members of our Brotherhood in key government positions throughout the world. We have access to everyone's records, no matter what country they live in. We can find whomever we need to. We travel this world with complete immunity, no matter what country we are in. And we maintain authority to deal swiftly with anyone who would disrupt the established way of life.

"So you see, Speaking Wind, had it not been for the Brotherhood, the Christian Church might not ever have come into the light. In fact, they might have disappeared from the face of the Earth altogether. We bring order to both sides. To the governments of the world, we assist them in maintaining authority over their population by ensuring religious and political lies are not spread. And, to the Christian Church, we provide them with a means of worshipping openly, without fear of reprisal. By assuring governments remain in control, we have niched a place for our Brotherhood that is beyond reproach, and those who assist us are amply rewarded. To date, we have discovered many of the hiding places for these so called ancient writings, and we know the location of others, but we have not uncovered them yet. We are waiting to see who will be drawn to them. We believe your brother has mistakenly uncovered one we did not know about, and he has unwittingly been led to believe what he found was truth. But, I assure you, it is not. All he has uncovered is a very old lie, one that could disrupt order for everyone around the world.

"I only want to speak to your brother, Speaking Wind, that's all. I just want to explain what he found is a lie...one that will do more harm than he can imagine. If you help us, I guarantee you will be handsomely rewarded. You can have money, political favors, or any job you want. You can write your own ticket and be set for the rest of your life. What about it, doesn't that sound good to you? After all, it isn't like I am asking you to do something against the church. This is only a small favor you would be doing, but your reward could be whatever you want. The information your brother thinks is true isn't. It can only bring disorder for everyone. If you could help to avoid this, and be rewarded handsomely, wouldn't you do it? What do you have to lose? After all, we only want to talk to him, nothing more."

"My brother tells me there have been two attempts on his life, Father Sanchez," I began. "Have you, or your Brotherhood, been responsible for that?"

"I believe your brother has a very active imagination, Speaking Wind. All we were trying to do was talk to him, and explain what he discovered is a lie...one that could bring disaster to everyone."

"I have known him all my life, Father Sanchez, and I know he doesn't have an over active imagination. If he said there have been two attempts on his life, I believe him...not you."

Father Sanchez looked at me with eyes burning bright with anger, ready to unleash it on me.

"Grab him!" he yelled to the three men. Immediately, my arms were held behind my back and I felt something hard press against my ribs from the man standing on my left.

"Don't move, Speaking Wind," the man to my left said. "My gun is pointed right at you."

"You'll burn in hell for this, young man! I'll make sure of it!" Father Sanchez said, as spit flew from his mouth.

Suddenly, there was a crash at the front door of Sadie's and Nahe walked in with two deputies. Another crashing sound accompanied theirs, from the back of the kitchen and out walked two more deputies, all wearing badges and side arms.

"You...you in the black vest standing by the table, don't move or I'll open fire!" Nahe said, pointing his revolver at me.

Without lowering his gun, he walked to the table and told one of the deputies to cuff me and take me to his truck.

"Thanks for holding him, we've been looking for this one all day," Nahe said, prying three sets of hands away from me.

I felt myself being transferred from one set of guards to another and a set of handcuffs fasten around my wrists. However, instead of being tightened to the point of hurting, they were loose.

"Hold them up with your hands," the deputy whispered very quietly in my ear. "We'll have you out of this in a minute."

"What do you think you're doing officer?" Father Sanchez said, pushing his way to my side of the table.

"Taking my man into custody," Nahe replied.

"But he is with us; you have no business here!"

"This is my prisoner, sir. Whatever complaints you have can be taken up with the judge. But I'm not releasing custody of him until he is tried in a court of law."

Father Sanchez walked directly in front of Nahe, his eyes squinting to keep his rage from pouring out.

"Do you know what this is, officer?" Father Sanchez demanded.

"Kinda looks like a passport, but I don't have much experience in those matters ya know."

"It is a diplomatic passport, and we are under the protection of your country's diplomatic laws. I tell you, this man is with me, and as such, he is accorded the same protection we are!"

"Then show me his passport."

"What?"

"Show me his passport, and I'll release him to you," Nahe stated flatly.

"I am not with these men, officer!" I yelled.

"Sheriff, if you please," Nahe returned.

"I'm not with these men, Sheriff. They're forcing me to go with them."

"Ya see what happens when you get into trouble? First it starts out small, then grows into bigger and bigger things. Look at you now. Bet if you could, you wouldn't have started this life of crime. But now we've caught up with you and you'll pay for what you've done.

"Now go to the truck with my deputy, I'll be there shortly."

"Tell me, Sheriff, just what has this man done?" Father Sanchez demanded.

"He stole chickens!" Nahe replied.

"What?!" Father Sanchez spurted out, shaking with rage.

"Stealing chickens! You have bothered me for this? You're taking him away for stealing chickens?"

"Two of them!" Nahe replied. "And around these parts, that's a pretty serious offense. Don't know 'bout you diplomats, but to us, that's food off our table. You know, a hungry family with kids n' all."

"I don't believe this!" Father Sanchez blurted out, as he reached insider his jacket for something.

Nahe waived his revolver in front of Father Sanchez. He wanted to remind him he was outnumbered, and not prepared for a confrontation. Father Sanchez looked around for anything to squeeze, then looked at me, then Nahe, and then his left eye began to quiver.

"Do you know who I am, Sheriff? Do you realize what I can do to you, and this whole town if I wanted?"

"Nope, don't know you, or what you could do. But like I said, if you want to tell me, you'll have to wait for court to convene."

"And when will that be?"

"In about a week from now, I imagine. Unless we have a serious crime take place before that."

"You mean someone might steal a pig? Bet that's gonna make the news!" I said, looking at Father Sanchez.

"Come on, criminal, you're at the end of your trail," Nahe said, as he walked me out the front door of Sadie's.

Father Sanchez screamed threats to us as we left, but the laughter from the customers was too loud to hear what he was saying. As we left the restaurant, I saw Father Sanchez through the front window. He reminded me of an exposed nerve, ready to explode. He was standing next to the table yelling, shaking, and pointing fingers at everyone. Most likely telling them what he could do to them. And all the while getting more and more angry, because his threats made everybody laugh harder at him.

"Glad I'm not that important, brother. Don't think I would like that much respect. Sorry 'bout pointing my gun at you, Speaking Wind, but I wanted to be ready in case one of those goons tried to get the draw on me."

"That's all right, Nahe. Talk about perfect timing! They were about to take me away. I mean really take me away!"

"Kinda figured that one out for myself, Speaking Wind," Nahe said, chuckling to himself.

"Okay, guys, everyone meet up at the old barn. See you there."

"Nahe, how did you know?"

"Remember the symbol you drew for me? The one you put on Bending Water's note?"

"Yeah, seems like everyone's been showing that to me lately. Why do you ask?"

"Found out what it meant. And when I did, I grabbed my deputies and made a beeline over here."

"Is it significant?"

"Boy, I'll say! Think you'd better be sitting down when I tell you. You won't believe what it means. Just the sight of it made an old man almost jump out of his skin about an hour ago.

"Get in the truck, I'll tell you on the way."

"Oh yeah, got a message from Cheeway. He told me where to meet him, but we gotta hurry!" Nahe said, starting the truck. "Here, take these keys and unlock your cuffs."

# CHAPTER 5

▼

# MYSTERY OF THE SYMBOL

Nahe began driving while I took off the cuffs.

"Here, Nahe, you might need these again."

"Did that really quick, Speaking Wind. Had much practice taking those things off?"

"No, Nahe, the deputy put them on so loose, I was afraid they would fall off before we got out of the restaurant. Here, the key's in them."

"You said Cheeway got a hold of you with a message? What did he say, where did you see him? Was he all right, or was he hurt? How did he look?"

"Whoa, brother. One thing at a time, okay? First I need to tell you about the symbol you drew for me. There's a lot behind that story, and I think you need to hear about it first."

"All right, Nahe, but first tell me if Cheeway is all right."

"He's fine, Speaking Wind. Says he'll be waiting for us in a special place. But, sit back for now and let me tell you what I discovered about the symbol. I believe who Father Sanchez really is will make sense to you when you hear this. Who were those three giants with him? Don't recall seeing any of our people get that big. Just one of them working as a deputy would do the trick. One look at them even gives me second thoughts about breaking any law."

"You should have been where I was, Nahe. Don't think you would be so quick to want them with you."

"Guess not, brother," Nahe said, leaning back from the steering wheel.

Then, he pushed his hat up, took a deep breath, and began his story.

"We gotta stop by the church on the way out. You okay with that, Speaking Wind?"

"What are you talking about, Nahe! We just got out of one mess with Father Sanchez and his three goons. You want them to catch us again?"

"Don't worry 'bout them, brother. They aren't going anywhere, not for awhile that is. You see, they're gonna be stopped for speeding soon as they leave the restaurant. Going to be a long wait for them though, been kinda difficult getting through to the DMV lately. Especially when my deputies know that already."

"How do you know they'll be speeding, Nahe? What if they are going slower than the speed limit?"

"No one knows what the speed limit is in certain parts of town, brother. Not posted, and left to the discretion of my deputies, if you know what I mean. So relax, we got enough time for this one stop. Even if they do find us at the church, we won't be alone. Got a lot of people looking out for us now. Seems like you and I must be the only ones who don't know about the symbol drawings. But we need to stop at the church to confirm what Running Dog told me.

"Not that I don't believe him, but I gotta see for myself. If I can get a few questions answered in the meantime, so much the better."

"Is that what made you come for me when you did, Nahe, and with four deputies?"

"No, Speaking Wind. Goes further than that. Guess we have time enough to go into that now. Remember Running Dog? He used to have a still in the mountains behind town."

"Yeah! I remember him. We would sneak up on him and say we were from the revenuer's office. Then laugh watching him break, or hide, all the stuff he made. But that was a long time ago, Nahe, and he was really old then. Is he still around?"

"Yup, in his eighties now, I guess."

"What's he doing now? From what I remember about him, he only wanted to make whisky and drink it."

"That's all he ever did, that one. Now, he just walks around town looking for things to eat. The shopkeepers turn their head the other way when he comes in. They know he doesn't have money to buy anything. And as long as he only steals what he needs for the day, they let him think he's getting away with it. Only one time I had to come down on him though. Was when he put a mask on himself and got caught walking into someone's house. Wanted to raid their icebox, that's all. What really made it funny though was he brought a handful of dandelions with him, something like a cat burglar from the movies would do. Guess he was gonna leave them when he finished eating their food, but he didn't get that far. When his belly was full, he went to the bedroom to leave his flowers for the owner. But when he walked in, the floor creaked and woke the owner up. Should a seen the look on his face when the lights came on! It was all I could do to keep from laughing."

"You were there, Nahe?"

"Was my house he broke into! When I heard the floor creak, I turned on the light and saw his face not more than two inches from mine. Thought he was going to kiss me, or something. That sent a real chill down my spine. Anyway, I had to lock him up, but after I had him wash all the dishes he used, then take out the trash. Didn't want to do anything serious to him though. He's really a harmless old man now, wouldn't harm anyone. Besides, don't none of us lock our doors at night, and if I made a big deal over this, it would have caused some of the people here to panic. You remember what its like living in a small town, don't you? Anyway, I kept him in jail for a couple of days and had him do some cleaning. Thought that was more than enough punishment for his crime. He hasn't done anything like that since. So, guess he learned his lessons."

"Don't think just seeing your face when the lights came on was enough punishment for him?"

"Would have thought that myself, but I believe Running Dog has been messing with the fire water too long. Don't think he has much of a brain left."

"So what's he have to do with uncovering the mystery of the symbol, Nahe?"

"Oh yeah, kinda get off track sometimes ya know. Here's how it started. We planned for me to wait behind the restaurant for you. Next to the back door I opened, remember? And I did, but when you were in there for quiet a while, I thought things were going smooth, or you would have made some kind of noise for me to hear. Thought I would take it easy and look at Bending Water's note again. The symbol you drew, plus the one she placed on it was drawing my attention. Like they wanted to tell me something. Anyway, I took her note and leaned up against the hedges behind the restaurant. I knew I was close enough to hear you if you got into trouble, and could have been there quick. I was holding the note in my hands to study the drawings closer. Then lowered the note to give myself time to think. However, as I was trying to remember where I had seen those symbols before, my fingers must have relaxed a little too much, and the note slid out and fell to the other side of the hedge. What I didn't know was Running Dog had copped some day old bread and thought he found a safe place to eat it on the other side of the hedge, right behind me. Well, it didn't take long for the action to begin. I heard paper crinkling, and thought one of the small animals had gotten a hold of the note. When I looked over the hedge to see what it was, I saw Running Dog looking at the drawings on the note. When I saw who it was, I started to ask for my paper back. But before I could, Running Dog looked up, saw me looking at him over the hedge, and made great efforts in getting away from me, while screaming as loud as he could. Shook me up, just seeing Running Dog in a panic you know. At first I thought something bit him, or someone put something bad in the breads he stole. But that wasn't the cause for his fear. It appeared to be me, and I couldn't understand why. Screaming at the top of his lungs he wasn't ready to die, he made one attempt after the other to get up, and run away. Just as he was about to get off the ground, he would fall back down with his face looking back at the note. Then, he would scream again, try to get up and fall down again. By the time he managed to get himself off the ground, he was covered with a lot of grass and mud. Thought he might be hurt, so I waited, and watched. When he was able to stand up, he looked at me and began making warning signs. You know, the kind all of us grew up knowing, when we want to keep an evil spirit away. He shouted at me a couple more times, then took off running. But at his age, running is like a slow walk to you and me. And I knew there wasn't any hurry to chase him. He couldn't have gotten far anyway, not before he needed to rest. But if I started chasing him, he would probably hurt himself, and that would not be good. So I shouted at him."

"Hold on, Running Dog! You're gonna hurt yourself if you keep this up."

"No! Not ready to die yet. Still young, not want to go!"

"Running Dog, if you don't stop now, I'm gonna take you to jail. Want that? Got a lot more cleaning that needs to be done."

"Okay, no more run. What you want with Running Dog? Come to take him away? Not want to go now, have plenty work to do."

"What you talking about, Running Dog? I just want to ask you a question, that's all."

"That all you want?"

"Yeah, I promise. But if you don't want to answer my question here, you can do it in jail while you clean. Is that what you want?"

"Running Dog not do anything wrong! You know that!"

"Been littering, Running Dog? That can get you a couple of days in the cooler."

"I not throw paper at me, you did! You want kill Running Dog, that sign you throw at me on paper, I know! That sign all people know. What you want kill me, Nahe? I no do you bad. Not no more."

"I picked up the paper and looked at it. Seemed like Running Dog knew more about this than I gave him credit for."

*"You know these drawings?"*

*"Running Dog know all bout them, Nahe. But why you don't? Everyone know bout those drawings since little kids. Look like I know more 'bout something than you, Nahe. Maybe you look at me with better face now, huh?"*

*"Tell me about these drawings will ya? Come sit with me. I won't make you go to jail."*

*"Not make Running Dog clean whole town again either, huh?"*

*"No, not enough cleaning for someone as fast as you. Come on, sit and tell me what you know bout these drawings."*

*"Drawing not for me, Nahe? You not want me dead?"*

*"Of course not, Running Dog, I just want to know what these drawings mean. I remember seeing them, or hearing about them. Just can't remember what they're about. Been along time since I was little, ya know."*

*"Okay, Nahe, I sit with you. Kinda like old times now. Times when Running Dog's friends still like him."*

"I really like old Running Dog, Speaking Wind. He only has one tooth left in his head now, and when he smiles, you can see it. It's right in front of his mouth."

"Running Dog finally sat down with me. That caused him, and me, to breathe a little easier. Thought I would have to take him to the hospital from a heart attack. Ya know, the way he reacted to the drawings and all. But now, he calmed down. Now that he knew I didn't make the drawings for him, that is."

*"Tell me what these drawings are about, will ya?*

*"Okay, Nahe, but only because you friend to people here, and to me now. But you no make trouble for me because what I tell you about the drawing sign?"*

*"Won't be no trouble, Running Dog. Just as long as you tell me straight truth. Understand?"*

*"Only straight truth, Nahe. I promise."*

*"Drawings very old, Nahe. Older than the alive ones can remember. But I remember what parents tell me bout them. Remember very well cause someone tried to use on me, long time ago. Wanna hear that story from me?"*

*"Not now, Running Dog. Just tell me bout the drawings and what they mean. You can tell me your story later. Don't have much time right now, okay?"*

*"Stay near those drawings and you have no time at all! Better to get away from them, Nahe, no go near one who make this drawing either. It bring big danger, not only for you, but for whole village. Drawings made by old white skins with black and*

*brown robes. Ones who used to say our people all gonna die and go to hell if we not do like they say. They gone long time now from lands, but not drawings. Drawings still around, still being used to make fear be born among the people."*

*"What do they mean, Running Dog? Do you know?"*

*"They mean death for whoever get one!"*

*"You mean from a long time before, when the black robes were new to these lands?"*

*"No! Mean now! They still come to some around here, Nahe. Just they come in different way now, not like before. But they still come! In old times, when men in black and brown robes first come to our lands, they not have many other white skins with them, so they not say truth for what they want. Only tell the people they come to save them, and want to see how they pray. People take them to many sacred places, and let them meet our holy men. These black and brown robes write something down on sacred places they visit, then give drawing of same thing to holy men. They not say what it mean, only say holy men must hold it till someone ask for it. When more white men come, black and brown robes feel more better 'bout their place among the people. They tell white men who wear the iron on their body, and ride the great animal where to find holy men who have this drawing. And, show them sacred places where they make the drawing in stone."*

*"Which drawing are you speaking of, Running Dog? Is it the one with the hooded man holding a sword, or the one with the cross inside a triangle."*

*"Only one drawing ever used to mark things and people for death, Nahe. It one with cross inside triangle. No other marking ever used."*

*"But what about the other one? The one with the hooded man holding a curved sword? Wasn't it used by them as well?"*

*"Yeah, but not for same reason, Nahe. Drawing of the man holding sword used to show who they were. The black and brown robes would show this drawing to white men with iron skin. That say they have power to know what needed to be destroyed, and when white men with iron skin see this, they bow to them, and do whatever they say. But white men with black and brown robes not carry it outside their robes. In those days, they carry it inside their pocket. Don't know why, maybe they not want it to be stolen or something. It all made of silver, and you know how much they like silver, Nahe. Many white skins kill to have it. But other mark, one with cross inside triangle, that dangerous one. When holy men show this drawing black and brown robes give them to white men with metal skin, we not see those holy men again. They gone from the people and no one know what happen to them. When black and brown robes take ones who ride the great animals to sacred lands where they carve sign in the stone, they destroy that place too. If they cannot burn or tear it down, they make it so dirty with their filth, no one can use sacred places again. That why cross in triangle danger-*

*ous, Nahe. It still mean you gonna die if it come to you. Mark still around here now. Go look at wall behind picture of crucifixion in big church, Nahe, it still there. Right on wall behind painting."*

"I looked at Running Dog, and could see he was telling me straight truth, Speaking Wind. If he wasn't, I could've seen it in his face. Just something I know from doing this kind of work so long, ya know. However bizarre his story is, we need to check it out. That's why we have to stop by the church, Speaking Wind. To confirm what running Dog and someone else told me 'bout."

"Someone else knew about the drawings, Nahe? Who?"

"Can't go into that now, brother, we're here."

Nahe stopped the truck and we went into the church. It was one of the really old ones and had walls thicker than a conventional doorway. There was a window at the top of one wall and the sun was shining in through it. The ceilings were so high, there appeared to be a floating mist as the sunlight passed between it, and the floor.

Once inside, we looked for the picture Running Dog told Nahe about. For that was the confirmation he needed, perhaps to believe there was any significance to the symbol drawing and convince himself this was not one big hoax. I, too, felt the need for confirmation. It seemed like I was living a dream, or nightmare, from all that had happened already.

"There it is," Nahe said, pointing to a huge painting of the crucifixion. "Come on, help me take it down will ya?"

Nahe and I lifted the huge painting off its hook and lowered it to the floor. We were careful not to damage the painting, as it was one of some worth. But our efforts caused us to kick over one of the stools next to us, and the sounds brought another visitor.

"The silver is in the rectory, gentlemen. That is, if you don't think you already have enough," came a voice from behind us.

When we turned to see who was speaking, Nahe put his hand up in a gesture of greeting and spoke.

"It's me, Father Juan. Just looking for something, that's all."

"Well, Nahe, if you wanted to see something, why didn't you ask me? You know I would show you anything, nothing to hide here. What brings you here today, and who is this with you? He looks kind of familiar."

"This is my brother, Speaking Wind. He has come for a visit. We haven't seen each other for many years and thought it was time to renew our acquaintance."

"Tell me, Speaking Wind, why do you look so familiar to me?" Father Juan asked, looking at me as one would look at a book. "Have I seen you before?"

"Perhaps some years ago, Father. I used to come here with Grandfather and Two Bears."

"Grandfather and Two Bears. Oh yes, now I remember. There was another young one with you, a boy by the name of…let me see…Cheeway! Yes, now I remember, all four of you would visit Nahe and his grandfather, White Eagle, didn't you?"

"You have a good memory, Father. Thank you for remembering us."

"What are you doing now? Grandfather, Two Bears, Cheeway, and you of course."

"No time for that, Father Juan," Nahe said, placing his hand on the old priest's shoulder. "I'm on a case and there might be a clue I need in your church."

"Oh yes, help yourself, Nahe," Father Juan said, as he looked around for anything else we might have taken down. "If there is anything I can do to help you, let me know. After all, I have served this church for over thirty years and know many of its secrets. As long as it doesn't violate my laws of confession, I will be more than happy to share whatever I know."

"Thank you, Father. If I find what I'm looking for, I just might need to ask you a few questions."

With that, Nahe turned and looked at the wall for any sign of the drawing or symbol.

"Here it is, I found it!"

Nahe took his hand and brushed away the cobwebs that had gathered behind the picture. As he did, the symbol of the cross inside a triangle became obvious. Beneath it was another etching in the plaster covered adobe wall. It was an exact replica of what was on the silver medallion Father Sanchez and his three body-guards wore on theirs.

"Now I will take you up on that offer, Father Juan," Nahe said, looking intently at what he had uncovered. "Look at these symbols. They must have been there for quite awhile to have all these cobwebs over them. Know anything about them? Or who might have put them there?"

I was entranced by what Nahe found, and didn't look at Father Juan immediately. However, when there was no answer, I turned to see what had happened.

Father Juan was standing behind me, staring at the etchings in the wall with a look of horror on his face. His mouth and eyes were wide open, and his breathing was short and shallow.

"You look like you've seen a ghost, Father," Nahe said, reaching for his arm. "Sit down, you look like your legs are about to give out on you."

As soon as Nahe said that, Father Juan fell to the floor. His eyes were open, but he wasn't moving. He just lay there staring at the ceiling, and the two etchings on the wall.

"Is he dead, Nahe?"

"No, don't think so, Speaking Wind. Think he just passed out. Come on, help me get him on one of these benches will ya?"

We picked him up and laid him on a bench. Then, Nahe went to get some water and left me alone with the old priest. Before Nahe could return, Father Juan began making moaning sounds. The kind one makes as they are regaining consciousness.

"Not here, please God, not here! This can't be real, not here!" Father Juan kept repeating, as his eyes began to focus.

"Here, drink some water, it will make you feel better," Nahe said, returning with a glass. "You hurt or anything? You had quite a fall, want me to call a doctor?" Nahe asked, holding his head up.

"No, Nahe, I'm fine…really. Just a bad shock is all, but I'm all right now. Help me sit up will you?"

"Sure you're all right, Father?"

"Oh, really getting dizzy now and I'm having difficulty seeing. Perhaps you should call a doctor, Nahe."

"Got better than that. Speaking Wind?"

When Nahe called out my name, I knew what he wanted me to do. So without hesitating, I placed one hand on the Father's head and the other over his heart. Then I called on the healing river of the Earth Mother to flow through him.

It didn't take long before he was able to stand up and see again, but the look on his face told me he was surprised at what I had done.

"Oh, I better sit down again. Two shocks in one day are a lot for an old man like me. What did you do to me, Speaking Wind? I haven't felt anything like that before."

"Just a quick healing, Father, the kind our people have done for as long as I can remember. Nothing to worry about though, just brought you into balance. There were a few places that needed a little help, and were causing you to feel dizzy and unable to see.

"How do you feel now?" I asked, looking deeply into his eyes.

"Better than I've ever felt before. I'm still a little light headed, but feel like I'm being held in my mother's arms. I feel very secure, thank you. Thank you for whatever it was you did. I know this is a gift from God, and I am grateful for it."

"God goes by many names, Father, but in truth, all names call to the same one."

"If you're all right now, would you answer a few questions about these etchings on the wall?" Nahe asked, sitting next to Father Juan.

"Of course, Nahe, just give me some time to get over the shock of seeing them here, and in my church. I had no idea they were real. I thought it was one of those made up horror stories to keep people scared of doing anything wrong. But from what I see, I know it isn't so. And for that, I am truly sorry for having doubted everyone who came to me with stories about this…this dreadful thing here.

"Whew! What a shock to see this here, Nahe! Right here in the very church I have lived in all these years, and under my nose. I can't believe what I am seeing, really!"

Reaching his hand out to the air, Father Juan pointed at the etchings on the wall, then to me.

"Speaking Wind, what a wonderful gift you have been given. Use it for good, don't let it go to waste."

"I will remember, what you say, Father, and will use it in the way it was meant to be used."

"Father, we don't have much time. Anything you could tell us about these etchings or what's behind them, would be helpful," Nahe said, looking at the old man.

"Very well, I will explain what I know. If you need to delve further into this matter, I can let you see some old church records that also speak about this," Father Juan said, as he placed his hands over his mouth. "But I never gave them a second thought. I looked at them as a parent would look at a fairy tale told to children."

After taking a few deep breaths, Father Juan began telling us what he knew about the two etchings on the church wall.

"It was a very long time ago, my friends. A very long time…we were new in this land and felt very much alone. For there was much work to do, and we had to convert a new race of people. For the most part, our order was put in charge of providing spiritual comfort to the king's soldiers. But soon, all that changed. And we could no longer remain simple spiritual providers."

Father Juan looked at Nahe and me with a face of bewilderment and confusion before continuing.

"This is where it begins then, this thing I believed was only a cruel rumor started by those who were lost in their own ignorance. When the new world was discovered, Columbus was given a charter by the King of Spain. He was not only to determine if the natives were hostile, but was to search out their pagan practices and destroy them. I guess it is safe to say he was the first who used what you see on the wall in these new lands. At least that is how the story has been told to me.

"However, Columbus was not true to his charter. He began instigating more trouble than he needed to. After all, he wasn't in the new world more than three months before he started shipping men and women back to Spain as slaves. In his chronicles, he spoke of the indigenous population here as a farmer would speak of their heard of cattle. And all this caused his quick demise as the once highest head of state for all of the new world. Not more than seven years after his discovery, he was taken back to Spain in chains. He was forbidden to ever set foot in the new world again because of a treasonous act he had done. But, as the story goes, a very powerful group of men secretly met with the King and convinced him not to kill Columbus. They said Columbus was doing their bidding, and should not be punished for helping them keep the faith, and government, intact. Because if Columbus had not done what he did, not only the church, but also the royal way of life, would be in jeopardy. It has been said, this group of men knew the exact location of the New World, but would only allow one country to claim it. They chose Columbus to do their bidding for them, you see. What we've been told about Columbus going from King to King looking for a backer to his expedition is not entirely true. I've been told he went from King to King looking for one that would agree with conditions set by this powerful—and secretive—organization he represented. And his time was spent showing them what they had to gain if they agreed to their conditions of discovery. And, from all accounts, those conditions were made by the secret organization who spoke to the King of Spain on his behalf. Apparently they wanted to keep this new discovery to themselves. It had something to do with what they were searching for. And, if there were too many people settling the new lands, they might get in their way, or come across whatever it was they were searching out before they did. And for them, that would not do. They were prepared to do whatever it took to keep that from happening. One of their conditions was to be given unquestioned rule over the new lands and the natives there. They were willing to give whatever King they chose the major share of all wealth discovered. And they would only retain a small portion of it. They said they were more interested in discovering new things than acquiring wealth. I believe they already had enough wealth, and power, if they could speak to Kings that way. And like so many of my order, when we first heard of this, we were skeptical. But look at how the new world was handled, my friends. Why did it take over a hundred years before another country established major settlements here? It wasn't like they didn't know where this great land was! They had maps and sailors who knew how to get here, but they didn't come. In those days, every King had spies in all courts. They knew what every royal was involved in. And, I am sure the way to the new world was not as closely guarded as history makes it out to be. I don't think they were all that concerned with the armies of other countries either, especially since they spent their whole life fighting among themselves. No, I think there was another reason. One that caused the Kings of the time to fear going against a power greater than they could fight. I believe it was this secretive group of men who were responsible for this. The ones who somehow put those symbols in my church. They were said to have gone to all the Kings of the known world and told them if they attempted to settle the new world before they were given permission, they would be overthrown and their country given to someone else. Another who would do what they were told. I'm still not sure what all that means, my friends. But it goes with what I have heard about these markings, and their use."

Father Juan took a moment to look at Nahe and me. I could see the look on his face was one of anguish because of what he was about to share next.

"I don't know how to say this without sounding like some kind of demon," Father Juan said, holding his hands over his heart. "It is not pleasant, and may cause you some pain. Are you sure you wish me to continue, Nahe?"

"Yes, Father, keep going. If I don't find what I am looking for, there could be someone very special hurt from this lack of knowledge."

I put my hand on Father Juan's shoulder.

"It's all right, old one, those wounds have been healed for Nahe and me, now. We don't hold anyone responsible for events of the past. But we need to hear what you know so it doesn't repeat itself again."

When I said this, Father Juan gave me a look of confusion.

"You mean what I am telling you has a possibility of happening again? Today?"

"Could be, Father. But we won't know till we hear what you have to say," Nahe returned.

"Very well then," Father Juan said, as he looked at the etchings on the wall again. "This is the hard part of the story to hear. It's been said, this group of powerful men were an established order within the holy church. But they were more concerned with politics than religion. They came to the new world just after Columbus had been forbidden to ever return. They sent members of their order to establish positions of power among the new inhabitants, but there is more to it. What they came for was to discover how the natives worshipped, then report back to their brotherhood who would send them instructions for what they were to do next."

"You mean they sent word to the church in Rome or Spain, Father?" Nahe asked quickly.

"Neither, Nahe. I heard they received their instructions from another place, a place their order was centrally located, but was much more powerful than the church, or any monarch in the world. It has been said they would often decide which King would win a battle, long before it would take place. They were said to be involved in religion, politics, currency, and food distribution, and even the personal lives of everyone in the world. Their order was said to have recorded everything that's been discovered from the first day of our civilization. And they used this information to black mail the Kings and Queens of the world to do their bidding."

"You mean if the ruling monarchs would not go along with them, they would release what information they had on them?"

"Kind of, Nahe, but much worse," Father Juan continued. "They were said to have such unlimited power over world affairs, they could completely shut off any countries food and make their population starve to death. Next, they would spread rumors about the King, or Queen, telling the people their rulers were responsible for them not eating, that the food they were supposed to have was being hoarded by the ruling family, or being sold to another country for a profit. And, they would authenticate what they said by providing credible witnesses or documents, proving to the masses what they said was true."

"And that's how they did business then?"

"And now, from what I have been told, Nahe. But let me go back a little. I seem to be getting off course."

Father Juan took a deep breath, looked at the symbols on the wall again, and then made the sign of the cross over himself.

"You've heard about all the killing when the Spaniards first arrived, haven't you? Well, it wasn't the priests or their following who did this, Nahe. It was the men who wore the two symbols you see on the wall of my church. And what I see before me, tells me that I, too, have an equally great burden to carry for all of that too. My telling you about this, in a way, eases my guilt for not having listened to what the natives here have been saying all these years. Perhaps what I share with both of you will make the pain I feel a little more tolerable. When we first came to the new world, there were approximately twelve million natives living here.

And in less than one hundred years, only half that number remained alive. Do you know why?"

"Most was from disease wasn't it? The ones that plagued Europe for centuries," I offered.

"Yes, this is what history tells you. But what wasn't recorded is the order of men who wore the symbols you see on the wall before you. They were responsible for most of the death that took place among the natives. They came up with a plan to bring members of various tribes into towns that were infected with a killing plague. We were told to go out and look for a village that had been marked by them. They told us they had sent missionaries into those villages and began the conversion process to Christianity. All we needed to do was bring a few of them into our town, baptize them, then allow them to return to their village with gifts of blankets and food. Thinking we were doing a great service to the church, our priests would go to the marked villages and return to their city to do just that. Not knowing that bringing them into our villages would infect them, and giving them blankets and food to take back would infect their whole tribe. Our priests were told the key members of a village, or tribe, would have a piece of paper with them. And on this paper would be the same mark they had marked the village with. When we found them, we were to bring them back and baptize them. But, in those days, so many were being brought in, the process could take several weeks. Eventually the natives said the white men had invisible bullets which they would shoot their enemies with, and they came to our towns so they could be baptized and live in peace with us. But the invisible bullets did not make a connection for what little we knew of the disease we were spreading. But the men with the symbols did, and there was a journal discovered near Santa Fe that was said to have spoken about it. It was said to have been written by one of these mysterious men. It was a detailed account of the number of native villages that had been successfully wiped out because of their success in infecting them. It also said this method could only be used for a short time, because the inhabitants would eventually develop an immunity. But at present, this was the most effective method of killing off the ones who knew too much, for at least two generations. After that, they would have to employ more conventional means, and mentioned that making a religious war against the natives was being considered."

"What do you mean when you said they wanted to kill the ones who knew too much, Father Juan?" I asked, looking at Nahe. I knew he, too, made the connection of why Father Sanchez and his three men were looking for Cheeway.

"They were said to be looking for hidden sites in the new world. Something about those places seemed to cause them to fear what might be found in them. I don't know what it could have been or why they were looking for them. I only know they considered these places dangerous to mankind, and would do anything to discover where they were, and I believe, kill anyone who knew about them."

"Kinda like Coronado looking for the seven cities of gold, isn't it?" Nahe said, looking at Father Juan.

"Actually, Nahe, it was that secret brotherhood who funded his expedition and sent their own members with them."

"You spoke of the markings these men would make on a village. What markings were these, Father?" I asked, as I looked at the wall carved with the etchings.

"The one with a cross inside the triangle, Speaking Wind. They were said to make this mark on everything they considered dangerous. What they would mark would be destroyed. Either by an infectious disease we would unknowingly give, or by the Conquistadors who were directly ordered to destroy by the secret society."

"These men they marked, Father, was there anything special about them?"

"Yes, there was one prerequisite before they were marked. They had to be a holy man of the village."

"Not a leader?"

"No, Nahe, they weren't interested in leaders. They knew that position could change quickly among the natives. But their holy men, once recognized by the village, were in that position for life, and the people would listen to them without question."

"So they marked the holy men for death using that mark? What about the sacred sites they used to hold ceremony? Surely they couldn't infect them, could they?" I asked.

"That was a real trick, according to what I have heard," Father Jaun explained. "They waited until a village was extremely infected, then they would send one of their doctors to visit. The doctor would use the disguise of coming to heal them, but the truth of the matter was, he wanted to locate where the natives were going to pray. When he did, he would use the same mark, the one with the cross inside the triangle. He would tell the natives this place was the cause of their sickness and when they left, the soldiers would destroy it using any means they could. By then, the holy men were all dead from the disease we gave them. So there was no one the natives could speak to for direction. There was only the sick, and the dying, no one else."

Father Juan held his head down for a moment, reflecting on what he had shared. Then, he took a deep breath, looked up at the etchings on the wall, and continued.

"It has been said, this powerful group of men have always been associated with the Holy Church. They have been with our movement for as long as anyone can remember. However, from what I have heard, they are not like us. Not like we who have dedicated our lives to spreading the teachings of Christ. Rather, they are intent on controlling things. Like making sure what we say does not affect the authorities. It's almost like they are keeping an eye on us for something they haven't found. They seem to be afraid of what it can do to them, or who they represent."

"When you say they aren't like you, Father, what do you mean?" Nahe asked, sitting next to the old priest. "Do you mean they don't wear the same kind of clothes, or they can't give mass like the other priests?"

"Oh no, Nahe, they can do all of that. If fact, I have been told they are trained in the seminary, just like the rest of us. They can give communion, hold confessions, give last rights, and perform any priestly function that I can. But, even though they can do all of that, they choose not to. I have done some research on them and found out their order was started around the first century A.D. They are more political than religious, that is, among the Catholic Church. If it wasn't for them, we wouldn't have been so fortunate with having the financial resources we have today. But even though they can do all the things the other priests do, that's not what I meant. From what I have heard, everyone in their order seems to lack compassion for their fellow human beings. That is something which is just not in them. After all, compassion is what our faith is based on, but they don't reflect this…to anyone. Oh yes, I have heard they train in other religions too. One priest told me he saw someone who wore a crucifix with the same drawing on the wall, working in a Baptist Church one week, then in a Jewish Temple a week later. It didn't make much sense then, Nahe, but now that I see what is on my own church wall, it does. You see, this group of men call themselves The Brotherhood. They believe themselves to be a religious order whose sole purpose is to keep the masses in check by feeding governments information they can use. You know, information that could undermine authority, or something like that. But there is more to this mystery. There have been accounts of people who spoke of things considered dangerous by them, and they disappeared without a trace. When they vanished, there were no questions asked, and the men who have been living in the vicinity posing as priests, rabbis or other religious leaders, disappeared as well, leaving no trace of ever having been there. I've heard accounts of other priests running checks on these men when they first came to their parish. They said when the priests first arrived; everyone had information about them. When they ran credit checks, using their names and social security numbers, they were listed with outstanding credit ratings. But when they left, presumably when their job was done, there was no trace of them to be found. No listing of either their name, or social security number, could be found. It was like they never existed."

"Only heard about them in this country, Father?" Nahe asked, as he got up to look at the symbols on the wall again. "Or have there been accounts from priests in other countries as well?"

"All over, Nahe, not only in this country, but in as many as I have acquaintances in. They all tell the same story about these mysterious men appearing, and then disappearing without a trace. I don't have working relationships only with priests from the Catholic Church, Nahe. I have friends in all religious persuasions, Christian and non-Christian. And, over the years, they have all told me similar stories."

Father Juan looked at me with a questioning look in his eye.

"Is there something more, Father?" Nahe asked.

"Yes, Nahe, there is," Father Juan said, looking up at the etchings on the wall again. "Does the name Father Sanchez mean anything to you, Speaking Wind?"

"Might!" I said, as I jerked back on the bench. "Why do you ask?"

"He and three men came into the church this morning asking questions about you and Cheeway. I don't know what they wanted, but he said they were supposed to meet both of you at Sadie's around noon today. He said they were from an archdiocese in Mexico and were entrusted to give you information. It seemed to be important from the tone of his voice."

"What makes you think of them now, Father?" Nahe asked. "Do you remember something about them? Something I can use?"

"I don't know what you are working on, Nahe, and I don't want to. But when I spoke to him, I noticed he was wearing the same design that's on the wall beneath his crucifix. You know, the one with the hooded man holding the curved sword...Does all of this help?"

"Yes, Father, very much. We gotta go now. There's a lot we have to do."

"Nahe!" Father Juan said, standing up. "What about the painting? I can't put it back myself, and I don't want the parishioners to see what's behind it. That would be like displaying a swastika in the holy lands. It would cause a panic, if you know what I mean."

"Oh, sorry, Father, we'll put it back now."

However, when Nahe and I lifted the large painting to re-mount it, we ran one of the corners into the wall and chipped off the plaster where the two symbols had been carved exposing the original adobe.

"Wait a minute, Speaking Wind!" Nahe said. "Put the painting down, I want to look at something."

"What is it, Nahe?" Father Juan asked. "You didn't find more symbols, did you?"

"No, Father, but I think there is something you need to look at. This adobe here, it seems to be out of place!" Nahe said, as he ran his fingers over a portion of the exposed wall. "It's more than twice the size of the others, and seems to have been put in place without mortar."

"It's loose, Nahe!" I said. "Look, I can move it with my fingers!"

"Can we see if it comes out, Father?" Nahe asked. "Might be something behind it."

"As long as you don't ruin anything, Nahe," Father Juan returned. "Please keep in mind this is a very old church. These walls date back to the fifteen hundreds, and they can't be replaced if you ruin them."

"We will be careful, Father!" Nahe returned, as we moved the large adobe back and fourth.

Soon, it slid out of the wall, exposing a hole that was about two feet high, three feet wide, and two feet deep. Nahe pulled out a flashlight from his belt and looked inside.

"There's something in here, Father! Looks like it might be a book or something like one. Can't tell for sure because there is a lot of dirt on it."

"Let me see, Nahe!" Father Juan said excitedly.

The hole in the wall was too high for Father Juan to see into without standing on something. We put one of the church benches next to the wall to let him stand on it.

"Can I see your light, Nahe?" Father Juan asked. "Yes! I can see what you're talking about now. I believe it is a book! Help me get it out!"

We painstakingly pulled the object from the wall. When we removed the dust that had gathered over it, we saw it was not just a book; rather, it was a book that had been put together a very long time ago, and one that appeared to have been done in a hurry.

The front and back of it were made from thin pieces of wood. There were three holes drilled into the wood and leather straps were inserted to make sure it would not come apart. Then, the whole thing had been covered in a thick wax like substance, perhaps to keep it from being ruined by the passing of time, or weather.

Apparently, the writer did not know how long it would be before someone would discover it. And, he wanted to make sure whatever he wrote would be found intact.

Father Juan went to the rectory to get some ice. He said that was the safest way of removing the wax without disturbing the contents of what was inside.

Soon, we had the wax removed and opened the wood cover. What we found amazed Father Juan so much he had to take a moment to catch his breath.

"Something wrong, Father Juan?" Nahe asked. "You gonna be all right, or should I call for a doctor?"

"Nahe!" Father Juan whispered. "I have lived in this church for over a quarter of a century. And, in that time, I have seen more than my share of life and the disasters that creep into it. But in the last couple of hours, you and Speaking Wind have convinced me of something I always told my parishioners. When you think you have seen all life has to offer, you can still be surprised!"

"You mean the book is important, Father Juan?" I asked.

"It is a treasure, Speaking Wind," he returned. "Look at the date written on the front. It says, the fifteenth of August, in the year of our Lord, 1536. That was about the same time this church was built."

"Any idea who wrote it, or why?" Nahe asked, as he looked at the opened portion. "And what kind of writing is this? I haven't ever seen anything like it before!"

"It's Latin, Nahe!" Father Juan replied. "Much of the writing back then was like that. As for why it was put inside this wall, we won't know about that until I read what's inside. Now let me see if there is a signature on this. Oh no! This can't be!"

"What is it, Father?"

"The name here, Speaking Wind! It's someone I know!"

"Does he work in the church with you?" Nahe asked.

"No, Nahe, that's not what I meant!" the priest continued. "This manuscript was written by a Father Juan Rudolfo. He was the priest I took my name from when I was ordained. But his life has been shrouded in mystery!"

"What do you mean, Father?" I asked. "Could he be the one who put the two symbols on the wall?"

"Could be, Speaking Wind, but I don't believe he was a part of The Brotherhood! Not from all the kindness he had shown to the natives when the Spaniards arrived. Let me give you a little history about him. My namesake, Father Juan

Rudolfo, was one of the earliest of his order to come to the New World. He was loved by the natives here, but not by the government in Mexico, or Spain. He, and his best friend, another priest by the name of Father Paul Saiz, arrived in Mexico City and found the government was allowing many atrocities to be done to the natives. The Spanish government was in the throws of questioning many of the Aztecs at the time, so those who survived the final battle were not killed, just questioned. However, the natives who had no connection with the Aztecs, they were considered expendable and many of them were tortured to death, or experimented on. All in the name of science, or religion. But the Aztecs were being saved for other reasons. They were being questioned about the location of more gold and precious stones. So, Fathers Juan and Paul were not too involved with how they were being treated. But they were quite upset with how the other natives were being treated, and wrote a petition to the Governor General in Mexico City protesting this treatment. But their petition was ignored and sent back to them with a note saying they should concentrate their energies on converting the natives to Christianity before they died. For that was their role in the New World, and if they persisted in meddling in state affairs, they would be sent back to Spain and another order would take their place. However, that did not stop them. They sent another petition to Spain, but the results were the same. That was when they decided to become personally involved with the questioning of the Aztecs. They believed if they could not help the other natives, they might be able to influence the methods being used to question the Aztecs. But during one of their interrogations, something unusual happened. There was an old Aztec man who had been brought in from their captor. Because of his age, they held him for a long time before they got around to questioning him, long enough for some of the other priests to introduce him to the process of Christianity. They told him about God, and how his son Jesus was the savior of all mankind. But the old man told them he already knew about that. He said none of what they were telling him was new. For he had studied from a group of priests who knew about that because they found it in an ancient city, one that had been built long before anyone could count time. At first, the priests did not believe the old man. So they questioned him on things they thought he could not know, not unless he was telling them the truth. But each religious question they would ask, he would answer correctly. But he went one step further. Rather than just giving them the answer they knew, he added to it. He was telling them things they had not heard of before, but all of it made perfect sense to them. Things like a more detailed history of what life was like for the Hebrews in the Old Testament, and what life was like for the Jews in the New Testament. And soon, the old man gave up the role of being converted, to one of teaching the priests things they did not know. When Fathers Juan and Paul heard what the old man had to say, they quickly dismissed the other priests and vowed them to an oath of secrecy. They knew if word got out that this man knew the location of ancient records that spoke of their own beginnings, the government would destroy them. They knew all too well how the officials regarded the natives, how they believed they were beneath them, in every way. But if the government officials knew what the old man had said, they might change their minds about them, even consider them to be a threat to their authority, and destroy this ancient city the old man told them about. And they wanted to explore it before that happened. So they arranged a pardon for the old man and asked him to take them to the ancient city. But some of the priests did not keep their vow of silence and the government officials caught wind of what they were about to do. They could not stop Fathers Juan and Paul from searching, for it was within their rights of religion to do that. But they would not let them look for it alone, not without a large group of soldiers to go with them. They left under the escort of three hundred soldiers, and five hundred native bearers. But when they returned a few months later, there were only a handful left. The rest had either been killed, or killed themselves. But no one knows what really happened, except that they did find an ancient city, but no one would talk about it. That's about all I know about the city, Nahe. But I will say that whatever they found caused the Spanish Government to radically change its mind as to how they regarded the Aztecs. From that moment on, the government spent every available resource at their disposal destroying all Aztec records. Especially anything that made reference to an ancient city. And even those who were being held for questioning as to the location of more gold, were killed. Seemed like whatever they discovered in that mysterious place posed more of a threat than their greed for gold. And for the Spanish government in those days, it must have been something monumental for them to change their attitude so quickly. Soon after their expedition returned to Mexico City, both Fathers Juan and Paul disappeared. No one ever heard from them again. It was like they vanished from the face of the Earth. But this manuscript we found tells me at least Father Juan made it this far. And, I am sure once I translate what he wrote, we will know more about what he found before he died."

"How long will it take you to translate it, Father?" I asked.

"Perhaps I can do it now, Nahe, let me see…"

The priest opened the book, but just as he turned the first page, his mouth fell open. For the pages had not fared well through the centuries and began falling apart the moment they were touched.

"All I can read is what is on the first page, Nahe! If I attempt to turn another page we could lose even that!.........I was right, this was written by Father Juan. He says there had been many attempts on his life, and he fears the worst for his friend Father Paul. He says he left Mexico City at night and made it to this mission where he found safety among the brothers. But he knew that would not last long. It says he believed a powerful organization within the whole church would soon find him, and when they did, they would end his life. He mentions the ancient city. Says they found something more valuable there than all the gold in the world. But this treasure was not in the form of metal, but ancient records...an account of everything the Holy Church is founded on was recorded in that city, but some of it contradicts what the church has been teaching about Christianity. There is a reference he makes to a second version of the Holy Bible. And he believes it is more complete than the one we use today. But that's all I can read, my friends, the rest will remain lost in time due to the deterioration of the remaining pages."

"Sounds like what the priest found could be the same ancient city Cheeway found, Speaking Wind," Nahe whispered.

"Cheeway found an ancient city, Nahe? Where?" Father Juan asked.

"It's not public knowledge, Father," I said.

"Well, tell me this then. Did he find it in the Yucatan, near Campeche?"

"I don't know, Father. You see we are going to meet him soon and I'm sure he will tell us then."

"Then I must go with you," Father Juan said. "I must, and I won't take no for an answer. Perhaps I can be of assistance. You might be surprised."

Nahe and I thought about it for a moment, then agreed it might be advantageous to have Father Juan come with us. For he did have knowledge about the ancient city, and might be able to fill in whatever blanks Cheeway might have found.

"One more thing, Nahe, I would like to bring a friend of mine, Father Joe. His background in this sort of history could prove invaluable as well, and he is much younger than I. So if we need more man power, he could be helpful."

"What are you planning, Father?" Nahe asked. "I have known you for many years, and know you don't do anything on just a whim."

"Just this, Nahe," the priest replied. "You have been chased by Father Sanchez, and he represents the dark side of the church. I believe, in order for all of you to have a more objective perspective, you need Father Joe and me with you. You know, someone from the light side to even things up! Most of us are not like this Father Sanchez, or his order, Nahe! And perhaps our presence with you will remind you of that. If Cheeway has found the ancient city, the ramifications could be universal. Especially if The Brotherhood Father Sanchez represents wants to suppress what is there, like they have throughout the centuries. I believe you will need us with you. I am not speaking out of idle curiosity, but I am speaking from my heart and spirit. May we accompany you?"

"Very well, Father, you can come. But let me warn you, we have to travel fast. That Father Sanchez and his three goons are really hot on our trail!"

# CHAPTER 6

▼

# THE MEETING

Nahe and I returned the painting on the wall, then got in the truck, picked up Father Joe, and continued our drive to the old barn where I had left my rental car.

Fathers Juan and Joe sat in the back as they had much to discuss about what had happened so far. That left Nahe and me alone in front to discuss things.

"Is this a dream or what, Speaking Wind?" Nahe said, putting the truck in gear and backing out of the drive.

"If it's a dream, Nahe, I wish I could wake up. This is really getting involved," I returned. "Where are we going now?"

"Back to the old barn. My deputies will be there by now, and we gotta put our plan together.

As we drove back to the barn, I noticed Nahe looked perplexed by what Father Juan had told us. I, too, was having difficulty believing what I heard. It sounded more like something from a murder mystery than something we were actually living through.

"Ever wonder about stuff like this before, Speaking Wind? You know, things like Father Sanchez and his goons being real?"

"Not in the present, Nahe. I thought all those things were long gone from this world," I said, as I watched the passing scenery. "But when you think about it, it wasn't that long ago when our people were treated badly. Like not being allowed into stores, not being able to walk on sidewalks, things like that, you know."

"What are you getting at, Speaking Wind? What does that have to do with our situation?"

"Just this, Nahe. If we tried to tell others about the terrible things our people were going through, when we were young, no one would have believed us. They would have thought we were crazy, or carrying a chip on our shoulders. We would have been labeled troublemakers and either ignored, or put away."

"Yeah, I see what you mean. Like the stories Father Juan heard about the markings, he thought they were started by superstitious people and had no basis.

"That what you're getting at, brother?"

"Yes, Nahe, that's exactly my point. Just because we don't have first hand knowledge about something, doesn't mean it doesn't exist. And for both of us, I think all this has provided a great lesson, one that will benefit us well down the road."

"I agree, but we still gotta come up with a plan to keep Father Sanchez and his three goons away from you and Cheeway. At least for awhile."

Nahe was looking at me for confirmation to what he said. Suddenly, I saw an old woman standing in the middle of the road and I knew Nahe hadn't seen her.

"Look out! You'll hit the old woman!"

Immediately, Nahe turned his eyes to the road and saw her. She was waving frantically for the truck to stop, but when she saw it was too late, she froze and faced us with both arms up.

Unable to stop without hitting the old woman, Nahe swerved into a ditch on the side of the road causing both of us to hit our heads on the dash. It seemed that a large cloud of dust stirred slowly inside the truck. I couldn't tell for how long.

"Must have got knocked out, you okay?" Nahe said, rubbing the top of his head.

"Yeah...think so," I returned, feeling dazed. "What about Fathers Juan and Joe? Can you see if they are okay?"

"Yeah, I think I see them moving."

"Sheriff, need you to know something," came a pleading voice from the old woman. She was standing next to Nahe's side of the truck and was not about to wait for him to get out before telling him what she had to say.

"Evil come to our lands, Sheriff! Evil from the past! You gotta do something 'bout it before it make people die again!"

"Wait a minute, grandmother," Nahe said, trying to calm her while getting his bearings. "Let me get out of the truck first, okay?"

Nahe and I got out of the truck, then helped the priests. After inspecting ourselves to make sure nothing was broken, our attention returned to the old woman.

"Truck on fire, Sheriff. Better do something, I think, huh?"

The truck started smoking and Nahe told the old woman to stand back in case it decided to blow up. Then he reached inside the cab and pulled the hood release while I lifted it up to see what was causing the engine to smoke.

Nahe ran back with a fire extinguisher and began spraying the engine.

"Looks like this old friend isn't going to take us any further today, Speaking Wind. Hope the radio still works. I can call in for someone to pick us up."

When Nahe turned it on, it still worked. He called into the station for assistance and gave them our location. But when the dispatcher asked what his destination would be, he told them he wasn't sure yet, but would radio it in when he got there.

I knew this was not standard procedure, but from all that had happened today, not much was, and I was glad the dispatcher was not uncomfortable with that. I knew Father Sanchez and his three bodyguards were resourceful. If Nahe had given our destination over the radio, they would be there, waiting for us. Just like they were at Sadie's.

When I told Nahe what I thought, he looked at me with one of his half smiles.

"Don't have much trust in my deputies, Speaking Wind? Told you they'd be holding those four for awhile. Think they missed them or something?"

"They are very resourceful, Nahe, and we don't know the full extent of their support base here. But one thing I do know, I won't underestimate them again, and neither should you."

"Sheriff ready to listen to me yet?" the old woman said, with a quivering voice. "Already checked on priests you brought in truck. They all right, just need a little rest."

We had forgotten about the old woman with all that had happened. Then turning, Nahe tipped his hat and told her she had his full attention.

"Sheriff Nahe friend of people, I know this. Talk to many people 'bout you. I Molly Two Socks. Live in house over that hill," the old woman said, pointing the way with an old and bent finger.

"Live on land from time I was born. Know all 'bout things of our people. And 'bout evil that come back, and I know why. That why Molly Two Socks come look for you, Sheriff friend. You need to know what goin' on here. Wanna know this thing, Sheriff? Wanna know what Molly Two Socks see?"

"Yes, grandmother, I want to hear what you've seen that wears the face of evil. But why don't we find a good place to sit before you begin," Nahe said, as he pointed to a clump of trees next to the road. The grass looked brown, but soft, and seemed inviting after our ordeal with the accident.

"We gotta be where our driver can see us, grandmother. Will you sit with us and share your wisdom?"

"Okay, Nahe, I do this for you."

"We go back long time, Nahe, our people do. All things already been written 'bout, we know how they s'posed to happen. And this evil thing no different.

"Molly Two Socks see everything that come to this land, Nahe. Not see with these eyes," she said, pointing to her eyes.

"See with these!" she said, as she moved her hands from her eyes to her heart.

Nahe and I looked closely at the old woman. We noticed she had not opened her eyes. Then we knew, she didn't see with her eyes, because she was blind.

"Grandmother, do you need our help getting back to your home?" Nahe asked, holding one of her hands.

"No, Nahe, friend of the people. Molly Two Socks no need help to get any-where. Can see better than you and Speaking Wind. I see all things, ever since lit-tle girl. See you play with Speaking Wind and Cheeway from seasons long ago, now back together again. This good for all people, it time for this to be. Not be afraid of evil, it not win. Grandfather and Two Bears make sure of that already!"

"Grandmother, I didn't think you remembered me," Nahe returned.

"Molly Two Socks remember all three of you. Let think you getting some-thing over on me from long time ago. That when you eat fruit from tree friends that grow by my house. I know you not have money to buy food to eat, specially for young growing boys. Also know Grandfather and Two Bears not let Speaking Wind and Cheeway do things that hurt anyone's way of living either. I know none of you raised to be greedy and take more than you need. Molly Two Socks have enough to eat and keep life in her too. So let you feel you get away with sneaking from me. But I knew I see you then. Just like I see you now. Remember what Grandfather and Two Bears teach you. Everybody here on Mother Earth to support each other and share freedom of living. That way, everyone get lessons they need. Then, there be none who take that away from them. That freedom of living, Nahe and Speaking Wind. That part of what life all about. Okay? You understand me good now?"

"Yes, grandmother, we understand you. Very well!"

"Now Molly Two Socks say what she see on land today. See face of great evil return from past. But face supposed to return now. I know this because of what written by Ancient Ones and told to me by Grandfather. This time for mighty things to happen now, things like you never see before. This because doorway been opened. And when doorway open, it bring back all ancient knowledge for everyone to hear 'bout again. It bring back way of knowing who everyone is, and not allow shadow of illusion to blind people no more. Glad to see you bring both priests with you, Nahe. They part of this too. You not know that yet, but will soon! Doorway been opened by Cheeway, and evil is making great effort not to let people know what come through. Evil been guarding places where ancient knowledge been kept. They know places where much ancient knowledge stored, but they not know all of them. Evil face want destroy them, but must find them first. Know when this knowledge come back to life among people, evil not live much longer. And this make evil much afraid. But it afraid because it believe itself to be evil, not know no different. It not know this way was supposed to be. Ancient knowledge not supposed to be know by everyone yet. But time comin' real soon. Cheeway know when that time is, no worry about that. But evil come by house short time ago. It tell me it not stopped by your deputies, Nahe, it escape and looks for you now. So, Molly Two Socks come straight to road here. Know you come by this way and been told you not know 'bout them getting free from trap. Was told you need to know this so you aware there still big danger by evil who look for you. That why I stop truck way I do. I know you not hit me, know your heart better than that. Also know truck gonna get hurt in stop, but not you. Truck had to be hurt so Molly Two Socks can tell you what you need to hear, and remember. Otherwise, if truck no get hurt, Nahe be in too much hurry to take time to listen to what he need to hear. Cheeway safe for now, but not be safe for long. He need strength from all four of you very soon. But got one more thing to tell you 'bout evil. No think it without power, it knows how to be invisible when need to. That how it get away from you sheriff deputies, Nahe. Now, it angry with all of you, and Cheeway, for trying to stop it. Better go now, other truck comin'."

When the old woman said that, there was a sound of an approaching vehicle. She was right; it was one of the Sheriff's trucks. The one Nahe had radioed for.

"One more thing, Nahe. Speaking Wind need plenty help now. He been away from path of seeing for long time. He been too long with white people who still blinded by illusion. No make bad face for him when he stumble, Nahe, help him back up. It not take him long to remember who he is, he still quick learner."

When she finished, Molly Two Socks started walking to her house. Looking at the sureness of her walk, I did not doubt she knew where she was going, with more clarity than I did.

Thinking about her and how she said Grandfather had already taken care of the evil, I asked Nahe what he remembered about her.

"She's about as close to a spirit walker as one can get without dying, Speaking Wind. Her medicine is strong, and well known 'round these parts. But I didn't recognize her at first; she's changed a lot. Don't know why, but I get the feeling that when all this is over, Molly Two Socks time with us will be done too."

"Guess we'd better listen to what she told us, shouldn't we?"

"Yeah, Speaking Wind, that would be a wise thing to do," Nahe replied, keeping his eye on the approaching truck.

The truck pulled up and the driver opened the passenger side door for us to get in.

"Hi, Father Juan!" the driver said. "I'm surprised to see you out here."

"Nahe was kind enough to give us a ride to visit someone in need of our services, deputy."

"Got some bad news, Sheriff," the deputy said, leaning toward the passengers side of the cab. "Those four men you wanted us to detain, they got away."

"What ya mean they got away?" Nahe returned, in a demanding tone. "I told you to hold them, didn't I?

"We did, Sheriff. Had their car stopped and everything. Even had them sit in the back of the patrol car, but didn't help. They disappeared and we haven't been able to find them."

"Disappeared! How can someone you have in the back of a patrol car disappear?! Can you explain that?"

"We followed procedure completely, Sheriff. We put them in the back, locked the door and radioed DMV to run a check on their plates. I was in the car radioing when it happened, Sheriff. When I got off the radio and looked back, they weren't there. They were gone, and the strange thing about it is both doors were still closed and locked. Don't know how they did it. By all rights, they shoulda been there, but they weren't! Don't know what to tell you, Sheriff. We did all we could. Just wasn't enough!"

"Nahe, remember what Molly Two Socks told us about them knowing how to use invisibility?" Father Juan asked.

"Yeah, what about it?"

"I don't think your deputies are at fault. If they know the secret, they could leave anyplace they wanted, and not be seen."

"Maybe, but this worries me. Where will they resurface next, and what can we do to detain them? Makes all this seem more dangerous. Everything's changed now. Not sure if we can give Cheeway the protection he needs. What do you think we should do?"

"Continue as we have, Nahe. Can't outguess things we don't know about," I returned.

Nahe nodded his head and we got in the truck, then continued our drive to the old barn. We knew we had about ten minutes before arriving and decided to work out a plan that would throw Father Sanchez off our track.

The truck pulled into the barn, and I saw the four deputies that were at the restaurant earlier. We had used our ten minutes of driving time to come up with a plan we felt comfortable with, and now, we would share it with the men who were about to become a part of it.

When we got out of the truck, Nahe motioned for the men to gather near. We needed to tell them of our plan and get it started quickly. For all we knew, Father Sanchez could have already figured out where we were, and was on his way.

Nahe told the deputies the plan called for two trucks to circle town a few times, long enough for Father Sanchez to see them. They weren't to travel close to each other, that was to keep them from being seen in the same place, or at the same time.

He called for one of the deputy's to drive the truck and the other to lay in the back, covered with a tarp, but not completely. He explained our previous plan of getting to Sadie's unseen, and was certain they would be looking for something like that again. But instead of seeing me and Nahe, they would only think it was us.

The deputy driving the truck needed to look like Nahe, and he told them to get two of his jackets from the office and put it on, then put on a hat that was a little larger than they were used to wearing, one that will cover most of their face without impairing their vision. That would help their disguise. The other deputy would lie in the back of the truck covered with a tarp, but not so covered they would not be seen by an attentive eye. They were supposed to be seen, but only slightly while they make motions of looking out the back, from under the tarp, for anyone who might be following. After circling town a couple of times, each of them would head off in a different direction. One would go toward Colorado Springs and the other to Santa Fe. If they were seen by Father Sanchez, it would give the four of us enough time to head out and cover our tracks.

The deputies nodded their heads and started to head out when a forgotten voice spoke out.

"What about me, Sheriff?" the deputy who picked us up said. "You just want me to wait here?"

"Alvin, almost forgot about you," Nahe said, tying his hair in back. "You take Speaking Wind's car and drive out to Chaco Canyon. Spend the rest of the day there, then come back. You can park the car behind the jail then go home."

"What if I'm seen, Sheriff, want me to avoid them?"

"No, Alvin, if they see you, keep driving for awhile. You know, long enough to make sure they can't get back here before we have a chance to leave."

Nahe looked at the deputies and told the two who would be driving the trucks they would have to untie their hair. That way, they might be more likely to be mistaken for him by Father Sanchez. He told the other three to keep their hair tight, so if they were seen, they would be more likely to be taken for me.

Before anyone could start out, one of the car radios cracked a message.

"Dispatch to Alvin. Are you there?"

Alvin hurriedly walked to the truck and responded.

"Alvin here, dispatch. What you got?"

"Just wanted to let you know the black Ford Bronco is gone, Alvin. No one saw who took it, but we think it was the same four you stopped earlier. You know, the ones you said disappeared from the back of your car."

"We left the truck parked at Sadie's like you said. But one of the patrols reported in a few minutes ago that it was gone. You want us to do anything more on it?"

I looked at Alvin, then at Nahe when I heard this. Something didn't seem right and the look on Nahe's face told me he didn't feel right about something either.

"No, dispatch. Don't have any further instructions. Just stand by, when I meet up with the Sheriff, I'll let you know more," Alvin responded, looking directly at Nahe.

"What you mean when you meet up with the Sheriff, Alvin? You called in and said you were about to pick up him and three passengers about twenty minutes ago. You all right, Alvin? Something wrong?"

"No, dispatch, just got lost for a moment, that's all. Alvin out!"

Alvin put the mike back on the radio, then walked to Nahe. "Well, Sheriff, what's next?"

"Head out to Chaco Canyon, Alvin, I need to cover a few more points with the other men."

"Where you going to be, Sheriff?…In case something comes up."

"Don't know yet, Alvin, maybe right here in town, or up on top of the hills. Someplace I can get a good look at whatever is going on in the town, ya know. Why you ask?"

"Oh, just wondering, Sheriff. With all that's been going on today, no telling what might happen next," Alvin started walking to my rental car, then turned back to the Sheriff. "Going to take my truck, Sheriff? It's full of gas and will get you where you need to go."

"Yeah!" Nahe responded, looking intently at this deputy. "I'll take your truck.

"But one other thing," Nahe said, looking at everyone. "I want complete radio silence from everyone, understand?"

"What if we get in trouble, Sheriff?" Alvin asked. "What if we get stuck somewhere? After all, Chaco Canyon can really be a lonely place for someone stuck, you know."

"Only for an emergency, okay? Otherwise, keep off the radios…Take off, Alvin, we gotta put this plan into action now."

With that, Alvin climbed into the rental car and headed out to Chaco Canyon. Nahe turned to one deputy and told him he would switch trucks with him. Then looked at me and motioned we needed to start out.

The four of us drove out of the barn and headed to the back hills, away from the barn and town.

"Nahe, this isn't the way to town! I thought you were going to park on top one of the hills so you could see how the plan was working!"

"Not today, Speaking Wind. Too much has been shown. Been reading signs lately?"

"What signs, Nahe? The only thing I picked up was Alvin might have taken a little more authority than you wanted him to."

"Alvin seems to be another missing part for what's been troubling me, brother," Nahe said, pulling his hat down a little further. "Too many things been happening that shouldn't have. Like Father Sanchez and his three goons disappearing when they shouldn't have. Their truck being parked at Sadie's, when I had specific instructions for it to be left where it was, then watched. And Alvin saying he hadn't seen us, when he had already called in he was about to pick us up. Then there was Alvin's curiosity about where we were going, and his insistence on our taking his truck. Any of that add up to you, Speaking Wind?"

"You think Alvin is helping Father Sanchez?" Father Joe asked.

"Yup, but don't know for sure, Father. Only know they have been able to get by with a lot more than they should have. Makes me think someone's been feeding them information."

"But we've both known Alvin since he's been little, Nahe. What makes you think it would be him?"

"Just a hunch, Father, but I think we'll get another sign in a few minutes," Nahe said, looking at me.

"What sign, Nahe?" I asked.

"If I'm right, he'll figure a way to send another message over the radio. You know, Father Sanchez and his men do seem to be very resourceful. They are probably monitoring the air waves, listening to everything we've been saying on the police band.

"If I'm right about Alvin, he'll attempt to inform them of our location. When he does, I'll know I'm right about him."

"What if it's not him, Nahe?"

"Then he'll have a good trip to Chaco Canyon, that's all."

"But you don't think you're wrong do you, Nahe?"

"Nope!" Nahe returned, as we continued the drive away from town.

We'd been driving about ten minutes when it happened. Alvin requested assistance over the radio, and we listened.

"Dispatch, you there?" came his voice over our truck's radio.

"Dispatch here, that you, Alvin?"

"Yeah, it's me. Got trouble I'm afraid. Rental car I'm in is smoking, but don't see a fire yet."

"Need assistance, Alvin? I can send someone to tow you in if you want."

"No need, dispatch, I see someone driving toward me. I'm going to wave them down and ask them for help. That will save you a trip. I'm on the road to Chaco Canyon and you know how far out of the way that is. So just sit tight, I'll get back with you…Oh yeah. Dispatch, could you help me out with something else?"

"What is it, Alvin?"

"Tell the Sheriff I won't be able to follow his plan, okay?"

"What plan? I thought the Sheriff was with you."

"Nah, things changed! He's in my truck. You know, truck sixteen."

"Okay. Want me to give him a call on the radio?"

"No, were supposed to be in radio silence, dispatch. Only supposed to be on the air if we got an emergency."

"How you want me to tell him then?"

"Maybe you could send a patrol car to the hills just outside town and find him. Think he might be there looking over things."

"Got it, Alvin, you sure you're going to be all right?"

"Yeah, dispatch, I'll be fine. Here comes a car and it's stopping. See you when I get back to town. Alvin out."

"Damn!" Nahe shouted, hitting the side of the door with his fist. "Thought he might be the leak, just didn't want to believe it."

"So Alvin's working with Father Sanchez, Nahe? What do we do now?"

"Just as we planned, Speaking Wind. Now that we know who's been leaking information, it'll be easier to work around him.

"After all this is over, I plan on having a good talk to that one. But now, we gotta get to Cheeway without being seen. And, my brother, even though Alvin didn't mean to, I think he's giving us the time we need to make our getaway."

"Where is Cheeway going to meet us, Nahe? Is it far?"

"About a half day horse ride."

"Where is it?"

"The Unseen Cave of the Ancients. Remember that place? Been a long time for you, I'm sure. Even had to give Cheeway instructions how to get there yesterday."

"Yesterday! I thought you hadn't seen him before now, Nahe. Why didn't you tell me!"

"Knew there might be a leak in the department, Speaking Wind. Not for this mess with Father Sanchez, but for other things that just seemed to be too convenient. When Cheeway met me and told me about his problem, I knew I could not speak freely about it to anyone. I decided to play dumb till I could find out who was leaking information from my office. Had a lot of questions to answer for things that went on here, brother. Not that there was anything illegal done, or even trying to hide anything. But things that could have only been known by me and my deputies were being asked about by some politicians in Santa Fe. You know the paper work they generate when they ask a question? It's a lot!…Well, a lot of questions came up last week. Thought if someone wanted to keep me too busy to notice what was going on around town, that would be the way to do it. That's when I decided there might be someone within the department leaking information, but until I spoke with Cheeway, I didn't know why anyone would want to keep me tied up with paper work. Now I do!"

"So you think Alvin is working with Father Sanchez? Why would he do this, Nahe?"

"Money, Speaking Wind. Alvin's been buying a lot of new things the last few days. Things I know his salary can't afford."

"Father Sanchez offered me money if I would work with him, Nahe. More, he said, than I would ever need. Think he made the same offer to Alvin?"

"Yup, and from what I've seen, he took it. Now he's on Father Sanchez's payroll."

"Guess it's better to know who is in the playing field then. Easier to work your way around any obstacles, huh?"

"Yeah, guess you're right, brother. Still bothers me though, you know, I've known him for a long time."

I could see Nahe had many things to think about. Especially concerning Alvin. I knew his talk with him was not going to be an easy thing to do. I knew Nahe did not pull punches either, and Alvin would feel Nahe's impact from his words and actions.

But now was not the time to think about that. I knew the Unseen Cave of the Ancients was inaccessible by car, or truck, and I felt uncomfortable about riding a horse.

"Nahe, horse back is the only way we're going to make it to the Unseen Cave?"

"Yeah, unless you want to walk there. But I don't think we have that much time before Cheeway returns. He told me he needed a few days before meeting us. Something about translating some ancient records. But think of it, riding horses again, and together. Kinda like the old days, isn't it?"

"Yeah, Nahe, kinda like the old days all right! Just hope I still remember how to ride well enough to make it!"

# CHAPTER 7

▼

# THE SET-UP

Cheeway and his investors spent the next few days putting their provisions together, obtaining visas, and permission to do a site search in an area they could only guess at, then getting Roberts to contact his friend in the Yucatan to arrange their security, and finally, boarding their flight to the Yucatan Peninsula in Mexico.

"We're on our way now, Cheeway!" Jade said, as she took a sip from her drink. "According to the flight manifest, we should arrive in Merida sometime this afternoon."

"Hope your brother was successful in getting escorts for us, Jade. I'm really worried about Father Sanchez. You know what he has done already, and if that's any indication for what he is prepared to do, just to keep this city from being discovered…"

"Cheeway, you worry about things that haven't happened yet," Jade returned. "Are you going to be like this the whole trip?"

"I was there, Jade! I saw what happened to Mary, and the dig! I know what Father Sanchez is capable of doing! You don't!"

"But, Cheeway, what if his influence was only in that small town of Cuzco? What if his sphere of influence doesn't go any further, but he wanted you to think it did? A lot of priests in small towns are like that, you know! Especially in the south where you were. They gotta feel they can rule with an iron hand, if you know what I mean."

"I've seen the iron hand of religion everywhere I've gone, Jade. It isn't a stranger to me. But there is something different about the way Father Sanchez acted, something I can't put my finger on though. And it's making me nervous about what he might be capable of doing next."

"Come on, Cheeway, I know you'll feel better about this whole thing when it's over."

"Jade, if we find what I think we will, it won't ever be over. Not for any of us!" Cheeway returned, then looked out the window at the passing clouds.

"All right, Cheeway! I know something that is sure to take your mind away from Father Sanchez. Here, look what I've found on this map!"

Jade had opened one of the maps they brought to one that only showed the locations of the ancient cities of Central and South America. There were no country borders or Common Era cities on it, only marks showing locations of cities that had been built thousands of years ago.

"Look at how these cities are always grouped together, Cheeway! Can you see the similarity of these to the ones we are going to?"

"You mean how most of them seem to be in groups of threes?"

"Exactly! There seems to be one difference though, and that is the distance the third one is from the other two. The two that look like they are directly in line with each other. You know what this can mean, Cheeway? It means if we are successful in our calculations, and uncover the Ancient City of Prophecy, we will know these other ancient cities have been built for the same purpose. We will know their physical layout was meant to be a map for us, a map showing locations of other sacred sites, perhaps with the same level of impact on the world the Ancient City of Prophecy will have. What do you think of that, Cheeway? Wouldn't that be a great find? This revelation would certainly change a lot of thinking, you know!"

"I'm sure it would, Jade, but I'm still concerned about, Father Sanchez. Especially if you're right about the map thing."

"What do you mean?"

"Think about it for a moment, Jade. Father Sanchez wants to keep us from finding the city on the map stone. And it was most likely he who robbed the two previous expeditions, taking the talking stones Nauti gave them. Just seems like Father Sanchez is attempting to keep hidden whatever keeps coming up about knowledge of the past," Cheeway continued. "And, whatever his reasons, he means to do just that. But if we are successful in finding the Ancient City of Prophecy, and your theory can be proved, what then? At present, we have only been working with the possibility of one city, and so far, only Father Sanchez has been involved. But what if you are correct and we discover other ancient cities around the world have been laid out as a map for us to follow...a map showing locations of more ancient wisdom and knowledge than we, at present, can understand. How many more Father Sanchez's will we force to come into the open, and when they do, what will they do to keep that information from being known?"

"You're talking about the conspiracy theory, aren't you? The one Stevens brought up back in Colorado Springs."

"Yeah, Jade, that's what I'm getting at. If Father Sanchez is associated with the group Stevens called the Illuminati, and if such a group really does exist, I'm sure they are extremely well financed and have people all over the world. After all, if they exist, they've had thousands of years to establish themselves everywhere."

"And in all the governments too, Cheeway?"

"Yeah, Jade, even in the Mexican government."

"You think Roberts' friend could be a part of it, Cheeway?" Jade asked, looking him squarely in the eyes. "Then what about me, what about Stevens, and what about everyone we know! Think they could be a part of it too? And what about you, Cheeway? What proof do you have that you're not a part of the Illuminati! Don't you see where you are taking yourself, Cheeway? If you don't stop what you're doing, pretty soon you'll believe all of us are in this thing, and against you! That kind of thinking won't lead you anywhere but down the road of paranoia, and you won't find any answers there, Cheeway. What do you think? Who would have thought such a thing from Stevens because of his involvement with international politics, but you, Cheeway? That really takes the cake for me!"

"Yeah, guess you're right, Jade. Maybe I am getting a little out in left field with this whole thing. Perhaps it's all the thinking I've been doing about Mary, ya know. Maybe I am just looking for someone, anyone, I can pin the blame on. After all, we really don't know if such a group exists or not. So I'll tell you what, until I have proof in my hands that they are real, I'll say nothing more on the topic. That okay with you?"

"I think we will have a much smoother journey, Cheeway. Let's get some rest now. We'll be landing in a few hours. When we hit ground, we'll have to take off running. Lots to do you know!"

They laid their heads back and went to sleep. Cheeway was taken to places by the dreamers he would rather not have gone to. He was revisiting his last moments with Mary, just before she left him in jail, then drove out of town. He didn't want to remember that time, not just yet anyway, and woke himself up with a jerk, a jerk that coincided with the plane landing on the runway, and he knew they both landed at the same time.

"We're here, everyone!" Roberts said, from the seat behind them. "Look out the window and see if Hector is there, will you?"

"Who's Hector, Jade?" Cheeway asked, as he put himself between her and the window she wanted to look out.

"A friend of ours, Cheeway. He went to school with us. Now he's working at some important job with the Mexican government here. I know you'll like him. He's really a nice kind of guy. Always making practical jokes in school, you know the kind."

The plane slid down the runway, but they saw no sign of Hector. They deplaned, then walked to the baggage claim area. Hector was waiting for them, but he wasn't alone. He had three armed guards with him.

"Roberts! Stevens! Jade! Over here!" a voice shouted over a large crowd of people.

Once they got off the stairway, they could not see Hector, but followed the sound of his voice, and an occasional hand held up in the air. When they arrived, it seemed like old home week. And Jade, Roberts, and Stevens went through a ritual he was sure meant something to them, but not to him. Cheeway remained where he was waiting for the luggage while the others completed their greetings.

"Cheeway!" Roberts yelled out. "I would like you to meet a very special friend of mine!"

"It is a pleasure to meet you, Cheeway," Hector began. "I have heard a lot about you from Roberts. Please allow me to introduce myself. I am Hector Gomez, Assistant to the Director of Antiquities. If there is any way I can assist you, please do not hesitate to call on me. I am at your disposal."

Hector seemed to possess all the finesse of a diplomat, but something about him told Cheeway he was hiding something. He decided to keep a close eye on him and pay close attention to what he said.

"Why the armed guards, Hector?" Roberts asked.

"Oh, they're not for me. They are for you. You said you would need escorts, didn't you? Or did I misunderstand your message."

"Yes, I did request escorts," Roberts returned. "But I didn't expect to see them so well armed, and from the Army!"

"Won't they do, my friend? I can find others to take their place if you wish," Hector offered.

"They'll do just fine, Hector. Thank you!" Jade jumped in. "I thought you might be up to your old tricks again, that's all."

"You mean the jokes? I haven't had time to get any real good ones off in years now. How many has it been, at least five or six, hasn't it?"

"At least!" Stevens returned. "Time really moves when we are doing what we need to be doing, doesn't it?"

"You can say that again," Roberts said.

"What's all this about an ancient city you think you found? I'd really like to know more about it. Care to explain?"

"Not here," Roberts returned. "Did you bring a car, Hector?"

"Not a car, my friend. I brought much better than that. There are three new heavy duty vans waiting for us outside. Two for sleeping and one for the guards. Will that be sufficient? Or will you require more?"

"More than enough for our needs, Hector. Come on, we'll explain what we are searching for as we drive. Don't want everyone to know about it, you know."

"Where are we going then?" Hector asked, receiving a strange look from the four of them. "I need to tell the guards so they don't get lost. They are the drivers…understand?"

"Of course, Hector, you just caught us a little off guard! We're going to Chacmultun first, you know the way?"

"Yeah, I know it real good. Just picked up another group from there, not more than a couple of days ago. They said they were looking for some kind of an ancient city, too."

"Anything strange about them?" I asked.

"No, at least not for these parts, Cheeway. Just a priest with three men. He said they were his protégés, getting them ready for the seminary. He told me he wanted to give them one last outing before they began their studies.

"Why do you ask, anything I should know about?"

"No, Hector," Jade returned, as she looked at me, then Hector. "Just a few pre-dig jitters is all. You know how we get just before we begin one of our adventures. We don't want anyone else to know about it. If they did, they might get to it first, and then there would go our project."

Hector looked at Jade and smiled. But Cheeway could see there was something she knew that she wasn't saying.

"What was the priest's name, Hector? Did he tell you?" Cheeway asked, as he picked up one of the bags.

"I believe he said his name was Father Sanchez," Hector returned expectantly. "Mean anything to you?"

"No, Hector," Jade said, as she pushed Cheeway outside the baggage claim area. "Nothing at all. Let's get going. We don't want to keep the old ruins waiting, do we, Cheeway?"

On the way out, Jade called Cheeway's attention to a ring Hector was wearing. On it was an engraving of a hooded man holding a curved sword. She made a sign they shouldn't say anything, but would talk about it later, when they had private time, away from Hector.

"Going to stay with us through the dig, Hector?" Roberts asked, as he lifted his suitcase into the lead van.

"Off and on, my friend. You know how these kinds of jobs are, on call twenty-four hours a day, seven days a week. But don't worry, you'll know I'm around. I don't want anything to happen to my old friends. Where you're going is pretty isolated, but don't worry, the guards have radios. I gave them instructions to keep me informed every few hours or so. That way I can keep up with you without having to be there. You don't mind, do you?"

"Not at all!" Stevens returned. "Glad to have your oversight on our behalf."

"There was a time when you would have been safe in our jungles, Stevens, but that was a long time ago. Guess those days are gone forever now. Times here are really uncertain, you know. Especially when it comes to our government! Just last week there was an attempt to overthrow it, but we heard about it just in time and put a quick end to it before it got started."

"What happened to the men behind the plot?" Stevens asked.

"Guess they went back into the jungle to hide," Hector returned. "We have a lot of them out there now. You have to be very careful where you go. They would see the four of you as easy prey. Just be glad you have someone like me to take care of you. The guards and I, will make sure nothing bad happens!"

There was very little conversation for the duration of the trip. They arrived at the first site just as the sun was setting and began pitching camp in the twilight of their first day.

Cheeway didn't realize it then, but that was a sign of things to come. It was a sign telling them a dark night was about to begin.

"If you are all set, my friends, I will be going back to the city with one of the guards. I'll have him drive back here in the morning. That will give him a chance to get a little sleep. You okay with that?"

"Yeah, that'll be fine, Hector. Tell him not to worry about rushing back here though. We should be here for at least a couple of days. He'll find us easy enough."

"That's his job, Roberts, keeping his eyes on you that is. I'll send him back in a couple of days then."

With that, Hector and the guard got into a van and drove off leaving the other two. The guards looked like they were about to fall over from being so tired, and Roberts told them it would be all right for them to get some sleep. He assured them we needed to go over some information and would be up for the next few hours. In the mean time, they could get some rest. When we decided to turn in, he would wake one of them so they could guard the camp.

The guards didn't need to be convinced and handed Roberts a rifle then crawled into their tent and went to sleep. That left us with an opportunity to discuss what Jade had seen on Hector's ring.

"You want to begin, Jade?" Cheeway asked, as he put a few pieces of wood on the fire.

"Begin what, Jade?" Roberts asked. "You're not going to begin something really entailed, are you? We're really tired and if we want to get an early start tomorrow, we will need our rest."

"It's important, Roberts," Jade said quietly. "We gotta talk about it now. Tomorrow may be too late."

"Very well then," Roberts returned, with tiredness in his voice. "Why couldn't I have been blessed with a sister who was more interested in getting her beauty sleep than solving mysteries? What did you find now?"

"It could be a lot!" Jade returned. "I saw Hector wearing a ring with an engraving on it. One that has a lot of significance to our dig."

"You don't think it could be something he just picked up at one of the local markets?" Stevens asked. "You know how the natives are here, they see something that looks good and put it on everything they make."

"No, Stevens, it wasn't like that. It was an engraving of a hooded man holding a curved sword. Just like the symbol Cheeway saw. And, Stevens, exactly like the one you described to us back in Colorado Springs."

"What are you saying, Jade? Are you saying Hector could be one of Father Sanchez's clan?"

"Or working with him, and those he represents, Stevens. It just seems a little too convenient for him not to be. Think of what he told us before he left. How there had been an attempt of overthrowing the government here, but they found out about it before it had a chance of developing."

"Yeah? What's new about that? They have those kinds of things happening frequently in these parts, don't they?"

"So we've been told, but think for a moment. Think of what you told us about The Illuminati and how they trade secrets with governments, trade things like information for special favors. And in return, they give them important information that allows them to remain in power. It just seems too ripe here for that not to happen. A volatile government with a population that's ready to revolt. And then, seeing Hector's ring. That put the icing on the cake for me and Cheeway as well. I don't think we can trust Hector, or the guards either, Stevens. I think we better keep an eye on them, and when we find something significant, we better keep it to ourselves until we can discuss it privately. Away from them."

"I think Jade is right, Stevens," Cheeway said, as he looked at Stevens sitting across the fire. "She has a good mind at unraveling mysteries, wouldn't you agree? After all, it was she who put this whole idea of how to find the location of the Ancient City of Prophecy, wasn't she? I think we ought to trust her on this one too. What do you think?"

"All right then, what if you're right, Jade? How can we get rid of Hector and the guards? Remember what he said? They are expected to make contact with him every two or three hours on their radios. If they don't, he'll know something is wrong and come back with the cavalry."

"That's why we need to make a plan tonight, Stevens. We're alone now, but I don't know when we will have an opportunity like this again!"

"Jade's right," Roberts said, with a look of disbelief on his face. "We've got to do this now, or not at all. Got any suggestions, Jade?"

"Just this!" Jade said, as she motioned for us to come closer so we might not be overheard by the guards. "We act like we don't suspect anything for the moment. Each of us will do what we came here to do. I will look for writings on the ancient buildings within the three sites, Roberts will attempt to uncover any clues from the past civilizations that lived here, Stevens will do his share of relating anything we uncover to what he already knows about international cultures and customs and Cheeway will do what he has always done, look under the Earth for clues we need, places that will show us where to look for anything that might help us decipher the map stone's reference to the sitting cat. I will work at the measurements of the Sphinx and the pyramids and attempt to draw my calculations, then superimpose them within these three sites. Then, when we believe we have what we need, we make two maps. One map, we keep to ourselves and not show the guards or Hector. The other map, we show the guards or anyone else who wants to check our progress. But the second map won't have the same location ours will. We will do our measurements and include them as if they were correct, but they will be false, just enough to throw anyone off if they discover what we did and try to follow. And we show the position of the sitting cat for them as well, but instead of being in the correct position, it will be off by twenty-five degrees, and turned around. When we're ready to make our move, we set the false map out for the guards to take, and tell them the night before we solved the mystery of the Ancient City of Prophecy. If they are working for Father Sanchez, which I believe they are, they'll take the map and leave. When they go, we make our move out of here—out to a place known only to the four of us and begin our dig in secret and out of sight of Hector and Father Sanchez. By the time they discover we have given them a false map, we should be finished with our excavation and on our way out of the country."

Jade looked at us with an accomplished look over her face.

"Well, what do you think? Is it a good plan, or not?"

"Well, it's the best thing I've heard so far, Jade," Stevens said, as he periodically looked at the two guards sleeping in the tent. "I think it's going to work too. Even if they get a hundred men to help dig, they'll be floundering long enough to let us complete what we came here to do."

"What are they going to do when they reach that location and find we aren't there?" Cheeway asked.

"Why'd you have to bring that up, Cheeway?" Jade said. "I thought I really had a fool proof plan until you said that."

"Think I have a way out of that one, Jade," Cheeway returned.

"Of course, what's up your sleeve?"

"Remember how Hector said the jungle is full of rebels and outlaws? Let's do something to make him think they've taken us captive, holding us for some kind of reward from a U.S. government agency or a corporation. I think that will keep him from looking for us, for awhile anyway."

"Yeah, and we could leave him a note or something like that, couldn't we?" Stevens asked, as he reached for a pen. "I can whip up a draft for you to look at."

"No, Stevens, I really don't think that will be very convincing," Cheeway returned. "The kind of rebels here probably don't know how to write, and the ones who do…well, I don't think they would take the time to leave a ransom note.

"Hector will know when it's time to initiate our plan. Remember how he spoke of the guards? I'm sure they will keep him well informed, not only of our movements and whereabouts, but even the kind of equipment we are using as well. Let's do this when it's time for us to initiate our plan! We act real excited about having made our final measurement to locate the site where we believe the Ancient City of Prophecy to be. Then we leave the fake map out here on the table and turn in for the night. If we're right about the guards, they will take the map and run like the wind to give it to Hector, and whoever he's working with. That will give us time to leave, but not before destroying the camp and only taking with us those things the rebels would have taken, things that could bring money if sold on the black market. I believe that will be convincing enough for them to believe we were taken captive, and will give us the time to finish our dig. Besides, if they believe we have been taken captive they won't be in such a hurry to find us. Most likely, they would rather we were all dead anyway, wouldn't you think?"

"All right, Cheeway, now it's my turn to throw some water on your plan," Jade said, with a smile on her face. "What if only one of the guards leaves? What then?"

"How long did it take us to drive here, Jade? Near as I remember it had to be over six or seven hours. And when you multiply that time times two, for a round trip, we will be left alone with one guard for twelve to fourteen hours. Don't you think we could catch him off guard long enough to disarm him?"

"Then what do we do with him, Cheeway?"

"We will have to take him with us, Roberts. Can't kill him, otherwise we would be just like Father Sanchez. Want to be like him?"

"Certainly not, but you know he'll slow us down if we have to carry him with us."

"We take the vans, Roberts!" Jade said, growing indignant. "Remember? They would be one of the first things the rebels would want. Transportation is a big thing in this jungle."

"Oh yeah, forgot about that!" Roberts returned, with a reddened face. "Guess I forgot where we were, ya know."

"All right then," Jade concluded. "Everyone comfortable with the plan?"

Everyone silently nodded their heads in agreement with the plan we came up with. Now, it was time to put it into action. While they felt safe with their purpose, they knew if they didn't find what they were looking for soon, they would probably end up dead. Not from the rebels in the jungle, but from Father Sanchez and Hector.

For the next few days, each of them worked at what they had been trained for. And every hour they would gather to share what they found. The picture was coming together now, and they could see where it was leading. It was filling them with great excitement; even the guards picked up on it and, from time to time, would help out with the manual labor. Finally, they completed the last piece of the puzzle.

They told the guards they had solved the markings from the old stone map, and when they next spoke to Hector, they should give him our thanks for his help, and tell him we were ready to begin digging in the morning. They further wet Hector's whistle by telling them they believed they would have to dig very deep before reaching the remnants of the ancient city, and would need at least fifty more men to help.

The look from the guards was exactly what they anticipated. They began asking questions about the markings on the fake map, and what they meant. They said they were curious just in case something happened to us before the dig could begin.

The group obliged and explained, in detail, what each of the direction markers meant, where the ancient city was to be found, and how far we anticipated digging before we would uncover it.

We knew the information we gave them would keep an experienced team busy for at least two weeks before they suspected they might be in the wrong place. This would be more than enough time for us to uncover what we were after and then make a run for it.

However, our plan was not to be like we thought, and when we gathered for the last night, ready to leave the map where the guards could take it, we were met with a surprise, and an unplanned one at that.

"Señor! In the camp!" came a voice out of the thick jungle around us. "You, Yankee! What you doin' here? Come to give us your money?"

The three guards sprang up from their seats, cocked their rifles and pointed them in various directions of the jungle.

"Are we in serious trouble, señor? Or is this something that is meant to scare us away?" Stevens asked, as he held tightly to one of the guards arms.

"Please, señor!" the guard returned. "You are keeping me from aiming my rifle!"

"Sorry, got carried away with all this."

Stevens removed his arm but remained right in front of the guard and asked again if they were in serious trouble, or was this something to scare us away.

"I don't know for sure, señor," the guard responded. "I think this is the same group of rebels that tried to take over our town a few days ago. If it is, we all better pray! From what we've been told, there are a couple of hundred of them, and if they have good places in the jungle, they can pick us off when they want to."

"Why don't they just shoot now and get it over with? Why play this cat and mouse game?"

"If they fire into camp now, señor, they might hit something valuable. You know, something they could sell on the black market. They need money, señor, they need it bad. But they can't sell what they ruin with a bullet. Think they will wait for the sun to come up, señor. Then, they will kill all of us, one by one!" the guard returned.

Jade and Cheeway walked over to the guards to listen to what was being said. They didn't want to be left out of this discussion, especially when it meant their lives.

Jade had the fake map in her hands, and when the guard noticed it, he changed his demeanor, completely.

"You finished with your calculations?" he asked.

"All done, but a lot of good it's going to do us now!" she returned.

"The old city marked on the map?"

"Yeah! Think I should destroy it now?"

"Why you ask that?"

"Do you want the rebels to get hold of it? Or haven't you had time to think that far ahead of our immediate problem? If the rebels find the old city, they would probably destroy it, thinking it's someplace evil. I don't want that to happen, do you?"

"No, and Señor Hector left instructions we were to protect the map with our lives."

"The map!" Roberts returned. "What about us? Didn't he leave you instructions to protect us?"

The guard didn't respond. He just looked at him through his dark eyes. But before Roberts could say anything more, there was a loud explosion further down the road. As the noise from the blast faded into the night, the voice in the jungle spoke again.

"No use trying to get away, gringos! We blew up some trees and blocked the road you came in on. That's the only exit from here, and we'll be watching it, and you. Unless your vans can jump over six feet of fallen trees, you are trapped! My men are all around you, so if you try to leave by the jungle tonight, you won't make it. I gave orders to kill anyone who leaves before we can shoot you in the morning. Those two guards with you, don't you know by now they are no good to anyone? Tell you what, if you kill them before morning, I just might let you live. After I rob you that is. Think I'm going to sleep now. I want to be rested so I can shoot each of you in the morning. And don't make any noise! If I don't sleep well, it throws my aim off and I might not kill you with the first shot! Ha! Ha! Ha! Ha! Ha! Ha!"

The deep guttural laughing voice faded into the thick night air, leaving no clue as to its point of origin in the jungle. Panic was beginning to make its presence known by this time, and looking at the guards for assistance, Roberts circled the van looking for safe places we could hide, or places we could lie under to avoid from being hit by passing bullets.

"What about the radio Hector left you?" Roberts asked, emerging from behind one of the vans. "Why don't you radio him for help?"

"Can't do that, señor!" the guard said, pointing to one of the vans. "All the antennas have been taken. Probably while we were eating."

"Well, what are we going to do? Just wait here for death to find us?"

"No, señor!" the guard replied. "There is more we can do. We have orders covering such a situation. Señora, you said the map is complete? The location of the old city is on it too?"

"Yeah, that's what I said!" Jade returned, with a questioning note in her voice. "Why?"

"We must ask you for it now!" the guard said, holding his hand out. "Part of our orders, you know."

"You mean you were to protect the map, but not us!" Roberts said, with an angry voice.

"What are you going to do with it?" Jade asked. "You are just as trapped as we are, remember?"

"No, señora, with our rifles, we have a better chance than you of getting away tonight. Now, please hand me the map. It will buy you a couple more hours of life if you do!"

When the guard said that, he and the other one backed away then aimed their rifles at them. The first guard told the second to set a leather pouch on the ground near us then instructed Jade to put the map inside it.

"What's all this about?" Jade asked demandingly. "Are you a part of those other men in the jungle?"

"No, señora, we are not with them. They really are rebels, but we are soldiers who have been given orders to carry out! And that was to bring back the map when your work had been completed."

"You make it sound like there is another part to your orders. Is there?"

"Yes, there is," the soldier replied. "But first, I will ask you to put the map in the leather pouch. If you don't, I will have to kill you, then put it in myself. I am doing all of you a favor! Just do what I ask, okay?"

"What favor and what part of your orders are you not telling us about?" Roberts demanded. "You know I am a personal friend of Hector, and when he finds out what you have done, don't think either of your lives will be worth anything! Do you hear me?"

"Very well, señor, and I am sure the rebels in the jungle heard you as well. I think all you have done is seal your fate though. You see, they want to kill Señor Hector more than they want to kill you. And now that they know who you are, how did you phrase it, oh yes…a personal friend of his, they will probably save you for last when they kill all of you in the morning. These rebels are clever that way. But don't worry, someone will find your bodies and get word back to your countrymen in a month or two. That should be how long it will take to find you. As to the rest of our orders, señor, your personal friend Hector told us to watch each of you very closely. And when we knew you had completed your work, and located the place to dig for the old city, we were to kill you, then leave your bodies in the jungle. We were to say the rebels took your life, but now, we won't have to lie will we? And we all know lying is a sin, isn't it? Señora, if you place the map in the pouch, it will buy each of you a few more hours of life. And that will be a couple of hours you won't have if you don't give me the map—now!"

With that, the soldier pulled the bolt back on his rifle, and we heard a round slide into position. The other soldier did the same, then both of them stood there, looking at Jade and the map.

"What will it be, señora? Death now…or later?"

Jade walked up to the pouch and slid the map inside. The soldier picked it up, then placed it inside his shirt. He looked at us and said, "Good! I feel better now. For the last few days I was feeling bad about having to kill you. You know, you have been good to my friend and me, and we didn't want to do this. But we had our orders. And now, looks like we won't have to kill you. Those rebels out there in the jungle will do it for us. Isn't that better? After all, I would rather be killed by someone I didn't know. Seems to make it better for the one pulling the trigger. Now, señors and señora, we leave you. Thank you for your hospitality and I would usually say something like may our paths meet again, but I know they won't, not for us. The path you are about to take is much different than ours. But I will give your greetings to Señor Hector, if you wish, that is."

"Yeah!" Jade yelled back sarcastically. "You can tell him to go to hell, for all of us!"

The soldiers smiled, bowed, then vanished into the dark jungle, leaving everyone else with their thoughts and not much else to defend themselves with.

"We gotta make a plan!" Roberts said, as he looked into darkness. "And it has to be something we can do to save ourselves!"

"Think we're pretty much done for, Roberts," Jade returned. "Someone help me bury this map. We don't want the real one to be seen by anyone now!"

At least that part of our plan worked, about burying the real map, each of us smiled when we thought of the look soon to be on Hector and Father Sanchez's faces when they didn't find anything. In a way, this was their final act of knowing they got them back for what they had done to them.

The rest of the night was spent reviewing the things they had done, as well as all they had not done. For them, this was like the great review we go through when we leave this life and go into the next. The night seemed long. Cheeway had thought his last night would pass much quicker, but he was wrong. Each minute seemed like an hour, and he kept looking at his watch to see what time it was.

Finally, the sun came up and each of them had become comfortable with having their lives ended. You know, when you are at peace with your life ending, so many things appear different. Things you thought were important seem to pale against others, but the thought of the map being completed and not being able to uncover the ancient city was holding Cheeway back. That was the only part of his life he could not make peace with. He knew if he were to die that morning, he would have been robbed of his destiny, a destiny he planned long before his birth.

As he thought of the men who would be coming out of the jungle to rob him of this, anger began to rise within his spirit. Soon, he could feel every nerve in his body react to it, and he knew if he just sat here waiting to be shot, that somehow, he would be giving up.

Within a few minutes after the sun rose over the jungle, men began to appear. They were walking toward them aiming their rifles at the camp. Seeing them come like this was not good for Cheeway. He didn't know why, but he knew he had to do something.

Suddenly, he grabbed one of the burning logs from the fire, stood up and gave a war cry! That not only shocked the members of the party, but the men walking toward them as well. Then he began running toward the rebels, waving the burning piece of wood around his head. He knew this wasn't him doing this, but was the connection to many generations of our people coming to life within him. It was the genetic remembrance of how one should die, like a warrior, and not like a sheep.

Yelling his war cry, he ran to meet the first rebel. When he got there, he hit him in the head with the burning log and saw sparks fly in all directions from the impact. Without hesitating, he turned on the second, then the third, then looked for more to attack. He knew he was going to die, and found comfort in doing it in the way our people have done throughout our time on this Earth.

Suddenly, his attacks were stopped by someone very strong holding him around the body. He couldn't have moved if there had been ten of him, and turning his head to see who had been successful in this restraint, he saw a giant of a man behind him. He had not only restrained his attack, but was holding him in the air and laughing.

Cheeway could not understand this new turn of events and struggled to get free. But, the harder he tried to escape from the giant's bear grip, the more tired he got. And finally, the warrior anger within him stopped and the giant let him go.

"You must be Cheeway!" the man said, still laughing. "Look what you did to my brave men! Really caught them off guard, you did. I don't think they've ever seen anything like that before!"

He looked back and saw the men he hit with the burning log. They were rubbing their heads and having difficulty getting up. The others with them were laughing. Some were laughing and lying on the ground, like they couldn't get up on their own.

This new turn of events caused him great concern, and he knew if the warrior strength was not in his muscles, it would be in his voice. And he turned to face his executioner and said, "You do not take a willing spirit, thief! You rob me of my destiny! I will come back and find a way of cutting your destiny short as well!"

"Relax, Cheeway!" the laughing giant said. "We haven't come to kill you! We've been sent to rescue you from Father Sanchez's men! Got any food to eat? Me and my men are really hungry. We spent most of the night making sure your plan would succeed."

"What plan are you talking about?" Cheeway asked.

"The one you put together for the guards," the laughing giant responded. "We knew you would figure out Hector was in with Father Sanchez. It was only a matter of time. He's not real cautious about it, you know—the ring? So, we figured you would make a fake copy of the map and send it back to Father Sanchez with the guards. It was the only way we could see that you could get away from them. When we saw you bury the map last night, we knew we were right about what we thought you would do. That's why we let the guards go. We knew you wanted them to get back and report to Hector and Father Sanchez."

"Who are you?" Cheeway asked. "What are you doing here? And how did you know where we would be?"

"I'm sure you have more questions that that, but now is not the time to ask them. Look, I have to take care of those men you messed up, and we have to eat too. Let's all sit down, have some food and coffee, then I will tell you our part in this adventure while we share some tobacco. Got any?…You all right with this?" he asked, as he looked at Cheeway, his men, then at the rest of the party in the camp.

"Don't have much choice, do I?"

"Not really, Cheeway," he returned. "We are your only way out of here."

They walked to camp and joined the other members of the party. The giant of a man sat down and looked back at the rest of his men. Guess he wanted to make sure they knew what was going on, and he was in our camp with us.

"I thought there were more of you," Cheeway said, as he looked at about thirty men coming out of the jungle. "That's what the guards said."

"We have to keep them thinking we're a much bigger force, otherwise they get too brave and follow us into the jungle. Wouldn't be good for us, you know. We've been doing real good with the odds though. We have a good contact in their circle of influence. He says that soon there will be more like him and they will give us even more help!"

"What are you talking about?" Cheeway asked. "First you come and scare the living daylights out of everyone, make the guards leave, say you're going to kill us in the morning, and now you say you are here to help us? Do you take us for fools, or what?"

"Hold on, Cheeway," the man said. "Why don't you, Dr. Jade, Dr. Roberts, and Dr. Stevens sit here, next to the fire and I'll explain why we're here. I said we were here to help and I meant it. Didn't you think something was terribly wrong when you saw the ring on Hector's hand? You did see the ring, didn't you?"

"Yes, we saw the ring. We also made the connection between him and Father Sanchez. Both of them were wearing the same symbol. Even before you got here, we had a plan put together, one all of us felt sure would succeed."

"Ah, but you hadn't counted on them killing you when they got the map. Even though you were going to give them the false one, you thought they would take off and leave all of you alone, didn't you?"

"Well, guess you're right about that. We hadn't planned on being shot the minute we handed the map over."

"Don't you think I should get a little thank you then? If it hadn't been for me and my men, all of you would be dead now. All your work wouldn't have done any good, even if you had been successful in hiding the real map, which I know you wouldn't have. Because you haven't buried the real map yet, have you? And you, Cheeway, how would you have felt if I hadn't come here when I did. Would you still be in a position of being able to carry out your destiny? Or would you have ended your life as an angry spirit who gets trapped on this Earth with the other angry ones? Trapped here, unable to leave and return home. What about it, don't you think my men and I deserve some kind of gratitude?"

"Well, thanks then!" Jade returned. "Should we call you the cavalry, or what? We don't even know your name, or who sent you here. If you were more open about that, it might help break the ice. Then we might get into some really heavy conversation."

"All right then! My name is Manuelito Gaspar Vincente De Los Cavajadas, but you can call me Joe, okay?…Oh yeah, and these are my men, all of them. And now that we've been introduced, why don't you start with the really heavy conversation, Jade. I can call you Jade, can't I?"

"Okay, for starters. What's your men's names?"

"They'll tell you when they think it's important for you know."

"Who sent you?"

"Xumal."

"Who?" Cheeway said aloud. "Who did you say sent you?"

Joe, as he wanted to be called, explained that Father Sanchez had been in and out of their country for many years, and before him, there were others of his kind, the ones who wore the crucifix with the silver plate attached. However, about two years ago, there was another group who came here. They were said to have power over Father Sanchez's group and called a meeting for many to attend. Joe said there were people from all over the world at this meeting, and when it was over, there were great numbers of the village people missing. Not only from his village, but all the neighboring villages as well.

Joe said he and his men weren't always rebels. He said they only turned to it in order to stop what he called the great madness. So they could bring their lives and those of others, back into some kind of normalcy.

He said from the time of that meeting, everyone in his village lived in a constant state of fear. They were watched, and if they did anything wrong, they would be taken away and never seen again. Those who chose to speak out against people like Father Sanchez were killed.

Joe's father owned a bakery. He didn't make trouble for anyone. He just wanted to provide a living for his family and perhaps save enough to have one of the kids go to school in the U.S.

About two years ago, Joe said three men, wearing the crucifix and silver medallion walked into the store and gave Joe's father 'El Carta del Muerto', the card of death. It had his name and address on the front, and the drawing of a cross inside a triangle on the back. The next morning they found Joe's father dead. Two days later, the same three men came into his house and gave his mother, two brothers, three sisters, and Joe the same card. Joe said he was scared and ran into the hills that night. The next day, he heard his family had been killed. He didn't know who, or how, but all of them were found dead. Just like his father.

Joe said we could speak to any of his men and they would tell the same story about their families. None of them had any living relatives left, anywhere. So in Joe's own words, they had nothing left to lose. All they wanted to do was kill the people responsible for doing this, and if they couldn't kill them, they were determined to foul any plans they would make.

That's what brought Joe to find Xumal. He was seeking someone who was willing to tell him of Father Sanchez's plans so he could plan against them. Joe was aware of the dangers in asking someone like him for assistance. For he was one of the three body guards Father Sanchez always had with him. However, in Joe's mind, the risk was worth it. For if someone like Xumal would feed him information, there would be no plan made he would not have knowledge of.

Joe and Xumal met in the jungle. Joe and his men had raided one of the military convoys coming into the city. Hector and Father Sanchez were there and wanted to find who was responsible.

Xumal saw Joe's party, but said nothing. And Joe knew Xumal saw him, because he stopped long enough to look him right in the eyes, then left. Over the next few months, they had several more encounters like that. Each time, Joe felt something more from this giant of a man called Xumal.

At their next meeting, which had been arranged by Xumal, they spoke. Joe told Xumal he wanted to subvert Father Sanchez plans, or those he worked for. And, Xumal explained his position to Joe. Joe believed Xumal, and they had been working together just before Cheeway's party arrived in the Yucatan. It was a working arrangement they were grateful for.

Joe, Jade, Roberts, Stevens, and Cheeway were sitting in the camp discussing what to do next. Joe knew they had the real map showing the exact location to the Ancient City of Prophecy. And Joe's interest in their finding it was to ensure Father Sanchez would not.

Xumal had given Joe information about what the ancient city was thought to contain and knew the implications if Father Sanchez, or his kind, uncovered it first.

Joe had grown up with a Native American background, but hadn't received the training Cheeway had. However, he was familiar with the ancient histories of the people, and had heard of this city long ago. He said these histories told that where the Ancient City of Prophecy was located, not many people went. It was considered to be an evil place and would change anyone's life just by walking close to it. But neither he, nor his men, believed that and was sure it wouldn't be a problem.

"We got about eight hours before they come back, you know," Joe said, as he pulled some bread to eat. "I told you we let the guards go last night. They should find someone to give them a ride to town when they reach the highway. Got anything here you need for your work? If not, I'll have my men start breaking things apart."

We packed the equipment we considered to be crucial to our dig and left everything else in place. When we finished, Joe's men began breaking it up into small pieces so it would look like they had ransacked the camp.

Next, they brought in some chickens and told us to take off our clothes and put others on. They picked a few articles of our clothing, killed the chickens, dropped their blood on the clothes, and in other places around the camp, then ripped up what was left.

They said this would make it more believable that they had killed us, rather than taking us hostage. Joe told us if Father Sanchez thought we were dead, he wouldn't be in a hurry to find us.

Made good sense to us, and when they were done, it looked very convincing.

Before we left camp, Jade pulled the map out and showed Joe where we believed the site of the Ancient City of Prophecy was. He said he knew of this place and could have us there in a few hours.

Joe instructed his men to move the trees they blocked the road with and told some of them to ride with us. He told the rest to stay behind and remove any traces that could show where we had gone. He told those who remained behind where to meet him later. He didn't tell them where we were going; rather, he named a place that was quite a distance from it. Cheeway thought that was strange, and when we were in the van, he asked Joe why he did that.

"We can't be too careful! I think I might have one or two men that are sympathetic to Father Sanchez and what his kind is up to. I don't know for sure though, so I guess this little diversion will tell me."

"And you think by using us as some kind of sacrificial goat, you can flush these men out?" Jade asked, putting her hands at the back of Joe's seat. "Really think that's wise, Joe?"

"I'd rather find out early, Jade," Joe returned. "Wouldn't want to find out there were informants in my band after we uncover the ancient city, would you?"

"No, guess not. Sorry Joe. Guess we're all a little on edge from all that's happened."

"Don't worry about it, the men with us now can be trusted. When we reach the site, I'll post some guards, then have the others help you dig, or whatever it is you do. If there is someone in the band who is an informant, they'll want to tell Hector or Father Sanchez that none of you were killed. Then, I'll know and we can go on from there."

"How will you know, Joe?" Cheeway asked, as he looked out the back window. "I mean, if you're going to be with us, how will you know?"

"Won't be with you right off, Cheeway. As soon as we get there, I'm going to double back and wait for them where I said I would. I can see if any of them are missing long before they arrive. If there are, we'll simply disappear into the jungle and not be seen by them for a while. That's all."

That seemed to satisfy the group and little else was said for the next few hours. The van made its way deeper into the jungle, jockeying over narrow dirt roads that, as the miles passed, came to look more and more like mountain trails and less like dirt roads.

They followed their map as close as possible and about an hour after crossing a small river, and driving over terrain that offered little, if any, trail, the group found their speed slowed by the increasing jungle growth near the base of a mountain range. Suddenly, everyone in the van began to get very anxious, as if an energy shift had happened.

Look, Jade! What's that?" Roberts said, as he pointed off into the distance out the side of the van.

"That's it, Roberts!" she returned. "That's it! We made it! We're here! Joe, stop the van!

Joe stopped the van. Everyone got out, stretching their legs and arms, taking a better view of what their destination really looked like.

Still excited, Jade yelled out to the group, "Come on, let's get started!"

"What is that, Cheeway?" Stevens asked. "It looks like a big rock coming out of the ground."

"I don't think that's what it is, Stevens," Cheeway returned, as he pulled some equipment out from the back of the van. "I think what you're seeing is the top of a pyramid, but from this distance, I can't be sure. And there's something else about it…"

Cheeway's voice trailed off a for a moment, then, "Anyway, there's one thing I am sure of, there's great power coming from someplace near here. Maybe it is our pyramid. Anyway, we'll know when we get there."

Stevens smiled and put his share of the equipment in his back pack. All of us, including Joe's men, did the same.

Joe said he and three of his men would remain behind to cover our tracks, then hide the remaining two vans. When they completed that, they would return to the designated site and meet up with his other men, then return.

He told us not to worry about them finding us though. From the size of that big rock we were heading to, they couldn't miss us.

We started walking toward the great stone with our equipment. From the distance, they knew it was going to be a few days before they got there and after the second day of hiking everyone was beginning to wonder if what they had seen was a mirage.

Just before they completed the second day, the great stone disappeared behind some larger mountains.

"Still see the stone, Jade?" Cheeway asked, as he took a moment to wipe the sweat out of his eyes.

"No, Cheeway, but don't worry. Roberts took a compass reading just before it disappeared behind that mountain. As long as we keep true to the last reading, I'm sure we'll be there sometime tomorrow, or the day after."

"It didn't look that far from the road, Jade!" Stevens said, as he took the opportunity of ridding the sweat on his face as well. "I can't remember when I worked this hard at getting somewhere."

"Yeah!" Jade returned. "Too bad they don't have shuttles here, isn't it?"

The sun went down and so did we. We knew we couldn't have a night fire, so we huddled close to each other in an attempt to stay warm.

"Something funny about that rock formation," Cheeway said, as he pulled his blanket over his shoulders. "It doesn't seem to fit the time line here."

"What do you mean, Cheeway?" Roberts returned.

"The way it's made. Just doesn't seem to follow the same pattern of the other pyramids, that's all."

"How can you tell? We only saw if from a far distance."

"I know, Roberts. But even at a great distance, when I looked at it with the field glasses, it seemed to be out of proportion. Like the top wasn't in symmetry to the rest of it. Know what I mean?"

"No, but, if you can describe it before I fall asleep, I'll listen."

"That's okay, Roberts, I'm tired too. I really don't have anything concrete, just a feeling, ya know."

Before Cheeway finished his sentence, Roberts was snoring. And it wasn't much longer till they followed him into the lands of the dreamers.

By the afternoon of the third day, they reached what they thought was the last mountain rise between them and the great stone peak they had seen. They arrived at the top and saw a huge valley separated by two mountains.

When they looked at the mountain on the left, they saw the great stone structure. The one that looked like a great pyramid before. At first, Cheeway thought that was the place they needed to dig, but something inside him said that was the wrong place, that they should scale the mountain on the right, rather than the one on the left.

"What makes you think we should dig on the right mountain, Cheeway?" Jade asked, as she pointed to the great stone structure on the left. "Can't you see the obvious?"

"I see it, Jade, but something tells me that is the wrong place. I've followed these feelings all my life, and they haven't let me down yet. I'm going to start on the right mountain. If you want to join me, you can. Otherwise you can take some of the men and start digging on the other one."

"Think we should follow Cheeway, Jade," Roberts said. "He's done this sort of thing more times than we have and he hasn't disappointed us yet."

"I think he's right too, Jade," Stevens added. "My vote is to follow his intuition."

"All right then," Jade said, with a look of disappointment. "But I think we are going to waste our time up there."

With that said, they began the descent into the valley. Not as two separate groups, but as one. When they reached the bottom, they noticed that hand and foot holds had been carved into the side of the mountain. These went all the way to the top of the mountain on the right.

However, the mountain to the left did not have any. It was like no one used it enough to merit carving them.

From the size of the climb, they determined they could make it before night fall. They thought it would be safer up there than on the valley floor. That way, if someone were to approach, they could see them long before the people approaching could see their group.

When they got to the top, all of them stood still where they were. What they saw surprised them so much; they couldn't move or say anything to each other. All they could do was look in silent awe.

# CHAPTER 8

▼

# THE ANCIENT CITY OF PROPHECY

Before them stood a city, very old and covered with vines and undergrowth. It looked like it has been burned and destroyed at some time in the far distant past.

They started looking for clues as to who once inhabited this place, and set up small groups to clear away the debris so they could see as much of the city that still remained.

It hadn't been more than two days into the debris removal when Jade came running down one of the pathways yelling with excitement.

"You've got to come see what I found!" she said, trying to catch her breath with her notebook in one hand, and the map stone in the other. "You won't believe it! You just won't believe it! This entire place is just a cover for something else! Come see for yourselves!"

Everyone dropped what they were doing and ran to Jade. They didn't know what she had discovered, but knew it had to be something important from the tone of her voice and the way she was waving her hands in the air.

"What did you find, Jade?" Roberts asked, as he held her by the arm.

"You won't believe it! It's just like the stone map said! I found the same thing!"

"Jade!" Stevens said, as he stood in front of her. "Slow down, please! We can't understand you if you keep on this way!"

"Okay!" Jade returned, and took a long deep breath. "There, that's better now. I just got so excited about what I found, I couldn't help it…You know this symbol on the stone map?" she said, pointing to the symbol drawing we believed named this ancient city.

"Yes," Roberts said, as he looked at the map stone Jade was holding. "We've all seen it before, Jade, what's your point?"

"I found it! Right here in this very city we're standing in! I found it on the pyramid!"

"What pyramid, Jade?" Cheeway asked, as he looked across the exposed part of the city.

"The pyramid over there!" Jade said, pointing to the direction she came from.

But when they looked, no one saw anything that resembled a pyramid. They thought she'd lost her mind for a moment and had seen something she wanted to find so badly, her mind made it up for her.

"Jade," Cheeway said, as he held her shoulders. "There's no pyramid here. You sure you didn't just think you found one?"

"No, Cheeway!" Jade returned. "I found it all right, it's right over there. Come on, I'll show you! It's a really big find, Cheeway. Really big! You'll see, come on!"

They followed Jade to her pyramid, but as they neared, they still couldn't see what she was talking about. The pyramids of the Old Ones were built very large, not small. And there was no sign of such a structure where Jade was going. Each one of them began to think the heat, danger, and exhaustion had finally gotten to her.

"Okay, you guys!" Jade said with a look of confidence. "Here we are! Now tell me I didn't see what I saw."

They looked where Jade was pointing, but nothing of a pyramid was obvious, only a small stone platform that rose about two or three feet above the city floor.

"This is it, Jade?" Roberts said. "This is what you're calling a pyramid?"

"Jade," Cheeway said, as he reached for one of her hands to hold. "Why don't you sit down with me? All of us are really tired, and we haven't gotten much sleep."

"Cheeway, you of all people! I thought you would be the last one here to not know what this is!"

Jade turned to the rest of us and said. "Are all of you blind? Can't you see what's right in front of you? Look! Right here, where this thing is coming out of the ground! Don't any of you see something just a little strange about this stone?"

"Looks like it might have been the beginning of a pyramid, Jade, but whoever started it must have given up on it long ago," Cheeway returned.

"Cheeway! This is not any beginning pyramid! This is a completed one that has been covered up. Look closely, then maybe you'll see what I mean."

Cheeway bent over the stone to look at it closely. Jade was right, there was something strange about it. On the top, there was the same symbol marking the stone map had, the one they believed named The Ancient City of Prophecy. But what was such a marking doing on the top of this thing...this pyramid Jade believed it to be?

Next, Cheeway took measurements of the top and the sides. There was a very specific relationship to the sides, height, and top of pyramids that had been built. And those measurements changed with each civilization as they moved forward in time. The older civilizations used a different set of measurements than the more recent ones, and that was one of the clues used to determine the age of their structures.

However, when he measured the top portion of this pyramid and compared it to the sides and base, he was surprised to find a clue to what Jade had been speaking of, one that caused her to believe this pyramid was covered up long ago and that what they were looking at was only the top portion of an immense structure that had been built centuries earlier.

"Find anything unusual, Cheeway?" Jade asked, standing between Roberts and Stevens.

"Yeah, Jade, I do. The measurements indicate this structure is much bigger than what we can see of it. I mean, if the same techniques were used in constructing this pyramid, as you call it, then we are only looking at the top portion of one that is really big. I mean, really big."

"How big, Cheeway?" Roberts asked.

"Don't know for sure, Roberts," he returned, as he looked at the top portion. "But from the angle of the sides, I would guess it to be about as large as this mountain we're standing on. If that's the case, this city we are looking at was built over another. And when we find a way to get under it, we'll see the rest of this structure."

"Think it could be what we're looking for, Cheeway?" Stevens asked, as he looked at the small jutting stone structure before him in awe.

"From what I've seen of cities built over others, there is always a passage way left to go back into it. Most times, that passage was blocked off with something big, but not so big it couldn't be removed with a little effort."

"If someone wanted to build over a city, Cheeway, why would they leave such a means of getting back into it?"

"Guess it was their way of ensuring they didn't make any mistakes they couldn't correct. Things like not shoring up the city from the foundation, or something like that. Perhaps it was to make sure they could re-enter the older city and re-strengthen their holding places so the city on top wouldn't fall down on them."

"Any other reasons, Cheeway?" Jade asked, sounding as if she already knew the answer.

"Yes, Jade," he replied. "There are other reasons. One was to appease the spirits who once lived in the original city. Many believed when someone died who still had a lot of anger in them, they would be trapped in the gray world. That's the world of shadows where ghosts and the like reside. And, if they built their city on someplace that was like a sacred burial site, they could re-enter the original city and appease the spirits. Then they would be happy and not bother the current residents. But there's something else here, just can't put my finger on it right now."

"Like what, Cheeway?" Roberts asked.

"Well, like the size of what is exposed here. When one city built over a previous one, it was for one of two reasons. One, they conquered them, tore the original buildings down to the foundation, then use it to rebuild their own. The second reason, was if a really old one was discovered, one that no longer had anyone living in it, but was a strategic location, they would cover up the old city with earth then build the new on top. That left the original city intact, but directly under theirs."

"There is something else here, isn't there, Cheeway?" Jade asked, as she walked toward the top of the stone structure.

"Yes, Jade, but I don't have an explanation for it."

"Can you share your thoughts on it then?"

"Has to do with the size of this structure. If this pyramid was built using measurements of the older civilizations, it should be about as large as the mountain we're standing on. I know I told you that before, but here's what else I am wondering about. If the builders of this city did cover up the first one, why did they build so high? That's just not usual, not at all. It doesn't make sense."

"You say there might be a passage leading into the original city given these circumstances?" Stevens asked.

"Most likely."

"Any clues or markings denoting it? I mean, if we were to find it, would there be any kind of marking telling us this is the place?"

"It would most likely have a symbol representing the God of the Underworld on it. Here, I can draw one for you."

"What civilization does this come from, Cheeway?" Roberts asked, as he looked at the form Cheeway drew on the paper.

"From the Aztec. I believe they were the builders of this city on top."

"But what about the other writings I've found on the base of the pyramid?" Jade asked, as she pointed to one of the stones near the ground. "These are definitely not Aztec and there is something else, something like the writing on the map stone. We don't know what they are, or who made them. But if they were copied by the people who once lived here, couldn't they have also copied one of their signs to denote the entry to the city below, if there is one?"

"Perhaps, Jade, but we all know what those symbols look like, don't we? If we keep them in mind, as well as the symbol the Aztec's made for the underworld, I don't think we'll miss the entrance. I only hope they made one and if they did, that we can find it."

"Then, if we come across a doorway that might lead us under this city, it should have this drawing on it?"

"Something like what I drew, or a symbol similar to the one on the map. Even though there have been variations of it from other groups of Aztec, there should still be something we can recognize."

"Hold on," Jade said, as she held out the small map stone. "There's something else here I think you need to see. Cheeway, see if you can chip off a part of this pyramid."

Cheeway knew where Jade was going with this. He reached for a hammer on his belt then hit the top portion of the pyramid, but nothing happened. He repeated this several more times, but with the same results.

"Didn't think you would make a mark on it," Jade said. "Got the idea when I discovered a hole on the top."

Jade's last remark shocked everyone and when they looked where Jade had pointed and saw there was a small but distinct cut-out on top of the stone structure, no one moved.

"Looks close to the size of the map stone, Jade," Cheeway said, as he ran his fingers over the grooves.

"It is, Cheeway! This is where the map stone was taken from. Look at this!"

Jade brushed the remaining debris away from the indentation, then put the map stone inside. It was a perfect fit, not even a hairline of difference from how it fit inside the cutaway on the larger stone top. And when she placed it in the hole, it blended perfectly. It set so well, it took them a half-hour to pry it out again.

"Anyone need to see more?" Jade asked. "If not, let's get started!"

Each of them went to a separate part of the city and began searching. There was a great level of anticipation for what they might find, and the closer they thought they were to finding the entrance, the less anyone spoke, all except the guards who would look around them every now and then.

Even though Joe said they would not be bothered by the superstition of this place, there was something bothering them. The only thing Cheeway could relate it to was what everyone was feeling.

The ancient city had been vacant for centuries and whoever was here last had destroyed it, as much as they could, using whatever they had. However, there was an energy they felt that was very strong here. It was the kind that made me think I was late to a very important appointment, but there was nothing I could do to get there on time.

It reminded Cheeway of being late for school, how he would run and run to get there. He knew he was already late, but ran anyway. And as he ran, the feeling of being late grew within him. This was the feeling mounting within everyone on the mountain that morning. Cheeway sensed an urgency to everything he was doing, and because of it, he caught himself making mistakes, mistakes that could be deadly if he were not careful.

He wanted to see if the other members of the party were feeling the same way, and asked. Everyone responded that they, too, were feeling what he was. All but one, Roberts. Cheeway didn't hear anything from him.

Suddenly, his silence broke as he yelled.

"Come here, everyone! I think I found it!"

But that was the last they heard from him. As his last words trailed out, there was a rumbling sound followed by a great crash, then dust billowing into the air all around them.

"Cheeway! Over here! It's Roberts; he's fallen in! I need some help! I think he's hurt pretty bad!"

They rushed to the sound of Jade's voice and when they got there, all that remained of where Roberts had been digging was a deep and gaping hole. It was larger than anyone would have thought if only he had fallen through. From its size, they could have driven all three vans into it.

Jade yelled down, hoping to get a response from her brother. But there was none. Only dust and a few bats answered her calls.

"Cheeway, we have to do something!" Jade pleaded, as she pulled on his shirt. "He's hurt, we have to get to him!"

"There's a long rope in my pack!" Stevens said. "We can tie it off up here and lower one of us into the hole. What do you think, Cheeway? Think it's safe enough for one of us to go in?"

"Yeah, Stevens!" he answered. "But I better be the one. Think I'm better prepared than any of you."

They tied the rope to one of the great stone pillars, and then Jade, Stevens, and some of the guards held the rope as Cheeway tied it around himself. They lowered him into the hole slowly; he didn't know what he would find and only had a flashlight to see with.

They had lowered him about twenty feet when he noticed something strange. There was light around him. He had expected the hole to get darker the further in he went, but it was getting lighter. At first he thought the cave-in had caused another opening in the side of the mountain and he was seeing refracted sun light. However, when he accidentally dropped his flashlight, the texture of light told him this was not so. The light had a blue tint to it, something he had not seen from the sun before, and its brightness was like the full moon at night.

Then he saw Roberts. He was lying next to another hole, one that must have been made when he fell. Cheeway didn't see any movement from him, and when his feet touched the floor, he let go of the rope and ran to him, cautiously. He didn't want to cause another cave-in that would have resulted in having the two of them injured, or killed.

When he reached Roberts, he felt a pulse and yelled to Jade he was alive. Immediately, there came three other ropes down, followed by a make-shift stretcher.

It was Jade, Stevens, and Joe. Guess he arrived just as Roberts had taken his fall. Perhaps it was the sound that caused him to rush here, or maybe it was something else. But something had caused him to wear a worried look on his face, and the amount of sweat that covered him was either from a hurried run, or nervousness.

However, when Cheeway shined his flashlight to look above them, his eyes were caught with another surprise, one that no one would have dreamed possible before now. They were in the middle of another city, one that had been built at least thirty or forty feet below the one on top. And above them loomed giant caved stones supported by many pillars made of stone as well.

It gave them the impression they were looking at a stone sky, for as far as they could see, there they were, being held up by massive columns of stone. From the size of them, they had to weigh close to a ton apiece. Then it dawned on them, what must have happened to Roberts was that as he dug, or pulled at something, that caused one of these stones to dislodge and fall through the floor, he must have lost his balance and fallen in with it. It made sense when they saw the hole next to him. If one of these huge stone blocks had fallen from its place above, its weight would have caused it to make the hole next to Roberts, especially if the city they were now looking at had also been built on top of another with the same design, and if that design was also built over the top of an older city, and not just on its foundation.

But the time to think of such things was not now, for Jade, Stevens, and Joe had arrived and were hurrying with the make-shift stretcher.

"Is he alive, Cheeway?" came a worried sounding voice from Jade. "Please tell me he is!"

"He's alive, Jade! Don't know how bad he's hurt though. He's still unconscious."

"Perhaps we should wait here till he comes around," Stevens said, as he watched Jade caress the top of his head. "Best one to tell us if he can be moved would be him, wouldn't it?"

"I agree, Stevens," Joe returned, looking at us with amazement from what had been uncovered. "But I don't think we have much time to wait here!"

"What do you mean, Joe?" Cheeway asked.

"When I got back, I didn't see any trace of my men. No signs of shooting either. It's like they just disappeared.

"Can only take that to mean they went back to Merida."

"Why Merida, Joe?"

"To report on us, Cheeway."

"I thought Father Sanchez and Hector would be long out of the town by now, Joe. You think they're still there?"

"If they thought all of you were dead, they would be. But, if my men were working for Hector and Father Sanchez, they'll be there by now, and telling them everything. Once they know you're not dead, they won't waste time getting out here."

"But they don't know where we are, Joe. How could they find us so quick?"

"We've been tracking in this jungle for years, Cheeway. They'll find us easy enough. Especially if my men are helping them!"

Hearing what Joe said, we busied ourselves in putting Roberts into the stretcher, then tied him down so he wouldn't fall out and pulled him from the hole. Once on top, he began to wake up and asked what had happened.

We told him what we thought happened, then explained how the great stone had gone through another floor beneath him, one that might have another city built under the one he discovered. But we hadn't explored that possibility yet.

"Well, go find out, Cheeway!" Roberts said, with a voice riddled with pain. "I'll wait here. I'm not going anywhere right now, you know."

"I think you're hurt real bad," Jade said. "We need to get you to a doctor! There's blood coming out of your nose, ears,…and your mouth. If I had to guess, I say there's been some internal injury. If we don't take care of it now, there might not be a chance later on."

"Go on, Jade," Roberts replied. "You think I want to miss out on what could be the greatest discovery of all time? I don't think so!"

"Think Jade is right, Roberts," Cheeway said, as he looked closer at the bleeding. "Think the wisest thing to do right now is to get you to a doctor, quick! The site can wait a couple of days. It's been here for thousands of years already, don't think a couple more days will make a difference."

"Better think about that again, Cheeway," Joe said. "If Hector and Father Sanchez find this place, it's all over. They'll destroy it—and you too. You know they will probably wait here with a couple of dozen soldiers until you return. They know you won't leave without completing what you began. And, when you return, they'll open fire on you and whoever is with you. They won't rest until everyone who knew of this place is dead."

"Then what can we do, Joe?" Roberts asked.

"Couple of my men can drive you to Campeche. It's not as far as Merida and they've got good doctors there. And they have a small airport, too. I'll stay with Cheeway and help him with whatever he needs. When we are finished, we'll meet you there and get you a flight home. With your injuries, Roberts, I don't think you would be much good out here. If we are discovered by Hector and Father Sanchez, we'll have to make a quick exit. And with the condition you're in, I don't think you would be up to that!"

"Guess you're right, Joe," Roberts said, with a regretful tone. "But are you sure you don't need me here?"

"I'm sure about it, Roberts," Cheeway returned. "The best thing you can do to help us is to get help for yourself. You know, we'll need your help once we're finished."

"Cheeway!" Jade said, as she looked up at me. "I must go with him!"

"Kinda figured on that, Jade; it's all right, I understand your reasons."

"But what will you do for a translator, Cheeway? I haven't had time to explain how to interpret the symbol drawing to you, or Stevens!"

"We'll figure a way past that, Jade. Don't worry. There's a lot of similarity in their writings, like you said. Perhaps they will be close enough to what I already know to interpret them good enough."

"No!" Jade returned hurriedly. "I would have to spend months to do that, Cheeway, and there's much more I know about ancient writings than you do at present. I have a better idea! Before we started, I thought something like this might happen, like finding this ancient city then not having enough time to decipher what we found. So, I took a few precautions, just in case my worst case scenario came true."

Jade reached inside her pack and pulled out several huge sheets of white paper and some long bars of charcoal like material.

"If, or should I say, when, you find the Hallway of Records, hold these papers over the areas you want to be translated. Don't let them move, or everything will be lost. When they are in place, take the charcoal and rub it over them. That way, we will have a duplicate copy to study later, when there isn't the threat of Hector and Father Sanchez coming after us. Do you understand, Cheeway?"

"Yeah, Jade, I understand. Kinda like how we used to make copies of pennies when we were young. Worked real well, but there is a problem with that. If the drawings got wet or were rubbed, they would smear and you would smear and you couldn't read them. What if something like that happens? There probably won't be another chance to get at them again ya know."

"I thought of that too," Jade said, as she pulled several spray cans from another pack. "This will stop them from being smeared, or destroyed by water. It's kinda like a decoupage spray. Once it dries on the paper, nothing will affect it. This spray will seal whatever it covers, and bends like rubber. That way, you won't have to worry about folding them up. It'll help us get them out of the country too, that is, if we're still being watched."

Cheeway knew Jade had the only workable plan for getting copies of the writings we believed were here, if we could get to the Ancient City of Prophecy before we were discovered. From what I had seen of Father Sanchez and Hector, they had a lot of resources they could draw on…and a network of spies everywhere. For all he knew, they were on their way here, rather than following the false trail they left for them. But whatever the outcome, Cheeway knew they had to make their best effort in locating the ancient city and the Hallway of Records that was said to be there.

Jade, Roberts, and a few of Joe's men went down the side of the mountain to the vans. They would drive to Campeche and get Roberts' injuries taken care of.

We, on the other hand, would remain behind to search for what we had come for.

Watching them leave, left Cheeway feeling hollow, like he was losing a part of his family. They had been together for such a long time, and being this close to finding what they had been searching for, only to have it pulled out of Jade's and Roberts' hands was hard to imagine. He knew it was something that did not set well with either of them, but he also knew they understood. If Father Sanchez did find them, they would have to move fast. And that was something Roberts could not do, not with his injuries.

Cheeway spoke to Stevens about a problem, now that there were only two of them to search the site. He told him if they were to carry out Jade's plan, it would take a third member to accomplish it. Her plan was to have the oversized pieces of paper held over what writings they found, then rub the charcoal over the paper to capture its image. But the papers she gave them were extremely large, and could not be held in place by one person, while the other made the charcoal rubbing.

Stevens agreed and recommended Joe accompany them rather than one of his men. Cheeway agreed and instructed Joe on the procedure they would be using, then asked him if he knew how to rappel. Joe agreed to accompany them, and informed them he was more than familiar with the technique, and, that he would assist either of them should the need arise.

Joe told his men to tie three ropes to the great stone pillars, and lower the other end into the hole. But, there was about to be another surprise, one that would cause us to hurry more than we originally planned.

Just as they had secured the lines to themselves, and were preparing to descend, one of Joe's men came running. From the quickness of his run, Cheeway knew he had found something important and motioned to Joe of his approach.

"Men comin', Joe! About fifty or sixty, I think! I see them over the hill!"

"How far, Juanito? Far enough to give us a chance of getting in and out of the hole with anything?"

"Don't think so! They ride horses, comin' real fast. Be here in a couple of hours!"

"What do you think, Cheeway? Think it's worth taking a risk to see if what you're searching for is really down there?"

"What do you mean, Joe? We've been taking nothing but risks since this whole thing began. What kind of risk you talking about now?"

"Just this!" Joe said, as he checked his rope ties. "They might be here before we can get out of the hole, but if they don't find us, they might think they have time to wait for us to get here. That is if they are really intent on catching all of you."

"So what's your point?"

"Just this, I think they've been told to wait until you get here, but if they had even the slightest idea you have already been here, they might attempt to destroy the place. Then, no one would ever be able to return. Not you, not anybody. I've seen what they've done to other spiritual places, Cheeway. What they can't destroy with their fires or bombs, they come up with a way of making it inaccessible to anyone. If you are willing to take a risk, here's what I suggest we do. It would allow us to look for a longer period of time, than if we just went in and left before they arrived. Wanna hear?"

"Yeah," Cheeway said. "What about you, Stevens, you willing to listen? No harm in hearing him out, is there?"

"Guess not, Cheeway, but remember, I'm not a risk taker. Not naturally that is. If it sounds like it might end up a disaster, I vote not to do it."

"Okay then," Joe said. "Here's what it is. We'll have the men help lower us down the hole. Once were at the first level of the city Cheeway found, we'll have the men throw the ropes down. Then we'll tie the ropes to the second level and lower ourselves down to the next. You did say there was another city level beneath the second one, didn't you, Cheeway?"

"Yeah, Joe, I'm sure of it. Saw a part of it when I thought Roberts fell further in."

"Okay then, we'll have the ropes we need with us. Next, I'll have my men hide in the jungle near here and when they see Father Sanchez's men leave, they can come back, lower more rope and pull us out."

"What do you think?" Joe asked, looking like he had just won at bingo.

"Only one thing, Joe," Cheeway said, as he tied the last knot on his rope. "What makes you believe they will leave if they don't find us here?"

"That's simple, Cheeway," Joe returned, with a large smile on his face. "Father Sanchez is the one to thank for that. His ego won't let those men do anything unless he is with them. And while his ego is very healthy, his body isn't. I don't believe he will be traveling with the men coming, not with his health the way it is. You know, he has to be carried in some of these hills. Guess he isn't strong enough to make it without help. I've seen this, and so have my men. If they find an old city here, and even if they find some clues we were here, they'll be too afraid to destroy it on their own."

"You mean they might not know we're here, Joe?"

"Don't think they do for sure, Cheeway. My man said they were riding here fast. That means they won't have a tracker in front of them. Riders coming fast mean they don't need a tracker. They already know where they're going. But they don't know if we got here yet."

"And you think they'll leave because Father Sanchez isn't with them, Joe?"

"Yeah, Cheeway, that's what I think. Even if they leave a few men to guard the place, my men can over power them. You see, these soldiers aren't a real problem that way. They work for pay you know, and we work from our hearts. Makes a big difference when you understand the concept."

"What makes you think they will only leave a few guards here, Joe? I mean, if there are fifty or sixty of them, don't you think that might leave more men here than your guards can handle? And if they do, what then? We would be trapped at the bottom of a hole we don't know anything about. Could be the end of our lives."

"From what I've seen so far, Cheeway, none of your lives are worth much anyway, seeing as how Father Sanchez knows all about the four of you. What's so different about dying in that hole, or some other place? At least my plan will allow you to see if what you have been searching for really is there. Even at worst case, you can know for sure before they kill you."

"Yeah, Joe," Cheeway said, laughing. "Guess you're right. Better to go down fighting like they say!"

"Go for broke, you two," Joe said, referring to Cheeway and Stevens. "I'll be right beside you. Already told you why this was important to me. If what you are looking for is down there, and we know we can't get out, we can at least do something to make sure Father Sanchez, or one of his kind, don't find it either, can't we?"

Cheeway knew Joe was right and saw Stevens nod his head as well. With this new alliance between the three of them, they began their descent, hoping to find what they had been searching for, and if they did, there would be a way to keep it out of Father Sanchez's hands.

# CHAPTER 9

▼

# THE HALLWAY OF RECORDS

They had to descend quickly, for the men on horseback would arrive in a few hours.

Joe instructed his men on the plan. They held the ropes in place while the group slipped into the dark hole beneath the first city. As they descended, Cheeway couldn't help but wonder if this would be his last great adventure. If Father Sanchez had his way, he would kill all of them and be done with it. To him, killing everyone was better than having anyone know what was contained within the Ancient City of Prophecy.

They were lowered about twenty feet into the hole, when Cheeway told Joe and Stevens to turn out their lights. That caused them to think he didn't know what he was saying, for he could see it from their faces.

"Come on, turn out your lights!" Cheeway repeated, as he switched his off, then placed it in his climbing belt.

"Why, Cheeway?" Stevens asked. "You afraid of being seen by someone? You know Father Sanchez probably won't even be with the men coming! What's so important that you want us to turn our lights off?"

"Just do as I say Stevens and you'll see," he returned, as they continued their descent.

Not more than a few minutes later, Stevens and Joe were holding their mouths wide open. Neither could believe what had happened. The minute they turned their lights out, the whole place was flooded with a light. Not a really bright one, but something like we see at night when the moon is full.

"Where is this coming from?" Joe asked, as he spun himself around on his rope. "No matter where I look, the light seems to be just as bright!"

"Did you know about this before, Cheeway?" Stevens asked. "Something you heard from Grandfather and Two Bears? Or from one of your peoples' ancient accounts of what this place would be like?"

"A little bit of all that, Stevens," Cheeway returned, as he kept his eyes trained on Joe. He reminded him of himself when he was a small child, and had experienced his first ride on the Ferris wheel. "I'd heard about the possibility of this light, but wasn't sure until I came in after Roberts. When I first saw him, I got so worried that he might be dead that I dropped my flashlight. Thought I would have to be brought back up to get another one, but after a minute or so, I noticed this light all around me. Kind of like I was being bathed in it."

"You think it comes from the spirit side of life, Cheeway?" Joe asked, sounding worried.

"No, Joe, don't think anything like that at all," he returned. "Think it might have something to do with the great pyramid we saw up there. Remember, the one sticking out of the ground a few feet?"

"But look now!" Cheeway added, pointing to the far side of the second city. "You can see more of it, and each of the walls seem to be giving off light too."

"Yeah!" Stevens returned. "Like its collecting the sunlight above and somehow transferring it down here!"

"Something like that, Stevens."

"But if the pyramid is sending out light, Cheeway, why aren't there any shadows...anywhere!" Joe said, as he held his hand over his chest making sure he hadn't missed something. "I mean, if light comes from one source, it has to be stronger on one side than on the other. And this light seems to be the same everywhere it goes! How do you account for that?"

"Because it's not just coming from the pyramid, Joe."

"But you said it was the only possible source for the light, didn't you?" Stevens replied.

"Yes I did, but that doesn't mean it isn't being reflected back from other sources as well."

"What are you gettin' at, Cheeway?" Joe exclaimed. "You think there's more than one pyramid here? Where? I can't see another one."

"Not another pyramid, Joe. Another source!" Cheeway returned. "Don't take things so literal when you enter someplace older than the time you have experienced. Big mistake to do that, Joe. You see, everything you've been taught about the past, well, it's not completely true. You know, history has been written by the side that won the last battle. And, they want to make sure they aren't seen as the bad guys, or as someone who knew less than the ones they destroyed. Puts a bad slant on things, if you try to relate what you've been told, to what you see when you actually enter one of the old places. Know what I mean, Joe?"

"Yeah, Cheeway, kinda thought that for a long time myself. But you still haven't explained about the light."

"Look around you, Joe, tell me what you see. Notice anything particular on the walls and tops of the buildings near you?"

"Bunch of shiny stones. Some big, others small. That what you mean?"

"My God, Cheeway, those are crystals set into the walls and houses!" Stevens exclaimed. "They're reflecting the light from the pyramid. No, wait a minute that can't be right. Not at this luminosity level! In order to have the same level of light on both sides of me, the light would have to be intensified many times. Are you saying these crystals are doing that?"

"Got another explanation for it, Stevens?"

"But, that's not possible, Cheeway. Crystals just don't do that!"

"You doin' what Joe was, Stevens? Relating everything you see here to something you've been told by someone else? We got a lot of bad history from that kind of thinking, Stevens, the bad history that allowed so many of the ancient sites to be destroyed because they weren't supposed to do what they did…You know where I'm going with this?"

"Yes, I do, Cheeway. I apologize."

When Stevens said that, he looked at Joe hanging from his rope. Joe was nodding his head, the way one does when they know someone has been caught up in their own deception, but they don't want to say anything to make them feel worse.

Without saying anything further, they lowered themselves past the floor of the second city and into the third. Before they entered they expected to see the light get brighter, but it didn't. It seemed as if it knew how much light was needed, and kept it at that level.

"Look, Cheeway, this city looks much different from the second one. And the second one was a whole lot different than the one on top. What do you think the reason for this is? Why are these cities still intact? Didn't you say when another culture built over a previous one, they would level the old city to use its foundation? Why is this here, and the way it is?"

"Don't know for sure, Stevens. I can only guess they felt the energy here, and believed it was a place to be honored. You know, just like the theory Jade came up with when she identified the writings on the map stone and the three Mayan pyramids. But to go further than that would be speculation on my part. We'll probably know more when we get to the bottom."

"You mean this isn't the bottom, Cheeway?" Joe asked.

"Don't think so, Joe. Look at the hole. It goes down another level."

"Think that will be the end of our descent, Cheeway?"

"Hope so, Joe! Don't think our rope will go much further, do you?"

"Oh yeah," Stevens replied. "Almost forgot about that. Maybe the men are still up there and they can throw some more to us."

"Wouldn't count on that!" Joe responded. "Trained my men to follow directions real good, you know. Need to, doing the kind of work we do. No, when they saw we landed on the first level and threw our ropes down, they left all right. It won't matter if you yell till you're blue in the face, they won't be back till Father Sanchez's men leave. At least most of them."

"So what do we do if we find there is another level below the next one, Cheeway? I'm not too comfortable with learning how to fly, not at my age."

"Fly? What do you mean, Stevens! Think we're going to fly down another level! I think you've lost your mind!" Joe spurted out.

"We're not going to fly, Joe. I don't know what we'll do if we find another city level beneath this one. But we'll come up with something, okay?"

"As long as that something has a rope attached to it, I'm all right with whatever idea you come up with, Cheeway."

"Joe, wanna try something?" Cheeway asked.

"I'm not ready to fly, Cheeway!" Joe returned. "I have plenty to keep me occupied in getting down this rope right now!"

"Come on, Joe, it's just an idea. Nothing that will make you leave your rope. What about it, you game?"

"What have you got in mind?"

"Shine your flashlight at the top of that building behind you. I would, but I don't have the right angle."

"What's it going to do?"

"Don't know, that's why I want you to shine your light on it."

Joe agreed, but had to swing himself out a bit in order to see the building I spoke to him about. He swung far left, then far to the right. His second attempt allowed him to have a straight shot at the building mentioned. And, when he saw it, he pulled out his flashlight and shined it there.

As soon as the beam of light hit what we came to know later was a huge crystal, there came a tremendous blast of yellow light. It was brighter than we could make with our conventional lights today.

But it didn't last long, and I think the reason was due to the short blast of light Joe was able to shine on it. But while there was light to see with, they saw the crystal that reflected and then intensified it back.

It was mounted on top of a large building and supported by three huge stone legs. The crystal itself had to be over seven feet tall and in diameter, but its thickness could not be seen.

Cheeway was curious about the yellow tint of light that came from it and asked Joe if the lens of his flashlight was glass or plastic. He said it was plastic, and Cheeway thought he had the answer, one answer for the many unanswered questions for what they saw here.

"Joe, swing over to me and take my light, the lens on it is crystal. Then swing back and see if you can get another shot at the crystal on top of that building."

Joe managed to get another beam into the crystal and when he did, we were covered with a brilliant blue light.

"That's it!" Cheeway yelled. "They are designed to reflect and intensify light, but only to the nature of its source!"

"How do they do it, Cheeway?" Stevens asked again. "Look! I'm not getting into the old way of thinking. After all, I didn't say they weren't supposed to do that, did I?"

"Glad you didn't," Cheeway returned. "I think these crystals have somehow been engineered to do this. Like taking a small amount of light and intensifying it thousands of times. Don't know how, or why, though. But they do."

"Let's not do that again, Cheeway, the last time the light stayed longer. If Father Sanchez's men look down and see what they think to be daylight, they'll know something's going on down here. Perhaps so sure we're here, they'll come down to get us."

"You're right, Joe, can't let that happen. All right, we won't do that again. Not with one of the big ones. But did any of you see the other crystals around the city? Compared to them, the one we shined our light on seemed to be a dwarf."

"I noticed some heat out of the light, too, Cheeway? Anyone else feel it?"

"Yeah, Stevens!" Joe said. "But I felt more heat from the first burst of light, the one that had the yellow tint to it. Felt heat from the blue one too, but there was more. It seemed to me, there was a tingling sensation from it. Think of the energy we would save if we had one of them in each of our cities, Cheeway!"

"Energy! That's it, Joe! That's why they designed them like they did."

"You mean I answered a question for you? Guess I'm better than I thought I was, huh?"

"They are designed to conduct energy, that's why they designed them the way they did. That's also why they intensified the light shown on them."

"So they did this to save energy? I really don't think they worried too much about paying their electricity bill, do you?"

"That's not what I'm getting at, Stevens. Think of what possibilities come to mind, if you knew how to make crystals that would not only conduct energy from something, or someone, but intensify it thousands of times over."

"I don't know, Cheeway, maybe lighting up a whole city? What are you getting at? I'm not sure I'm following."

"Me neither, Cheeway," Joe jumped on. "Can you be a little more simple for me, too?"

"All right then," Cheeway said. "What's light? It's energy, energy that's created when we bombard electrons with a charge. That's what causes the light filament to glow in our flashlight then be reflected out so we can see. But when we aimed that small beam of light on the crystal, it grew thousands of times more powerful that what we sent into it. Then it flooded the entire room. Now, we can measure thoughts. Not real well, but we have measured them. And, we know they too are a source of energy that's created by our brain. All of you with me so far? From what we have been able to discover about the thought process, the energy created from our minds is in measurable quantities. The stronger the thought, the more energy it creates. But, there's one thing about that energy, it isn't focused anywhere. It seems to disburse as soon as it comes into existence. And when the thought fades, so does the energy. It doesn't leave anything behind. However, what if these ancient people knew how to focus their thoughts in a way that could be centered into one of these crystals? We saw what it did to the light from our flashlights, what do you think it could do with focused energy created by a strong thought? It could even create something out of nothing, couldn't it?"

"But, Cheeway," Stevens said, looking at Cheeway as if he were constructing a science fiction scenario. "That would mean the people who lived here had more ability that we have today. How could that be? I mean most of what you're saying does make sense, but without our technology, how could they do it?"

"Stevens, have you ever heard the writing that says we haven't made any new discoveries; or the saying, 'there's nothing new under the sun'? We only think they are new because we hadn't seen them before. Well, I believe what we perceive as new technology has been around all the time. Only those who discovered its origins were too afraid to come out with where it came from. I believe they thought if people knew how much was known by ancient civilizations before us, we would feel as if we knew nothing at all. Think of the panic that would create! After all, ego is one of the culprits here, ya know. And ego tells us we are greater than any past generation. That is, until the next one comes along and pushes ours aside. No, Stevens, I believe life runs its course in a circular motion, not a straight line. I believe what we are seeing here is something that's been known of for a long time, only someone, or some group, has kept us from knowing about it. I think that's part of the reason Father Sanchez doesn't want us to leave with what we find here, whatever it may be. I believe he would rather kill us than have this information be known."

"Hey!" Joe screamed. "There is something painted just behind that building over there! Can you see it?"

"No, Joe, the light is beginning to fade. What do you think it is?"

"It's a painting of someone! Larger than life too, but it looks like it might be…No! That's not possible!"

"What are you talking about, Joe?" Cheeway asked, as he began to swing on his rope to get a better view of what Joe had seen.

"Hit the crystal with your light again, Joe!" Stevens yelled. "I'm going to swing near you, too. Perhaps if we had a little more light we could make out what you saw."

Joe did as Stevens asked. However, at the precise time he shined his light on the great crystal, Stevens had swung so close to the wall, we thought he was going to hit it. The light shown over the room we were in at the same time Stevens let out a blood-curdling scream.

"It's a monster, Cheeway! We gotta get away from this place…now!"

"It's not what you think, Stevens!" Cheeway said. "Look at it again when you swing back this way. You'll be surprised!"

Each of them looked at the wall painting in awe. For it showed a man, probably in his mid to late thirties, dressed in a tan colored robe, wearing sandals and a beard. His hair was dark brown, almost black, and very curly. Something that was not unusual for the natives in this region.

But there was more. He was standing on a hill with what looked like thousands of people all around him. He was holding his hands out exposing what looked like large holes in each of his wrists. And his feet, while clad in brown sandals, also showed two more holes above them, one in each ankle. Then the front of his robe was open, and in the middle and a little to the left, was another hole.

Behind him were three crosses, large enough for a man to be mounted on, and a picture of a white dove over his head.

"Think the Spaniards were here before us, Cheeway?" Joe asked. "They made their paintings on many things they did not understand. As if they thought they would be protected if they did something like that."

"Don't think the Spaniards did this, Joe," Cheeway returned.

"Why you say that?"

"They didn't have the technology to do something like this is why. Next time you swing near it, take a closer look at that painting. You'll see it isn't a painting at all, but a mural made out of colored and polished rocks. Look how they set each piece inside the wall of the cave. There isn't even a line I can see that separates the different stones. And the angles some of them are cut makes me think we would have a hard time duplicating that even with our lasers cutting the stones. No, I believe this painting was made long before the Spaniards ever came here. Most likely by whoever was living in this third village."

"Do you think it is who I think it is, Cheeway?" Stevens asked.

"Looks like some of the pictures I have seen of the Christ after his ascension, Stevens. Is that what you are thinking?"

"Yeah, exactly. But how could they know?"

"Don't know, Stevens," Cheeway returned, as he allowed his swinging to come to a stop. "But whoever did this had a reason. Perhaps we will discover something when we reach the next level."

After that, silence filled their thoughts. Only the sound of their sliding down the ropes could be heard, until they saw the end of their descent, and the great stone that had caused the passage way to be opened, resting on the bottom.

"Look! I think we're almost there!" Joe said, with a sound of relief.

"Yeah!" Stevens returned. "Not any too soon either from the look of what's left of my rope."

When they reached the bottom, they were standing in what appeared to be the last village. The one that had been built at the same time the great pyramid they saw on top.

And, the amount of rope they had remaining was not touching the ground, but was, in fact, about two feet short.

"Glad we made it," Cheeway said, as he looked over the first city of the ancients.

"You think this is it, Cheeway? Think this is the Ancient City of Prophecy?" Stevens asked.

"Looks like it, Stevens. But we'll know more when we have a chance to look around."

"Why is it so different?" Joe asked, as he rubbed his neck, relieved to know they had not entered a bottomless hole.

"What do you mean, Joe?"

"Look at the buildings, Cheeway! They don't look like anything I've ever seen before. They look like a bubble city—or something like that. But nothing I've seen, even from the old places, is like this, nothing at all."

Joe was right. The buildings were not similar to any kind of workmanship they had ever seen either. The city on top, as well as the two they just passed through, had similar structures. They were built using straight angles for their design. But the buildings in this city were not. They were oval, like someone used a circle, or bubble for their design.

"I don't recall anything ever being built like this, Cheeway? How about you?"

"No, Stevens, I haven't."

"Kind of gives me the feeling of being underwater, ya know. Like all this was built to provide support for a really heavy environment."

"Yeah, I know what you're talking about, Stevens. Like a drawing of what an underwater city would look like. That's what you're getting at?"

"Quiet!" Joe said, as he held his hands out. "There's something making noise back there. Think anyone else could be down here with us?" he said, as he reached for his gun.

"Don't think so, Joe, but don't know for sure. What are you listening to anyway? I don't hear anything."

"Guess it comes from living in the jungle for so long," Joe said. "You know, like listening for sounds of anyone approaching when you can't see well. But there is a sound, and it's coming from back there."

Joe directed his flashlight's beam to the rear of the city, but it only went a short distance. From what they could see, this city had been designed to have a much larger population than the ones they just passed through.

As Cheeway followed the beam of Joe's light, it vanished long before the remains of the city did. They knew it went well beyond anything they would have time to explore. Not if they were to remain ahead of Father Sanchez's men.

"What a waste this is!" Cheeway said sadly, as he followed his beam of light to other sections of the ancient city.

"What you mean, Cheeway?"

"Just this, Joe. I've been an archeologist for as long as I can remember, and have always dreamed of finding a place like this...to be surrounded by all the secrets of a civilization long dead to be revealed by the one who discovers it, you know. And now, we won't have time to investigate any of it. All were going to have time for is to look for the Hallway of Records. And even at that, it's doubtful we can find it before those men arrive."

"What about coming back later, Cheeway? You know, when the heats off you."

"You really think this site will be left intact, Joe? Especially when those men tell Father Sanchez what's here?"

"How they gonna destroy something as big as this, Cheeway? Blow it up?"

"Perhaps, Joe, but we got to use what time we have to our own advantage. Let's fan out and see if we can find something that looks like a 'Hallway of Records'. Okay?"

"Just one question, Cheeway," Stevens said. "It would really help if you told us what it might look like."

"Sorry about that. Guess I got a little carried away. Here," Cheeway said, drawing some symbols on two pieces of paper. "This should be something we might find on a door, or column near a place of importance. Might be something entirely different, being as this civilization is one we know absolutely nothing about. But there's a good possibility of something like this being near it."

Before they fanned out, they picked the most easily seen point in the city to meet at. They knew the chances were high of another cave-in, and if one of them couldn't return, the others would know where they last went to.

They partitioned the city into sections. Then each of them would explore that area. They agreed to meet again every twenty minutes. That would give all of them an opportunity to share what they found.

If something hopeful turned up, they wouldn't have lost anything but twenty or so minutes before they could get to it, and do what they had come here to do. And that was to record the writings in the Ancients' Hallway of Records.

By the time they had came back to the designated location for the second time, Joe returned with something extraordinary. He found a long cylindrical piece of crystal, one he said had great power in it. He said when he shined his light on it, accidentally, because he didn't want another blast of light to blind him, this crystal acted differently. Rather than radiating its light in all directions, it focused into what he said was a strong beam, only going in one direction.

Joe said it was brighter than ten of our flashlights, and would probably last a lot longer than our batteries. If he was right, this would alleviate one of their worries, and that was what they would do when the batteries gave out. They hadn't brought extras, as the weight of them would have been too much for the descent.

Cheeway shined his light on the long crystal; it emitted a beam to the front of it. He held his light on it for just a couple of minutes before it was time to take off on their next search, and he asked Joe to see how long it lasted before the light faded.

They met twenty minutes later and Joe was still using the light from the crystal. It hadn't dimmed one bit. Cheeway asked Joe if there were others like this one. He said there was and led the way.

They only had an hour or so left in the batteries. And while the light being emitted from the pyramid and other crystals was good, it wasn't strong enough to read the intricate inscriptions on the stone doors and pillars of the ancient city. They needed their flashlights for that. However, if they shared three of the crystals, they could save their batteries.

They found where Joe discovered the first crystal and charged two more. These gave more than enough light to see with, and that's when they found it. Right above their heads was a black stone structure. So black, it couldn't have been seen using their flashlights.

"Look! There's an inscription above the doorway, Cheeway! Can you read it?" Stevens asked.

"Kinda!" he returned. "Says something like We Are The Watchers From The Shadows And The Light."

"What you think it means, Cheeway?" Joe asked. "Mean someone is watching? You know those sounds I heard a while back, might be one of them, you know."

"Don't think what you heard then was from any person, Joe. My second search took me in that direction, you know, where you heard the sounds coming from. When I got close, I could tell it was the sound of waves hitting the land. Seems like this city goes back a lot further than we thought, but the rest is underwater."

"I think this is close to what was on the map stone, Cheeway!" Stevens said, with a look of confidence.

"As a matter of fact, I know it is!" said Cheeway.

Stevens paused for a moment, looked at Cheeway, and then placed a wild expression on his face. "This is it! We've found the Hallway of Records! This has to be it; no other building here is made of the same stone, or the same way! Remember what Jade told us, the Hallway of Records would be vastly different than any other building near it? Well, this is it! Look at this stone! It's all black! It looks like the whole thing was made out of one solid piece of black jet stone, or crystal. It's nothing like I've ever seen before. What do you think, Cheeway? Times getting away from us. Those men should be arriving here any minute."

"All right, let's go!"

Without saying anything, they entered the black stone building. What they found inside was the same kind of stone, but it was so highly polished, their lights gave it the impression of a mirror, but a mirror with writing in it.

What they were looking at in the long and narrow hallway, appeared to be what they had been searching for. For the description left by our ancestors described a place such as this. They told us the narrow hallway was created to remind us of the limited choices all mankind would have, once the time of the living prophecy would begin.

Cheeway looked at the long black stone walls and saw many different kinds of writings, but they were not limited to the walls, they were also on the ceiling and floor.

Then, in the far back of the hallway, he saw the place he had been looking for. At the far back of the corridor, and set in a place of its own, was something written separately from the other writings. He knew it was what he had heard of, the three warnings telling what could be done to change or alter the coming earth changes.

However, when he attempted to speak to Stevens and Joe, nothing came out. Not a sound. He thought he had lost his voice and tried again, but with the same result, no sound. Nothing at all. He saw Joe move his mouth and point to something up ahead, but he too was without sound. Then, Stevens saw what was going on and took his knife and hit one of the walls, but with no effect. It was as if whoever built this Hallway of Records did not want sound to disturb it. Whatever their reasons, and however they did this, was well beyond any of them. So, from that point on, they used gestures to signal what they needed to do.

They began making rubbings on the paper Jade left. First, from the walls, then the ceiling, floor, and finally to the far back wall where Cheeway thought the three warnings were recorded. As soon as they completed one set of rubbings, they took them out of the hallway and sprayed them. They didn't want to take any chances of having them smear, not before they had a chance to interpret them.

As soon as they sprayed one and it dried, they used the other side after marking it with a reference number showing where it was taken from. They did rubbings of the entire Hallway of Records. Then folded them up and placed them in a leather pouch.

Then, they exited from the hallway hoping to leave before Father Sanchez's men arrived. However, as soon as they returned to their descent area, they saw it was too late. Their pursuers had arrived and were lowering themselves down on ropes.

There were more than a dozen men lowering themselves to the floor. They were armed federal troops. Had it not been for the sureness of danger, Cheeway would have laughed. They reminded him of something he had seen in the movies. You know, the ones with all of those policemen trying to go someplace but getting in each other's way.

But that feeling did not last long. Soon, he heard a voice that filled him with fear. It was Father Sanchez; he had come with these men!

"Get down there! Quickly, Captain Fuentes!" a voice yelled. "I don't want any of them to escape!"

Father Sanchez was being lowered in a make shift chair. It didn't seem too stable though, because each time he yelled to Captain Fuentes, he would spin around and look like he was about to fall out.

"I'm coming, señor!" Captain Fuentes returned. "Where do you want my men to begin looking?"

"Down here, you fool! Why else do you think I would be here?" Father Sanchez yelled out.

Father Sanchez arrived at the bottom of the ancient city's floor, as did Captain Fuentes and about a dozen or so of the armed guards. Once they removed their ropes, they gathered around Father Sanchez to receive instructions.

However, that was not to come immediately. Father Sanchez looked like he was waiting for someone else to arrive. From where they observed, the ropes move once again, the way they do when someone is coming down them. Then, Father Sanchez yelled again.

"Hurry up! You want them to get away?"

Cheeway saw four people scurry down the rope then rush to Father Sanchez. They were the three bodyguards, and Hector, Roberts' so-called friend.

As soon as they landed, Father Sanchez began his orders.

"Everyone know what you're looking for? Any questions? If you do, now is the time to ask!"

"You mean the two men you showed us the picture of, Father Sanchez?" Captain Fuentes said.

"Good of you to remember, Captain, but did you forget about the third one. He calls himself Joe and is the leader of the band of rebels that has been raiding your towns. Can you remember what he looks like? Or must I show you his picture again?"

"No, señor, I remember! And so do my men," the Captain returned. "Just one more thing. You said we were to capture them. What if they resist? They might have weapons on them!"

"If they resist, kill them! But bring everything they have in their possession to me! No one is to look at what they have, just put it in a sack and bring it back here as soon as you can. Remember what I told you about this place! This is where the work of Satan, himself, was trapped long ago. If any of you were to look upon what was written about him, you would be marked for the rest of your eternal life and would be condemned to burn in hell...forever! There would be nothing I, or the Holy Church, could do to save you...or your families! Each of you bears a great responsibility. You are responsible for keeping the devil's own work trapped here, where it has been sealed, away from all mankind, for thousands of years. If they reach our world, I fear what would happen to all of you. Nothing could save you from the terrible curse God himself would place on you. Nothing! Now, begin your search, but remember, don't touch anything. Satan's fingers are long and could touch your spirit if you did. I will bring members of my order here to study this place of evil at a later time. Then, we will destroy it so it can't infect our world again. This is a holy mission and you men are fulfilling a holy destiny by following me. Each of you will gain great rewards in heaven...if you succeed. Now go, we have to find the ones who would release this evil back into our world!"

At that moment, Cheeway felt the icy hand of Father Sanchez sign his death warrant, and the two men with him. But why, he thought. Why would he have been allowed to get so close to achieving his destiny and be stopped just short of accomplishing it?

Stevens and Joe watched the men going in and out of the ancient stone buildings. As they continued their search, one of them would accidentally touch something they shouldn't and let out a scream, then almost run over their other comrades getting back to Father Sanchez, wanting to be blessed with holy water.

He must have gone through a gallon of it, as the men ran to him every time they touched something they thought they shouldn't. Cheeway thought he would run out of the stuff, but he saw how Father Sanchez was replacing it. He would pick up someone's canteen of drinking water and pour it into his small glass container when no one was looking.

However bizarre this all seemed, Cheeway knew there had to be a way out of this trap. Then, just as most of the soldiers were in another part of the city, there appeared a huge shadow over him.

He waited for a moment, hoping it would go by, but it didn't. He peeked around one of the large fallen stones to see who it might be and was met with what appeared to be a giant, a man who stood over seven feet tall and was as broad as two men put together.

Before Cheeway could warn the other two, the great man giant stepped around the overturned stone and stared at all three of them. Cheeway thought he had marked their end and anticipated him yelling to Father Sanchez that he found them. But he didn't.

Rather than giving their position away, he bent down so they could see his face. Then put one of his huge hands on Joe's shoulder and made a sign for us to remain quiet.

"Know another way out of here!" the great giant of a man said. "It's over there, next to the temple with the sun face on it! Do you see it?"

Silently, they nodded and that brought a pleased look to his face.

"I will go there and leave this glove at the entrance. Remember to look for it. Without it, you will never find your way out. When I signal you, that will mean I have distracted Father Sanchez and the other men away. When you hear my voice, take off! Got that?

"You! Cheeway!" the man giant said, as he held an old vase out, then removed an old parchment. "This is for you. Was left here hundreds of years ago by a priest named Father Paul. It tells what he discovered in this ancient city and will explain why The Brotherhood lives in such fear of this information ever being known. It is too late for the three of you. Each of you has been marked for death. But there may be a chance for Speaking Wind to carry this information with him. And, when the time is right, for him to tell others of what you have found here today."

The man giant then reached for Cheeway's leather pouch and shoved the parchment inside. With that accomplished, he disappeared into the shadows without a sound. Something very unusual for a man of his size.

Who this man was, Cheeway hadn't a clue. But the look that was on Joe's face said he knew him and trusted him enough to go along with his plan. Cheeway strapped the leather pouch across his back and waited for the giant's signal.

The giant made his sound and all of Father Sanchez's men ran toward him, and away from the temple he instructed us to enter.

Silently, they crouched their way to the temple's entrance and looked for the giant's glove. They found it, then entered a very long and dark tunnel within. After more than a few hundred yards, they saw what looked like a large stone doorway, one that had been built into the side of the mountain itself.

They shined their light on it and could partially interpret the instructions the original builders left. It said to push down the last of seven crystal faces on the wall, and something else that mentioned they should not take long to go through the doorway.

They located the seven crystal faces and pushed the seventh one in. There was no resistance and when the door opened, there was no sound. It opened with the ease they would have expected from a door that had been built just a few days ago. But all of them knew this had been built many thousands of years before.

It seemed the more they discovered about the ancient city, the more they regretted not being able to study it. It was almost enough to make them cry.

The door opened and they went through. Good thing they hurried, for just as soon as the last one left, the stone doorway slammed shut again, leaving them standing outside and free. But when the doorway closed, there was no visible sign of it being there. It was as if the side of the mountain swallowed it up.

But they were out of the mountain now and away from Father Sanchez and his traveling band of death. However, they exited on the other side of the mountain and had no horses, vans, or a clue as to where they should go.

"Should be something here, Cheeway," Joe said, as he pushed some of the brush away. "Yeah! Here it is. I knew he wouldn't just leave us out here without anything."

Joe rose from the brush holding a map and a compass. There were three knives next to it and a small note that said they should go to Campeche. It also said Jade and Roberts had been successful in leaving and the same people would help us leave too.

"Joe!" Cheeway said. "Who has done such a thing for us?"

"Xumal did!" he returned. "You remember, the one who came and asked me to help you out of the mess back there in the jungle."

"Xumal? Was he the giant we saw a moment ago? The same one who helped us to find this other exit out of the mountain?"

"Same one, Cheeway. He says he's going to protect you from Father Sanchez. Something about you being one of the Watchers who's returned. Don't know what all that's about, but he's sincere in his efforts, wouldn't you say?"

"Yeah, Joe! Real sincere!"

"What do you know about him?"

"Not too much, just what I've heard from others, mainly. Why?"

"Because, if he's sincere about helping me, think it would be a good idea to know as much about him as I can. Don't you?"

"Sure, Cheeway!" Joe returned, as he started walking in the direction of town. "You know, it's going to be awhile before we get there. More than enough time for me to tell you what I know about Xumal. Don't know if we'll have much time when we get to Campeche though. If you don't mind keeping up with me, I'll tell you what I know about Xumal and Father Sanchez on the way."

"Really appreciate that Joe."

"Me, too," Stevens said from behind us. "I think I need to know more about the one who pulled our bacon out of the fire too. There might be something we can do for him in the future. You never know."

"All right then, let's get started. But, we have to hurry. Won't be long before Father Sanchez discovers we aren't in the old city. And when he does, he'll most likely track us pretty quick!"

With the map and compass, they began the journey to Campeche. They were successful in finding the people who helped Jade and Roberts get away and provided them with a means of leaving the country as well. They said Roberts was doing fine when he left and his injuries had healed enough for him to make the trip home without being in too much pain. Then they bid farewell, telling the group if they ever had need of them, how to contact them. Joe said the same thing and made a prediction they would return, very soon. And when they did, he and his men would be waiting to assist.

# CHAPTER 10

▼

# TRANSLATING THE
# ANCIENT WRITINGS

Cheeway and Stevens flew into the Denver Airport and saw Jade waiting by the baggage claim. Joe told her which flight they were on and when it was scheduled to arrive.

"Good to see you two again!" Jade said, as she reached for two of their bags. "Have any trouble with customs in Dallas?"

"Not at all," Stevens replied. "It was like we were regular people again. No one chasing us and no armed guards to put up with."

"It's really good to be back, Jade," Cheeway said. "But there is still a great heaviness over me from what we had to leave behind. Think Father Sanchez and his goon squad will try to destroy everything we found."

"Don't worry about that now, Cheeway," Jade returned. "Roberts and I have put together a really great lab. We can work at translating what you brought back. You did manage to bring something back, didn't you?"

"Yeah, Jade, got it right here in my leather pouch," he said, patting the pouch strapped to his side. "Couldn't have left without this, ya know."

"All right then, let's get everything in the van and get going. Roberts is waiting, and you know him, he's as nervous as a first time father!"

"Where we going, Jade?" Cheeway asked, as he placed the last piece of baggage in the back of the van.

"Out to the country, Cheeway. We found a really secluded cabin to rent. Put enough down on it to keep it for the next few months. Didn't know exactly what you would be bringing back, but we wanted to have enough time to uncover whatever mystery you brought. Think three months will be long enough?"

"Think so, Jade, but if we had time to bring back everything we wanted, you would have needed a couple of lifetimes," Stevens replied, as he looked out the window.

"You too, Stevens?" Jade asked.

"Me too, what, Jade?"

"You regret having to leave the site before you could do what you wanted?"

"If only you had been there, Jade. Only if you had seen what we did, would you feel the same way. There's more there than anyone can imagine!"

"Maybe we can go back some day. What do you think?" Jade suggested.

"Don't know about that, Jade," Cheeway replied. "I think Father Sanchez and his goon squad have already taken care of that decision. Don't think there will be much left when they get through with it."

Silence filled the van that Jade drove from the airport. They saw the mountains just outside of Denver coming closer as the last remaining buildings of the city disappeared behind them. They turned onto a small road that led them to the middle of a great grouping of trees. Seeing that, Cheeway felt the peace of life begin to fill him once again, something he had not felt for some time.

It wasn't more than an hour later the van stopped and they got out. When Cheeway looked at their new home, he knew what Jade said was true. It was a two-story wood frame cabin with trees and a waterfall next to it.

He stood next to the van and listened to the sounds of birds singing, and felt the wind caress his face. He knew there wasn't any hurry now and let himself drink in the wonders of life that were reminding him of its balance…the balance that had slipped from him since Mary was killed.

"Come on, Cheeway!" Jade broke in. "Roberts is waiting inside and I am anxious to see what you brought. What did you bring anyway? Couldn't be too much if you're carrying it in that small leather pouch."

"Brought back rubbings of everything in the Hallway of Records, Jade. And something more. It's a piece of parchment that was given to me by Xumal, one of Father Sanchez's guards."

"You mean the one Joe told us about back in the jungle?" Jade asked.

"Same one. Said this parchment would uncover the secret of why the Illuminati are so intent in not having this information get out to the public. And, from what I can tell, it looks like he left an alphabet showing how to translate the old writings into Latin. Might help out you know."

Jade stood there for a moment without expression. She looked like someone had hit her with an invisible cannon shell. Then, without saying a word, she grabbed Cheeway's shirt and literally pulled him toward the house.

"Jade!" Cheeway said, demandingly. "You're going to tear my shirt!"

"Don't worry about the small stuff, Cheeway! I'll get you another if I do! And, if you hurry, I'll buy you ten more. That make you happy? Come on, we don't have time to lose. Got a lot of work to do. Why didn't you say what you were carrying before?"

"You didn't ask."

"Don't be cute, Cheeway!" Jade returned, as they entered the house.

No sooner were they inside when Jade yelled for Roberts to come running to the lab. Then she told the two housekeepers to remain outside and keep a look out for anyone who might drive up. She told them if they saw anyone coming, they were to get her immediately, even if she was sleeping.

"Cheeway, Stevens, good to see you made it back. I thought we might not ever see you two again," Roberts said, as he entered the lab.

"No time for that, Roberts!" Jade quipped back at him. "Come over here! Look at what these two dear angels brought back with them. Where is it, Cheeway? Come on, pull it out!"

Cheeway had seen Jade this excited once before and knew there was nothing he could say, or do, to calm her down. Not until she saw what they brought back would she find peace for herself.

Without speaking, Cheeway pulled the paper rubbings and the old parchment out of the bag. Then he explained the anomaly of not being able to hear any sound when they were in the Hallway of Records.

All of this held their attention, and from the look on their faces, Cheeway knew they had not ever heard of such a thing before. Then, Stevens relayed the story of the crystals and what they discovered from them, as well as the giant wall painting of a man resembling The Christ after ascension. He then went on to tell about the architecture in the ancient village and how vastly different it was from anything any of us had seen before.

"Now I feel worse!" Roberts said, as he slumped himself into one of the cushioned chairs.

"What do you mean, Roberts?"

"I've heard legends, well—just rumors really, maybe more myth than anything, about what you have actually seen. And I missed it, just because I wasn't careful and fell in a hole."

"Roberts, if it wasn't for you, we might not have found the city!" Cheeway said, attempting to sound reassuring. "Don't forget, Father Sanchez and his men were right behind us when you left. That didn't leave us time to do much of anything.

"If you hadn't fallen through the first floor, causing the stone to uncover two more cities below you, chances are, none of this would be on the table now!" he said, pointing to all they had retrieved.

"And, Roberts," Stevens picked up. "If you hadn't fallen, we wouldn't have seen what we've told you about. You would still be locked in a dark place wondering if what you had heard, or read, was true. But now you won't. Because of what you helped to uncover, you know it's true. There are such things from the ancient past and we are your proof!"

"Guess you're right, Stevens. But there's a lot that's still unanswered. Perhaps we can return there when the heat is off. What do you think?"

"I think we're going to have our hands full for a time, Roberts," Jade said, turning over the pieces of paper. "Cheeway, these numbers on the bottom of each page, do they reference the locations of these drawings?"

"Yeah, Jade, we numbered them so we could piece them together when we got out. Even though we didn't think we would at the time."

"Good thing Joe and his men came around when they did, huh, Cheeway?" Roberts asked.

"And Xumal, Roberts!" Stevens returned. "If it hadn't been for him, none of this, or us, would be here."

"That's twice he has saved our lives, Jade," Cheeway said. "You ought to see him though. You need a ladder to look at him eye to eye."

"Cheeway, let's talk about that later. Right now, let's get these rubbings where they belong. Think the room here is in proportion to the Hallway of Records? I mean, if we put these pages up where you copied them from, think we could re-create that place?"

"I think we could, Jade. Might be a little off though. You know rooms we live in are more square, but the Hallway of Records, and the other buildings we saw, they weren't built the same way. Something fundamentally different in their dimensions from ours. But, it might be close enough. If it isn't, we can make something up."

"Good!" Jade returned, keeping her eyes on the pile of papers. "You and Stevens begin rebuilding the hallway, and Roberts and I will work on the parchment you brought back. If there is a clue to translating the old writings in it, our work won't be difficult at all."

For the next thirty-six hours, they made working copies of the rubbings and put them on the walls, ceiling, and floor to mirror the ancient hallway.

Jade noticed one drawing that did not have a mark on it and asked what it was from. Cheeway told her it was a symbol that was over the entrance to the hallway.

She looked at it for a moment, then said, "That's what was on the map stone, Cheeway! Recognize it?"

"Yeah, Jade...I do."

"Wait a minute, there's something different in this one," Jade said, as she looked at the map stone again. "It says here something like 'We Are The Watchers', then it stops. But from the rubbing you found on top of the entrance, it says, 'We Are The Watchers From The Shadows And The Light'! Wonder why the difference? Got any ideas?"

No one responded, they were too engrossed in looking at all the symbols that had been placed everywhere in the lab. And, were wondering what they would reveal.

Only one of them could find the clues needed to unlock these silent voices of our past and Jade would have to be the one. The rest would be her assistants.

Several more days passed and all four of them remained in the lab. They ate there, slept there, and did anything else that they needed to do there. For them, that was their entire world. Nothing else existed.

Roberts, Stevens, and Cheeway worked in whatever capacity was needed to assist Jade in deciphering the coded writings. And at the end of each day, they would review their work, then record and archive it for later use, if there was a need.

Then, Jade confirmed what we had been told about the old parchment. On one of the papers, she found an alphabet that would allow her to decode the ancient writings.

The writing took the form of animals, plants, and the different seasons, and the parchment related it to Latin, a language Jade was more than familiar with. It took another couple of days before she had enough to begin translating the writings.

What she discovered was bigger than any of us could have imagined in our wildest dreams. And, it all made sense. Everything was put into perspective as well. Not just for events we had been searching for, but for every living thing in this world we know.

"Okay, everyone!" Jade announced, as she picked up a large notebook. "I'm ready to tell you some bed time stories now. Have a seat! Good thing we had that parchment, Cheeway. It gave us their alphabet. Without it, we could have been here years rather than days. Anyway, the way the writings were left in the Hallway of Records is significant. It seems they were written as a chronology of events. They begin from the time these people first arrived to when they left. And, the further back we go in the Hallway of Records, the more prophetic their writings become. Especially when it come to the prophecies they made and the reasons they knew they would occur.

"As for the writing on the top part of its entrance, the symbols there were similar to what they left on the stone map. We were right about what we thought they said. They read: We Are The Watchers From The Shadows And The Light. And just inside the entrance they explained what that means. The first dozen or so panels you rubbed from the wall mention a place the builders of this city came from. Nothing really specific, other than they make reference to a land with red earth. But that's the only reference to their home they make, other than saying this Earth is not where they are from. However, they refer to themselves as a race of helpers. That they came in vessels carrying the seeds of mankind, and records that were meant to assist us when our time here was almost over.

"Now, from what I have been able to make out, I can only take that as meaning one thing. And that is when we have polluted this Earth so much it can no longer produce food and water we can consume, I would say our time here is over. But they go further than that, gentleman! Much further! They say within these records, are ancient laws we were to follow. And they explain that if these laws were not adhered to, disaster would follow…disasters they knew about over forty thousand years ago! Now, I picked the forty thousand year mark from a map of the constellations they drew close to the entrance. And its position, in relation to the Earth, has not been aligned that way for about forty thousand years. So this is where I pegged the time they placed these inscriptions on the walls of their hallway.

"Now, what they call disasters, we call prophecy. I don't think any of you will disagree on that point. And they were certain enough to list them in great detail. I believe they knew what they left for us as a race of people would be ignored, or hidden. I also think they knew we would find this hallway of theirs, too, but only when we were close to what they refer to as the end of our time on Earth. They say they came here in great numbers, carrying the seeds of mankind so it could understand basic lessons. But each lesson that was ignored would attach a stronger emotion to it. So when it was presented to that same person again, they would believe that there was more than one. And, they refer to an ascension process that takes place the instant our lessons are completed.

"But they also make reference to this not being the first world they carried our seeds to. They say this had been done ten times before, and the result has pretty much been the same. There were a few who heard of the eleven laws left for them and made the effort of understanding, not just knowing them, then ascended to become one of the watchers. But the majority of these seeds had to be taken to the next place and their history was repeated. They say this process will be repeated over and over until everyone has learned.

"Another thing they make reference to is this," Jade said, as she set her book down. "They wrote something to the effect that whenever someone only knows something, there is a big hole in it. A hole, according to them, that is big enough to feel one can fall through it. And because of this, they fear their unknown. But when someone understands what they know, that hole isn't there. It seems like that is the balance they talk about us achieving...the knowing and the understanding.

"They make reference to great fear residing within the seed they brought here. Kind of like they've been watching us all the time, you know. So I looked for anything further they had to write about fear. They said it was like an aphrodisiac for the lost. As long as anyone felt fear, they would find ways to keep others from getting past it. Kind of like misery loves company, if you know what I mean. But they said in the final times for life on this Earth, there will be a return of those who wrote the eleven laws...that they would return and everything that was buried from the past would resurface again. But that, too, would cause many to fear what is to happen when this time comes. And, the ones who will feel the most fear will be those who have been controlling others from the dark corners of life. That particular statement seems more relevant to Father Sanchez. Right Stevens?"

"So, Jade," Cheeway said. "Think the group Father Sanchez represents fears what we found?"

"Yeah, Cheeway, I do. I believe they are the Watchers From The Shadows...the ones the original group trained to keep what they left a secret from mankind until it was time for the original builders to return."

"Who trained who, Jade?" Roberts asked. "Where did you find that? I don't remember you telling me anything about that."

"Well, I did, dear brother, but you probably had your mind in some other place when I did. I found that reference to their training other groups, just to the inside of the entrance. It was right at the beginning of their writings, like they knew this was the beginning for everything they left. But that beginning also marked their end. You see, when they first came here, they knew their time could not be long. It had something to do with the longer they remained, the more difficult it got for them to leave. Anyway, they saw a need to pick a few to train, to teach them what they left, so when this knowledge could be reintroduced, there would be someone here to know what to do with it. But something went wrong, terribly wrong! Now, this part of the writing gets a little foggy. There seems to be a different writing form they used here. And I can't translate it as well as I should. But I'm going to give you my best guess at what they wanted to leave, okay?"

By this time, Jade was holding everyone's attention so well, they didn't want to interrupt her by speaking, so they just nodded their heads.

"Good! Then here it is, at least the part I can translate. They mention three groups here. First, there are The Watchers From The Light, and they not only built this ancient city, leaving the eleven laws, and inscribed the writings in the Hallway of Records, but they were responsible for bringing our seed to this Earth.

"Then, there are The Watchers From The Shadows. They were trained on what all this meant, and shown the secrets of how they built what they did. The visitors left these people with an understanding of how to get through emotions that crowd out our common sense in life and get right into the lessons each of us need to learn. They told them where other records were left, in buried chambers, around the world, where they left the secrets to great technology for us to use, but only when the time was right and people would understand the intent of what they left. Otherwise, they would misuse these technologies and cause great disaster to fall over everyone.

"Then, they make reference to a third group called The Watchers From Within. And their purpose was to keep an eye on The Watchers From The Shadows, to make sure they would not fall away from their agreed part in this great plan. They would observe from within the group formed by The Watchers From The Shadows, and if anything went wrong, something like letting out information before it was time, they would stop it. In a way, this third group seemed to be stronger than the second, but it didn't turn out like that.

"After what appears to be an extensive effort in their training, The Watchers From The Shadows grew suspicious of The Watchers From The Light. It seems they believed they were withholding great amounts of information from them. So, they confronted them and found their suspicions to be true. The Watchers

From The Light told them not everything could be shared…that until their lessons had been learned, they would not be allowed to know everything they knew. And this brought a great rage to The Watchers From The Shadows. The writings say they killed The Watchers From The Light and the ones From Within. But before they completed this task, all locations where their technology and prophecy was located were moved. It was moved, as the writings put it, to secret places. I believe what they are referring to was that they had the technology to move entire cities. Like picking them up and setting them down in another location. And when they finished relocating their records in secret places, the original builders left.

"But there is another piece to this, one each of you will find most interesting. The writings say both groups of watchers will return just before the ending of time. And, they return with a specific marking. For The Watchers From The Light, they will have a red birthmark on the back of their neck. It is said to be located just under the hairline and looks like a map of something. That mark is said to be obvious when they are receiving information about who they are. And when the other group, The Watchers From Within, returns, they will have a mark in their right palm, one that can only be recognized by another of their kind. The writings say when these two groups of watchers begin to wake up, they will find all the secret places of hidden knowledge, and then bring it out for everyone to know. But when this ancient knowledge is learned, there will be no more secrets, anywhere in the world. Everyone will know everything!

"The writings say that until that time, The Watchers From The Shadows will have gained great status among all world governments, but their status will be a secretive one…one that will have allowed them to do their work unknown by other people. And when the ancient knowledge resurfaces, it will expose them and people will not only learn who they are, but also who has been controlling their lives throughout history.

"But this is only a small part of what makes The Watchers From The Shadows fear what we found, gentlemen. The biggest revelation is to be found in the parchment you were given, Cheeway. Having read what it contains, and finding the references it makes to these ancient writings, I can see why these Illuminati, as you call them, fear this information. They are feeling their secret life being torn away because of this. And I believe they are willing to do anything to keep this information from being known."

"But, Jade, from what you've said so far, I can't see anything that should make them afraid," Cheeway said.

"You're right, Cheeway, but you haven't heard what I found in the manuscript. The implications of what these ancient writings will mean to everyone will make them nervous. Think about this, a civilization over forty thousand years old who knew the answers to more mysteries than we can think to ask questions about. And they had technology more advanced than we have today. What happened to that? When people hear of this, they will know there is indeed a true legacy of mankind. One that has been around for a very long time. But why hasn't it surfaced before now? They will begin to see that someone, or some powerful group, has been keeping it from them, and they will ask why. As those questions surface, many will see everything that they have been told about the history of the world is, for the most part, a lie. Then they will question the need for authority. They will see that authority is not needed to maintain order in their daily lives, but has been used to keep them in the dark as to their true identity. And has been the sole instrument in keeping them in control. So much in control, they were made to fear ever searching for their own truth. That, then, is the real threat to the Father Sanchez's in the world, Cheeway. But it will begin when others, like ourselves, hear of what we have uncovered. For that will be the beginning of their end and that is what they fear the most."

"Like absolute power corrupts absolutely? And they most likely want to kill the other two groups of watchers before they remember who they are?" Stevens asked.

"Exactly!" Jade replied. "Whoever this secret group Father Sanchez represents is, whether they are a part of who Stevens calls the Illuminati or not, have ruled uncontested wherever they have gone. Think about that for a moment. If you had such authority over everyone, would you be willing to let it go? I don't think so. After all, they've become used to having their way with everyone. What are they going to do when they have to be like everyone else, not able to keep their precious secrets anymore? I think they will panic, just as Father Sanchez is probably doing right now!"

"Think he knows what we managed to bring out of the ancient city, Jade?" Stevens asked.

"I don't know for sure. But I bet he's dying to know everything we do. However, even if we didn't have the writings and the parchment, he would most likely want us dead anyway. You know, just by having anyone know places like this exist, provable or not, brings a real threat to his way of life. And, if he has the power base we believe his group does, chances are high he's still tracking us, hoping to kill us before we have a chance of telling anyone what we found. But, from what I discovered within the writings, there are great catastrophes coming to this

Earth if things don't change. Think for a moment, if you will. If this planet continues to decay at its present rate, what will be left in another ten or twenty years? The ones who left the writings thought of that, and left clues for what we could do to change it."

Jade stood in silence for a moment. It looked as if she was getting lost in her thoughts and was about to forget what she had translated.

"Jade," Cheeway began, as he looked at what remained of her pile of notes. "Looks like there's more you have to tell us. Is there?"

"Yes, Cheeway, there's a lot more," came her hushed response.

# CHAPTER 11

▼

# ANCIENT PROPHECIES
# THAT MARK THE END
# OF TIME

"It's like whoever wrote these writings knew what we would do. I mean, like making the choice of finding our way spiritually, that is."

"Why do you say that, Jade?" Roberts asked. "Something else you found in the writings that led you to believe that's true?"

"Yeah, Roberts, something like that. You see, when you go just a little further inside the panels, they speak of things that are going to happen on this planet, things that could very well mean the end of life here as we know it. And the funny thing about that is they are the direct result of what we have done to ourselves. It's like they knew the cause and effect for our greed and desire to control everything, you know?"

"Anything like the ancient prophecies of our Old Ones, Jade?" Cheeway asked.

"Yeah, Cheeway, almost all of it," Jade said, as she scratched the back of her head. "Tell you what! Let me cite one of these predictions they wrote then you tell me if it's close to what you were told by Grandfather and Two Bears."

"Of course, Jade, but where is it going? I mean, what does it have to do with uncovering more of these ancient writings?"

"Just this, Cheeway. For the longest time, I've heard you mention there was a strong connection to the ancient prophecies of the Pueblo people to an older culture. One that pre-dates anything we knew of, right?"

"Yeah, so far that is."

"Let's say that not only is their first prediction the same as what you were raised with, but all of them are. Then, we will know these writings were not isolated, but were spread among other cultures. We'll know a little more about what happened after the original people left. You know, if they were isolated completely, then we wouldn't have anything to worry about. For everything they speak of would be so new, no one would have a counter argument against it. However, if others knew of them, too, then people like Father Sanchez, in their time, would have created many arguments to convince people what they heard was not true. As for me, I can say this about these writings. What I have translated so far, I can relate to the Bible, kind of. But there is much more in these writings than there is in the Bible. Almost like this is the unabridged, or unedited, version of what we were raised with. And each of you knows I am not a religious person, but was raised with a Christian background. As such, I have read the Bible, both the New and Old Testaments. And what these writings speak about is close to what was written in Revelations and other parts of that book. But even more important, they explain why these catastrophes must occur and that made me fear what they had to say. I really wanted a way to tell myself what I was reading could not be true. Even though I know these writings pre-date the Bible by more than thirty thousand years, I found myself attempting to disprove what they said because of my Biblical teachings. I wasn't doing it on a conscious level, but I know that's what I was doing. I was attempting to validate something much older than my reference. And, my friends, that can be very dangerous. For what I was using as my reference was something, in relative terms, still in its stages of infancy. Now, if I did this, others would too. That is, if we know if these teachings were not isolated. Get my meaning, Cheeway?"

"Yes, Jade, I do. I see what you are getting at now."

"Jade," Stevens said. "You think we've been so conditioned, we can no longer think independently?"

"Yes, I do. I believe what I discovered about myself is something that resides in all of us. And I believe it stems from a society that controls others to do its will and not their own."

"Perhaps you're right, Jade," Cheeway offered. "Our people were told that in the end times there would appear two groups of helpers. And they would bring back understanding that would allow others to see on their own again. That particular prophecy also says if these two groups of people do not come, there will be no hope for mankind. All will be lost."

"That's exactly what I mean, Cheeway. If the group Father Sanchez represents is successful in keeping this from being known, that's precisely what will happen to everyone. All hope will be lost. But to them, to have their perception of power for one minute more makes it all worthwhile for them. I believe they are so afraid of losing control, they are willing to sacrifice us to keep it. Think about it, if they have been around for as long as they want us to believe, they would have had time to put tremendous mind blocks in everyone. Like desensitizing them to this information. You know, like social conditioning. They would have put it in our school systems, our histories, our prayer, and anything else they could find that would bombard people with reinforcement to their way of thinking, like getting us to believe if we did anything that deviated from the established norm, we would suffer for all eternity. I believe they have conditioned the populations of the world to be afraid of doing anything on their own. For if they did, they would be marked with certain death. Not only physically, but spiritually as well. All this has created a fear based society which each of us has been born and raised in. Think about that; think of what first comes to your mind when someone says you might doing something wrong. Not that it is wrong, but only that it might be. Don't you feel fear? I do and I don't think I'm different from anyone else."

"I see what you mean, Jade," Cheeway acknowledged. "Go on then, tell us something about the first prediction they left. If it comes close to what I was raised with, I'll tell you."

"All of you see what I'm getting to?" Jade asked, as she looked at the three of them. "I don't want you to feel I'm pushing my weight around. But, I really need to know if you agree with me or not."

There was only silence, but it was a silence that told Jade they agreed with what she said.

"All right then, here is the first prediction of their prophecy. I'll give them in order, not all of them though; I need more time to do that. But for those I have translated, I will give them to you as they were written. Once more thing, it seems the further I went into the back of the Hallway of Records, the more intense these prophecies get. So remember, this was one I found near the entrance.

"The first one speaks of four volcanoes. Two resemble identical children that are close to a larger one. The third one looks like a grandmother and she is awakened when the two children volcanoes go off at the same time. They cause her to awaken and blow a great population into the air. Then she, and all the land with her, sink beneath the great waters. But that's not all, it says here that when she erupts, she causes another great volcano to wake up. And this fourth one is called something like the grandfather. When he awakens, he also blows away many people, but more than that, he causes lands to shift and fall into the great waters as well. Once that is done, he is seen pulling on the leg of a great bird. Not a bird you and I are used to seeing, but one that breathes fire. Once awakened, he flies first to the great waters of life and sets all of them on fire. Next, he flies over all the known and unknown lands igniting them as well. Any of this seem familiar to what you have heard, Cheeway?"

"Yes it does, Jade," Cheeway said, as he rubbed his hands on a napkin to dry them. "I have heard of what you said. It goes back a long time though. It was left by the Anasazi. Grandfather and Two Bears showed us a spirit painting in a sacred cave. They said its origin was not known, but had always been there. One other thing about that painting, it wasn't made from paint. Its colors were from the stone itself. It seemed like the Earth Mother had painted this story for us using different colors within the rock. What you make reference to, we call the song legend of the Fire Bird. This is supposed to take place just before our last chance to change these prophecies. The two children volcanoes could be the ones we call the twins. They are located just to the west of Mexico City and are called Popocatepetl and Iztaccihuatl. Even though they have erupted before, they have done so separately. But, our prophecy says, when they erupt together, that it is the first of four signs we need to be aware of. For when they do, they wake the grandmother and she does not wake up happy. The grandmother is a volcano that was hidden from mankind long ago by a people who also knew of this prophecy. They thought it would take place in their time and made a great effort in stopping it from happening.

"From what I understand, they lived during a time very soon after the ones who wrote the Hallway of Records left. But there is no trace of their civilization from anything that has been found to date. They were, however, said to be a very large population base culture whose work with stones has not been matched. They were said to have spent generations carving out great stones and placing them inside the crater we refer to as the grandmother. She was not completely inactive then and would spew smoke periodically. This culture thought if they could seal up her mouth with stones too heavy for her to move they would avert the coming catastrophe and their lives would be spared. So they set into place great stones weighing several tons, at least as near as I can calculate. And they were so perfectly matched; nothing could escape from under or between them— other than the heat, that is. They created something that looked like a great stone bowl and the stones fit together so well, they did not allow anything to pass them. Not from below, nor above. Over time, the rains collected in this large stone bowl creating a huge lake. Miles across, as near as I can remember. But as it is with all things in this world, the culture that created it vanished, leaving no trace of them ever having walked the Earth.

"Later, the Maya found the lake and, feeling the heat from the waters beneath it, they believed it to be an opening to the underworld. Now remember, many of the southern people believed we stole our bodies from the underworld by trickery. And the Maya, not wanting to upset the dwellers of the underworld, made an island in the middle of the lake. On the island, they conducted sacred rites giving thanks to all creation for what they had been blessed with. They believed the results of their ceremony would travel past the waters of the lake and into the underworld. They thought if the dwellers could feel the good they were bringing them they would not be so likely to come and take their bodies back and allow them to continue their journey.

"After a period of time, the Maya left this area and the Aztec entered. The Aztec were originally a band of outcasts from many other tribes and villages. The name they took to themselves, the Mexica, means a mixture of people. And that's what they were, a mixture of many different people who had been cast out of their homelands. However, the Aztec had to be tough warriors. They were left in swamps next to the great deserts and to survive these hardships, they had to be tough. But when their numbers were large enough to form armies, they left the swamps and spread to the known lands south of them. They invaded many countries and took them over, making slaves of those they would conquer, or taking prisoners for sacrifice. But when they came to the great lake and felt the heat from the Earth beneath it, they too believed this to be a place of sacredness and expanded it to reflect their greatness. They made the island larger, then put in four roads that went from the shore to the island. After that, they built great buildings, but the healing from the waters was so great, they decided to make the island their capitol, believing themselves to be in concert with the underworld dwellers and their powers over life.

"Next came the Spaniards who conquered the Aztec and took over their capitol. They knew of the healing waters in the lake and believed it to be the work of the devil. So, they filled it with earth and stone, then built over it. They too, made it a capitol for themselves and called it Mexico City. However, none but the original builders of the great stone bowl knew of the existence of a volcano beneath it…the one we call the Grandmother. When the two twins erupt, our prophecy says they will awaken the grandmother. And when she belches out her heated rock, it will shoot out with such force, it will literally blow Mexico City into the sky. The result will be an immediate death for millions of people.

Cheeway paused, looking around the room at each of his friends, then said, "But there's more. It is said when she erupts, she will cause the Earth to tremble with such force, the tail of the turtle will fall into the oceans. The tail of the turtle is what we call Central America. That causes the grandfather to awaken, the grandfather we call Mt. Rainier, near Seattle, Washington. When he is awakened, he causes many people to be covered with a white smoke, one that takes away their breath, and they die. He has also acted, as a stopping hand to the moving from Earth, for his lack of eruptions in the past has been the only thing that kept portions of the Earth from moving out into the ocean. But when he erupts at this time, there will great pieces of Earth to sink beneath the water and there will be no life on them. Not life as we know it, that is. His actions wake the great Fire Bird who rises up out of the earth and blows his fiery breath over the waters in the Pacific Ocean. That causes the ring of fire to wake up from its sleep and all the volcanoes under the great waters to erupt. That is the ancient prophecy that has been shared with me, Jade. I believe it comes very close to what you spoke about, don't you?"

"Too close not to see its similarity, Cheeway," Jade responded.

"Jade, I think you're right about what you said before," Stevens said. "I don't think the writing you told us about was isolated, but what about the others? Do you think the rest of them were spread to other people as well?"

"Good point. Let's look at another one of their prophecies. The next one speaks of fuels being taken away. But I'm not too clear about the fuel part. After all, if these people didn't have the same kind of definition of fuel as we do, they might be speaking of something entirely different. And that could mean a lot to my translation."

"Go ahead with it anyway, Jade, I'm sure Cheeway will let us know if there is a relationship or not. You know, by telling us if there is a matching prophecy among his people. That way, we will know more about what you have discovered, and if that information has spread to other people too."

"Yeah, I guess you're right. All right then, here it goes. This one speaks of a time that comes just after the third warning sign is given."

"Wait a minute, Jade, what do you mean third warning? You haven't said anything about warning signs before."

"Well, Roberts, there are three warning signs in these writings. I hadn't mentioned them before because they are at the far back of the hallway. Forget about that now; I'll go into them later. That is, if it's all right with all of you."

"Yeah, that's find, Jade. Just remember, we haven't heard everything you've read, okay? We don't want to get lost in this you know," Roberts said.

"Anyway, this prophecy speaks to fuels being taken away. Every kind of fuel known will go underground, far enough that no one can get to them. Then it speaks of something like a global hunger that kills millions of people everywhere. And due to the fact that there won't be fuel to make their machines work, the dead will lie where they are. Some will be eaten by others, but most will just rot away. And from the decaying bodies, new diseases will appear. Some will be known, but many will be new. And there will be no cure. Furthermore, they say these diseases will ride with the winds of the world, spreading plague everywhere. No where will there be a safe place from them. Not even for those who live under the Earth. According to what I have deciphered, many will go underground to live, but they die too. And their deaths will be more painful than those who remain above the ground.

"Seems like there will come a time when the fuels re-emerge from below the Earth, but when they do, they are set on fire by the burning rocks. I take that to mean there will be an increase in volcanoes going off and when the fuels come back out, they ignite as they touch the lava. They say, during this time, many will run to find safety from the flames. They show them running to the oceans to keep from being burned, but when they get there, the water will be gone. And in its place, will be layer upon layer of the dead. So thick, they can walk on them, but so will the flames. Then, those who went underground to live, the writings say they will be trapped by the burning rock. And their lives will be ended because they cannot leave, and their air will vanish.

"However, just before the final death of all mankind, there appears a deliverer from the sky. Everyone sees him and he will appear holding both hands out. It says something about him doing this so everyone will know who he really is. And, that's all I could decipher from this prophecy. There is more, but I can't understand it yet. I'm sure I will in time though. What about it, Cheeway?" Jade asked, as she set down another of her notebooks. "Does this one sound familiar?"

"Yes, Jade," Cheeway replied. "All of it does, but I am surprised at its accuracy to what was originally written on those walls over forty thousand years ago. I was told our ancient prophecies were accurate, but until now, I didn't realize how accurate they were! Yes, Jade, this writing has been known by our people as well. We speak of it as the last day for all life and it goes like this:

"The Old Ones said when this takes place, everyone living will have been given a choice of what to do. Whether they will complete their destiny, or ignore it and listen to others, rather than themselves. There will come a time, when all the fuels of the Earth are taken away from us. We will no longer have them to use, nor will we be able to find more. And this will cause our great transportation systems to fail. That means no one will be able to travel further than one hundred miles from where they are. And no food distribution systems, electronics, heating and cooling, will be functional. This causes many to panic, believing their life has surely ended. But we are told there will be some who will not be affected by this time. They have awakened to their spirituality, not religion, and will find safe places to go, places our people call The Safe Lands.

"The waters of the world, with the exception of The Safe Lands, will be contaminated. They are said to have three sets of brothers in them and these brothers sound like bacteria from what I can tell. But no matter how hard people try to get rid of them, they remain in everyones water around the earth. Those who drink water will be infected with a terrible bacteria. It will cause them to dehydrate through the sweat of fever and their bowels will run very loose until their time is over. In the beginning, only the very young and very old will be killed by the three brothers in the water. But soon, our prophecies say everyone will succumb. But in The Safe Lands, there will be water to drink and food to eat. And in those places, the Spirit Wind will see there is no need to infect the people there because they have attained their spiritual balance and understand what is happening to the Earth. You see, they do not fear these earth changes, they realize the Earth Mother is in her final stages of ascending into her next world...the fifth world of peace and light.

"But for those who still need to learn lessons, they will not be allowed to remain on this earth. They will be taken to another world, where all of this will be done again. But for those who have learned, they will ascend when the one we call The Great Messenger returns and asks everyone his question. The question is, do you, or do you not, need to continue with your lessons. Those who understand their spiritual nature will leave for The Safe Lands just before this last prophecy begins. But those who have not been willing to read the signs, they will remain where they are believing they are safer in large groups and big cities. But they are not. In this time, there will come great earthquakes and floods. They will change many things on the Earth, but one of the most significant things they will change, will be the removal of all fuels from everyone. There will be no fuel to run their cars, trains, planes, computers, refrigerators, heaters, or air conditioners. Anything requiring traditional forms of energy will be taken away. They say when this time comes, mankind will have use of another source of energy. Like the kind we use from nuclear fission, but the great earthquakes and floods will take that away too. They say the material used to create this energy will be spilled over all lands and it will cause much death to everything it touches. They say great numbers of people and animals die in this time and because there is no way of transporting them to be buried, they will leave them where they are. But as they decay, they not only infect the lands they lie on, the rains also take their infections into the Earth. When they do, they enter the water tables and there will be no safe water to drink. For anyone drinking these contaminated waters, more contaminated than the water with the three brothers, they will die within three days. But their death will be different; their tongues will swell until it stops the air from reaching their lungs. And those who remain in the large cities, they will run out of food to eat. For all the distribution and growing of edible things will have passed. We are told by then, the infections from all the dead will reach levels unknown before. And their diseases will rise into the air and be carried to all places by the Spirit Wind. Once a person is touched by the disease carrying wind, they begin to decay while they are still alive. But since there will be no food to eat, people will kill them, cut away their infected parts and eat what is left on them.

"Our prophecy says when this time comes, it will be better to leave behind everything you once knew. For during this time, mankind will revert to cannibalism and will consume the weak, dying, helpless, and the young. They do this to survive, but they will not survive. Soon after the fuels begin to rise above the ground again. And everyone believes they have been saved. But the fuels rise in such great quantities, they cannot contain them and they flood the lands. Then, there is one last great earthquake before the molten rock comes pouring out of the Earth. And when it touches the fuels, they ignite, creating a great fire over all the Earth. Those who believe they can find safety in the oceans will run to them, hoping to escape the ensuing flames. But when they reach the great waters, they find nothing there but dead bodies of people, animals, and fish. So many they cannot find the water beneath them. When they turn and see the flames approaching them, they know their time is over."

There was a hush in the lab when Cheeway finished. What he had shared affected everyone.

"Are there more prophecies, Jade?" Stevens asked.

"Yes, Stevens, a lot more."

"Are they as bad as the first two you and Cheeway spoke of?"

"Worse," Jade returned, as she looked at the remaining writings. "Seems like the further in we go, the more intense they get. Probably could have translated more of them though, but to tell you the truth, I didn't want to. Not now anyway."

"I can't blame you, Jade," Cheeway said, as he stood looking over the long corridor of writing they put together. "Even though I have heard of the first two before, they hadn't really affected me. Not like they do now."

"Jade, is there something else there?" Roberts asked. "Something more reassuring than what we've been speaking of?"

"Yes, there is," Jade returned. "They left us something that gives us hope. But it was at the far back of the hallway, the place Cheeway said looked as if it had been kept separate from all the other writings."

"Wanna go into it now? Or is it something you would rather do later?" Cheeway asked.

"No, Cheeway, I think we need to go into it now. It might be the only thing that does give hope. And I believe we need that now......all right, here it is. But there is one more thing I saw when I began to translate these writings. Something like a subset to the other writings we found. On top of them was another symbol. I don't know if you or Stevens saw it, Cheeway. It was a drawing of a triangle with an eye looking out of it. And the writing under it said something like this: Know that whoever reads this, the Watchers From The Light and From Within have returned. And we are watching you."

"All right, what does that mean?" Stevens asked. "It sounds a lot like big brother or something."

"I think they're referring to Father Sanchez's group. They probably thought they would be the first ones to discover this place and wanted to remind them they weren't alone anymore. If there aren't anymore questions, gentlemen, I'll continue," Jade said. "I promise, it does get better. At least a little."

CHAPTER 12

▼

# THE THREE WARNINGS
# FOR MANKIND'S LAST
# CHANCE

"You know, if it hadn't been for what I saw on the far back of the hallway, I would really be feeling bad now," Jade said.

"You mean from the intensity of their prophecies, Jade?" Cheeway asked.

"Exactly. From what I translated, I felt I was being condemned—or something like that."

"How many more have you translated, Jade?" Roberts asked. "We really should be working with all of them."

"Yeah, I know that, Roberts. But they still make me feel depressed. It's kinda like watching your own execution, or something like that."

"But, Jade," Stevens interrupted. "They are only prophecy. Something that hasn't happened yet. So why are you letting them affect you like this?"

"It's what I found just before I began working on the three warnings, Stevens. Something caught my eye where the other prophecies stopped. The writings made a reference to the first warning and when it would take place."

"Because you know when it will happen, you're upset?"

"No, Stevens, not because I think I know when it will happen. It's because it's already happened and nothing was done about it."

"What?" Roberts exclaimed. "You mean the first warning has already taken place?"

"Yes," Jade returned. "And the second will soon be here. That's why I'm feeling this way. This isn't something that's going to happen years from now. It's here now, today, in the present. It can't get more personal than that, can it?"

"Jade," Cheeway said, as he looked at the writings on the back part of the re-constructed hallway. "Can you get back to what you were saying before? You know, about the three warnings and what they say we can do about all this?"

"Yeah, Cheeway, I just got carried away, that's all. It makes it a lot different when you know that what you're reading has already begun. At least for me it does. The originators of these writings must have known what we, as a race of humans, would inevitably do with our lives, and to the world we live in. They had to in order to make these prophecies as accurate as I believe them to be. But they wrote three warnings as a last chance for all mankind…as some kind of dim hope in the far distant background of life. They say all of us, collectively, could change what is already happening…these ancient prophecies that tell of the events that will take place, all over the world. They write that during the first two warnings, we can still do something to alter, or even stop, many of these Earth catastrophes from taking place. But when the third warning arrives, nothing more can be done. All we can do is head to the hills, if you catch my drift.

"The first warning, as I have said, has already taken place. And, when you hear about it, you will believe as I do. It came and went and no one did anything. It was like it wasn't even seen, you know. The writings say just before the first warning appears, mankind will believe its technology is greater than anything ever conceived before. Because of this false belief, many will turn their backs on what little humanity remains with them. They will believe more in their technology than in the one who gave them life. And this will cause them to ignore the first warning sign for things to come. The writings say mankind will hide behind their technology so they won't have to look at the misery that accompanies the first warning. And when they do, there will be a great cry from those being affected, but no one will take time to listen. The first warning speaks of thousands of people starving to death. And I believe this has already happened in Africa. Remember the news casts we were shown on television?"

"Yes, something about rebels starving their entire population, wasn't it?" Stevens offered. "In their attempt to overthrow their government, they kept all the food for themselves and let their own countrymen starve to death. I remember seeing pictures of their young and old alike dying in streets and villages. That what you're talking about, Jade?"

"Exactly, Stevens," Jade returned. "And all of us saw pictures of them on the nightly news, but did nothing about it. This first warning says we could have prevented the coming earth changes then. It says all we had to do was return to the earth, and walk in balance with our environment. It says when this great starvation happens, everyone in the world will see it. Think of what all of us have access to—the international news on television. The first warning says when they see the great starvation, they must make their first of two choices to stop the impending disaster coming to them. They can re-learn to live in balance with the earth and stop poisoning her as they have been, or they can choose not to hear the screams of the starving people crying for help. But if they choose to ignore their cries, they will have closed the first warning and made way for the second. The first warning says when it is complete, the earth will be on the brink of being so polluted, or poisoned, there will only be a few more growing seasons left when food that is safe to eat can be grown. For during this time, the Earth will be almost ready to return to us all the poisons we buried into her. The earth will first return it to us in the food we eat.

"Now, just think about that for a moment," Jade said, as she sat on one of the tables near the writings. "Haven't there been a lot of reports on the quality of food sold in stores? Seems like there hasn't been a week go by that we haven't heard of something bad popping up in our food. And what about the sudden emergence of genetically modified food in the grocery stores? Why has there been such a push to create and distribute this into our system? Do the large industrial farms know something that most don't? We hear about whole countries not being allowed to sell their cattle, poultry, or other farm products because they are infected. And this isn't just happening in our country, but it is taking place all over the world. We've all heard of mad cow disease. Given the present rate of decay in our food chain, I can see what these ancient writings are speaking of. I can see the truth is right here with us now. Think about it. The writings saw if we turn our backs on those starving people, which we did, the earth would begin returning our poisons to us through our food.

"Gentlemen, that's already begun. But think about this, the writers of the ancient prophecies said all we had to do was return to our balance with our environment, nothing more! And if we had, the prophecies they wrote in their Hallway of Records, would have been altered, or even stopped. It would have really been simple, if we had only taken the time to listen, you know?"

"I can see where you're going, Jade," Cheeway returned. "I remember a time, not so long ago, when I could drink from any of the streams in our mountains without fear. I could have walked up to the kitchen sink and poured myself a glass of water, and that would have been that. But when I go into the big stores now, I see aisle after aisle of bottled water. When I think of what you said about the earth returning our poisons to us, I wonder just how long the bottled water will be safe to drink. Don't think we can live very long without water to drink."

"Yeah, Jade," Roberts said. "Even if we attempt to steam our water, you know, like boiling it and collecting the steam as it rises. If there were poison in it, it would most likely rise with the steam. There won't be any safe water left to drink, other than what's found in The Safe Lands that Cheeway told us about."

"It's really sad, " Jade replied. "We could have stopped all these things from happening. All we had to do was stop poisoning the earth and return to the old ways of living in balance with her. That's all we had to do and none of this would have been necessary."

"But we didn't, Jade," Cheeway replied. "And I'm sure it's too late to go back and undo our past. What do you think?"

"I think you're right, Cheeway," Jade returned. "And that leads us to the second warning, gentlemen. The second one that says we still have time to alter the coming disasters. This one speaks of a time when mutations start appearing in all living things. There will be persistent rumors of babies being born with missing fingers, eyes, brains, or other parts of their anatomy. And there will be others born with extra parts to their bodies. But that's when the second warning is pretty much in full swing. In the earlier parts, the writings say we will see smaller life forms being born this way. There will be a call for everyone to take notice, but many, who are influential, will say it's nothing to be concerned about. They will say because they are just small animals, they have no bearing on human beings. But they are wrong. The writings state the reason for this happening is because the poisons we buried in the earth have found their way into the water tables all over the world. And everything that consumes water will be infected. They mention when we first see the smaller animals being born this way, those who see them will already be infected, and their offspring will be born to them with missing, or extra, parts. They say, from the first observation, there will be less than one generation left before the second warning ends. But, if we do not turn away from it, we can still change things. Then the coming earth changes will not be completely devastating to all mankind, and we could still survive. They say the way to avert the coming earth changes during the second warning is to rediscover our spirituality. For if we do, we will understand what we must do."

"But, Jade," Stevens said. "There are so many churches now. You think they want us to build more?"

"I don't think they are speaking of religion, Stevens," Jade returned. "After all, look at what religion has already done to everyone. It keeps them living in a constant state of fear. It holds them captive under its arm of control, telling them if they don't do such and such, they will be punished for all eternity. No, I don't think that's what they are talking about."

"Look, Stevens," Cheeway said. "I've grown up around religion and I have seen what it's done to an entire race of people. When I was little, my brother, Speaking Wind, and I were forced to attend a Catholic boarding school. They used us to perform labor for the neighbors. You know, the ones who had a good name in the church. They would pick us up in the morning and return us when it was time to be instructed in their religion classes. We must have worked at almost every farm and private home near us, doing things they didn't want to do, and for no pay. All in the name of religion. They told us we weren't worth saving, but by our doing this work for the righteous ones, as they called them, we might atone for our sins and get close to their heaven. We were not taught how to read or write, Stevens. We were beaten for opening our mouths, for speaking our own language, or talking openly of our spirituality. That to me, is what religion is. Though it may not be as obvious today, it strives to do the same thing. All of us are taught there is only one God, right? And we learn the teachings of the one that religion is named after. But look at the people in any of those churches today. Doesn't matter what country you're in, or if it's Christian or not. But when you look at the teachings that started them, then you enter one of their churches, or places of worship, I bet you won't find anyone there practicing what they say it's all about. No, I don't think the writings are referring to religion, Stevens. I believe they are addressing spirituality."

"Maybe it's my upbringing, Cheeway, but I thought they were the same."

"Not from what I have seen, Stevens. Religions are more like intolerant belief systems. They may teach tolerance of others but none truly practice it. Look, maybe this can help explain it to you. Whenever you see religion, ask yourself this question. Does it tell its followers they are different from any other way of worship? If they do, I assure you they are not spiritual, for they strive to keep their followers separated from everyone and everything that does not believe as they do. The religious people speak of great evil waiting to nab them, making them fear doing anything wrong. But they only fear doing things that are wrong in the eyes of those who preach to them. And religion says those who are not righteous will go to hell, a place they will suffer greatly as they atone for their sins. But the righteousness they speak of, only they can attain. No one else can attain it if they don't believe and worship as they do. If I believed this, Stevens, I would be a religious person, but I am not, and so I don't. You see, those who follow the path of religion speak of things that cannot be true. On one hand, they speak of a loving God, but on the other, they speak of a God who will punish you if you don't do as the preachers say. I would like to know who gave them the only ear to hear the words of Creator! I certainly didn't and I know of no other who has. But they tell their followers only they know the way to salvation, when the truth of it is each one of us has our own way. And unless we can be free to follow it, we will have to repeat all of this again…in another time, another place, and on another Earth.

"But let me get back to comparing the difference between religion and spirituality. You see, I get a little wrapped up when it comes to religion. I have seen no good, at least for me, come from it. Spirituality, as I understand it, does not teach separation of any kind. It teaches if you see someone doing something that does not agree with you, then you shouldn't do it. What they do is from their path and we must each walk a path of our own. You must believe they know what they are doing, either consciously or within their spirit. And if you interfere with what they need to learn, you not only stop them from growing spiritually, but you are stopped as well. Then you take on their responsibility as well as your own. Spirituality must be free, Stevens, for only by being free can we find our own way back to Creator. And Creator is just one being, the only one who created all of us. Doesn't this make us all brother and sister? According to the religion people, it doesn't, not until we agree to be like them. But to the spiritually enlightened, they agree that all of us are equal to one another. That there is no difference between any of us. Only some have things to do that may not be the same as what you have to do. And when you encounter someone like that, the best thing to do is walk away, but walk away with understanding and not anger.

"Basically, Stevens, religion keeps people separated from life by controlling them. And it controls them by making them believe they are not capable of doing anything right on their own. Once they agree to that premise, they are laden with fear. And fear is what keeps them in tune with their religion. But spirituality allows people to be free. If you wish to pray to a rock, or a tree, or even a passing cloud, that's all right. For the spiritual path teaches everything we see has life within it, the same life we have. It was created by the same Creator. It is a part of us and we are a part of it. So, I believe what the prophecy is saying we can do is this. It is telling us if we return to our spirituality, we can affect the coming earth changes. For if we are spiritual, we will find our freedom and allow others to find theirs as well. If we return to our spiritual way of life, we will see that all things are created from the same unconditional love. And by finding that love within ourselves, we have something to share with our brothers and sisters. We will not have to worry about someone stealing what we don't have, a temporary love that only lasts as long as its glitter shines. Then, when it no longer shines, it is thrown away, and so are we. I believe if we, as a race of people, return to our spiritual origins, we will see a way out of this. We will see a way of keeping certain destruction from wiping all of us out."

There was a brief moment of silence among everyone when Cheeway finished. Not even Jade had anything to say.

"Jade?" he asked. "Did you follow what I said? I mean, you're so quiet about it."

"Yeah, Cheeway. I followed well enough. It's just that I hadn't ever heard you speak like that before."

"Hope I haven't offended any of you by my words, have I?"

"Not offended," Jade returned. "Enlightened perhaps, but definitely not offended. I believe you have tuned into what I have translated from these writings. And I would gladly step aside to let you speak further on the matter."

"No, Jade, you can hear me anytime. But we need to hear more of what the writings say. However, there is one more thing I would like to share with you. It's a gift of peace.

"*When you drop all the rules, you will find your spirituality*. This is not complicated, but it really gets the point across.

"Okay, Jade, your turn now."

"All right then, but I don't believe I can get as deep as you did, Cheeway. Wow!"

"Jade," Roberts said. "From what the second warning speaks of, can you tell when it will arrive? I mean, since the first one came and went already, is there any mention of how much time will pass before it begins?"

"No, Roberts, not that I have been able to determine. But you gotta remember it's going to take several months to wade through all of this. It's not like reading an article out of the paper, you know."

Without going further, Jade turned back to look at the ancient writings. They could tell she was looking for something she thought was there.

"Maybe this will answer your question, Roberts," Jade said, as she pointed her finger on a curious symbol. "This looks like their representation for passing time. And it's located between the first and second warning. That could be our answer. Yeah…I think it is. I think the answer to your question is…seven years, Roberts," Jade returned, turning to face Roberts with a look of accomplishment. "It says that in this drawing of seasons. I see twenty-eight of them and to me that can only mean seven years. Of course, they might have used a different base count for their mathematics. You know, base six or base twelve…or base whatever. Now, that would change the count on most everything we've seen so far. But, after looking at how specific they were about some things, it looks like we're correct on the time count interpretations. A lot of references are repeatedly made to the seasons, you see. And they keep indicating four in each of those. This, along with some of the other writings we've been through, show a combination and length of four seasons to be similar to, if not the same as, one of our years. So, I believe that seven years is our answer…Now, for the third warning, gentlemen."

When Jade began this last part of the interpretation, she found a chair to sit in. For reasons that were only known to her, at the time, she did not want to remain standing.

"This is a real heavy one and it tells us the ending of the second warning to the entry of the third will be less than one year. You see, there are only three seasons between the second and the third. I didn't catch that before now. But when the third warning begins, the ones who wrote this say we should not attempt to do anything further. We should leave where we are and go into the hills. The moment the third warning begins, all gates and doors will close. That keeps everyone from leaving where they are at that time. Remember the part about no fuels? And where they are, will determine how they will meet their end. When the third warning begins, there will be such a great eruption of volcanoes under all the ocean floors, the waters will heat to almost boiling. The heat in the water will kill all life there. Next, the steam rising out of the oceans, and the smoke rising from the volcanoes, will block the sun and there will be darkness that will fall over the entire Earth. It will be so complete, people will believe the Earth has completely fallen away from the sun and they will never see light again. Then, the heat from the molten lava will be so intense, no one can get close to it. Afterwards, the cold from the winds, due to the lack of sunlight, will be so cold it will tear the flesh off all living things. But, there will be no place to run or hide. And when the end is in sight for all mankind, there will appear out of the sky a being they refer to as The Great Messenger. And he brings with him a question for everyone to answer. When he appears, everyone returns to stand before him. Even the dead come back. He asks each one if they still have a need to learn lessons. If they do, they are taken away to the next Earth where all of this will be done again. And if they have learned their lessons, they will ascend with this Earth into the next world, where they will be free of the pains of death and birth for all time.

"That does it for the gentle parts, my friends," Jade said, with a look of finality.

"What do you mean, the gentle parts? Sounded pretty final to me!" Roberts returned.

"There is more, dear brother! Much more, and it will explain why Father Sanchez and his Brotherhood, The Illuminati, are so intent on killing us just to keep what we have found hidden from people. The rest of the story comes from the old parchment Cheeway was given by Xumal. I hope you are ready to hear what it says, gentlemen. Because if I don't talk about it right now, I don't think I ever will. So hold on, here we go!"

# CHAPTER 13

▼

# MYSTERY OF THE PARCHMENT

Jade unrolled the old parchment Xumal had placed inside Cheeway's leather pouch. They could hear it crinkle as she opened it and she reassured us it would not be destroyed since she had sprayed it with a protective coating, one that would not only seal it from the elements, but would ensure its unrolling would not damage it.

"Cheeway, if you and Stevens only knew what you brought back with you. I don't think you would have taken this old parchment so lightly. As a matter of fact, I think you would have been rather paranoid just by having it in your possession," Jade began.

"This parchment is very old. It was written by a priest that went by the name of Father Paul. He dated it in the year of our Lord, 1534, and said it was done in a hurry because of its implications. Having read the contents, I'm surprised he put anything down at all. Considering it was written."

"You mean he wrote something against the government, Jade?" Roberts asked.

"Kind of, but more about religion. Remember, during that time, anyone thought to be seditious against either church or state was killed. So not many writings like this were made. Especially by a priest. You have to remember, when this was written, there was no authority higher than the church or state. They were considered to be the direct intervention to God, and anyone disputing that right was killed, but only after a long and painful period of torture. You know, the kind that makes the victim lie about why they did what they did. Anyway, this Father Paul writes that he and one other priest, a Father Juan, made this discovery together. He writes that they were the only two, who seemed to be concerned that the Spanish government and the church were allowing so many atrocities to be performed on the indigenous population. His parchment says they petitioned the governments of Spain and Mexico to stop this, but to no avail. They were told if they continued to meddle in state affairs, they would be sent back to Spain and tried for treason. Since that avenue was closed, they decided to sit in on the conversion processes of the Aztec nobles. The Aztec prisoners were being treated differently than the rest of the natives. The government thought they knew where more gold or gems were hidden and were not killing them as quickly.

"He writes there was an old man who had been waiting three months to be questioned. Since he had nothing to do, he would wander aimlessly around their capitol, Mexico City. That was when an order of priests began talking to him. They thought, since he had so much time on his hands, it would be good to start his conversion to Christianity. Father Paul and Father Juan, joined in. And that is what began, as he calls it, their long night of despair. The old man was once a member of the Jaguar Tribe. They were a very select warrior class of the Aztec, specially picked and trained from childhood. This man had been given the honor of guarding a special place…one that had been used by not only the Aztec, but the Inca, Mayan, Toltec, Olmec, and many other ancient tribes whose names go back so far, they don't appear in the oldest Aztec records.

"He further writes, when the priests began telling the old man about God and The Christ, he said he already knew about them, perhaps more than they did, from what they told him. But there was something in the way he said it that caused both Fathers Paul and Juan to believe the old man actually did know what he was talking about. So they began a long line of questions, asking him about things he could not have known, things that not only pertained to religion, but to the Old and New Testaments, both of which he should not have knowledge of. However, each of their questions were answered by the old man accurately and with additional information on the subject. They asked how he knew of such things, for they were unsure if he was who he said. Perhaps he was an angel sent to spy on them and what they were doing to God's children.

"But the old man said he had been trained by a group of Mayan priests that lived in an ancient city. They said the Aztec were so impressed by what they knew, they let them live, even after they came into power. And he had been assigned as one of the royal guards to ensure no harm would come to them. He told the priests everything that they spoke about was recorded in the ancient city. And he stated the information in the ancient city was more complete than what they told him. The old man said they only had a small part of the story. That the rest was contained within the ancient writings he had studied. Fathers Paul and Juan wanted the old man to take them to the ancient city. But they did not want the government to know anything about it. However, that was not to be, for the government in Mexico City did hear of their plans and assigned a large expeditionary force to accompany them. The government was only interested in gold or precious stones that might be found there.

"When the soldiers reached the destination, they were met by three old men who walked out from the mountain the city had been built under. The captain of the guard, thinking they might raise arms against his men, ordered them killed immediately. Fathers Paul and Juan were three miles back when that happened. Apparently they had traveled with the supplies so they could speak to the old man without being over heard by the Spanish guards. When they discovered what the captain had done, the old man hung his head and shed silent tears of regret. He said those three men who had been killed were the last of their kind. The only ones left who knew how to read the writings within the ancient city and now that they were gone, there was no one who could translate the records.

"The old man showed them the only entrance to the ancient city. They wrote it had been built over by three other cultures. But the original city was still intact and could be entered by using a hidden door that was opened by using a small crystal. Entering the ancient city, the soldiers began searching for gold and other treasures, while the two priests and the old man, explored as well. The old man showed them a hidden building within the ancient city where everything he had been taught was recorded. He called it The Temple of Mankind's Legacy. The two priests began their decoding process by asking the old man to tell them things he had been instructed on by the priests. Next, they asked him if he could point to a portion of the writings on the walls, places he could associate with what he was told. That, according to Father Paul, was what gave them their clues in translating the writings. And for the next few months, that is exactly what they did.

"However, when they told the soldiers what they found, most went insane and killed each other, then themselves. It was as if they had heard more than they could accept and that was what set their next course of action into place. The remaining soldiers returned to Mexico City to report to the government, while the two priests and old man remained behind. Fathers Paul and Juan believed mankind was not ready to learn of what they discovered. They believed mankind must evolve more in order to fully comprehend the truths they had found within the ancient writings. But they discovered what had been left within the ancient city was not complete either, for the writings spoke of another location where the rest of the information was recorded. Father Juan took the information he and Father Paul had translated, and went off in search of it. He only knew it was in the north and beyond the great desert.

"However, before he left, they discovered The Temple of Mankind's Legacy was a written account of everything that has taken place on Earth from the beginning of time. But as near as they could make out, the last entry was written over fifteen hundred years ago, then nothing more had been put down. And fifteen hundred years before then would have been about the time of the crucifixion of The Christ. That was what gave Fathers Paul and Juan a clue as to what these records contained.

"When the soldiers left, what was left of them, the two priests and the old man began translating what writings they could. The old man's presence was essential to let them know if they got their translations right or not, for he had heard most of what was within the temple. However, a few months into their work, another priest came to inform them they were wanted by the government for treason and sedition against the Holy Church. It had to do with what they told the soldiers about what they discovered. And now, their lives were about to be ended because of what they had said. The priest told them about a group of men who were behind this. They were from an order he had not heard of within the church. And if they remained in the ancient city, they would not live much longer.

"Most of the writings within The Temple of Mankind's Legacy had been translated, but Father Paul wanted to explore different buildings within the ancient city to see what else had been recorded. Fathers Paul and Juan decided to continue their work. But they knew what they found could not yet be known. For they had seen the effects it had on the soldiers. They decided to write everything down, then hide it. Perhaps at a later time, humanity would be ready to hear of these things. Father Juan went north to locate the other site, where the rest of the written history had been placed, while Father Paul remained within the ancient city with the old man. Both priests knew they would eventually be caught and killed, but decided it was more important to complete this work, than to save their own lives. And they did just that, according to the parchment. Father Paul sealed the ancient city, with himself and the old man inside, by taking the crystal out of the side entrance to the mountain. Without it, no one could enter and they were not about to leave. Not without completing their work. After that, the writings stop. They don't say what happened to the priests, or the old man. I can only guess they continued working till their death. But at whose hands, it doesn't say."

"That's all very intriguing, Jade!" Stevens said. "Meaning no disrespect for the parchment, and the work the priest did, but it doesn't say anything about what they found. I mean, if all they did was write about their adventure, it doesn't sound like that would have been life threatening for them, or would have been reason enough for a group of people to hunt them down and kill them."

"He's right, Jade," Cheeway continued. "If all those priests did was talk about their situation because of something they found, but not say what it was. How does that help us?"

"Because they did write about what they found, gentlemen," Jade returned. "All of it. The writings in the parchment say everything written in the Old and New Testament are also recorded in the ancient city. However, they found what is in the Bible, is not complete. There are many parts omitted and much of it was changed. They say the way it reads today gives way to people being controlled because the information is so vague. But what they discovered in their translations gives way to something else entirely. They say the writings in the ancient city are so complete, when mankind reads them, they will understand the original meaning. But it comes with a warning. Whoever reads them will change. For they will no longer be willing to follow the direction of another person, but will find their own way in life.

"Oh yeah, there is something else," Jade continued, as she held several pages of the old parchment in front of her. "It says here, there were not ten commandments, there were eleven. And the ten we have always been taught were altered. According to the two priests, someone, or some group, has taken much of what was originally written and changed, or removed it!"

"Do they say what the original commandments are?" Roberts asked, with his eyes full of excitement.

"Partially," Jade returned. "Ill read what they left, then you can make up your mind about the next step."

"What next step, Jade?" Cheeway asked.

"You'll have to wait till I get done, all right? The priests were very attentive in listing the commandments next to what they believed corresponded to them from the Ancients' writings. But they say these commandments were meant to be a guide for living, not an iron clad rule…something like they were left for those who wanted to get past the harshness in life. Anyway, the commandments go like this:

"The first commandment they cite says: You shall have no other God before me! And the ancient writings say: Regardless of how another's actions may seem to you, they are doing what they must do. Just as you cannot change what you do, neither can they. For each of you has a specific purpose on this earth and it can only be found by doing those things you feel you must. For this law has been written by The Creator of all life, and to look away from it, is to look away from him.

"The second commandment the priests cite says: You shall not make for yourself an idol in the form of anything in heaven above, or on the Earth beneath, or in the waters below! And the ancient writings say: The Creator of the Universe lives within each of you. You honor him when you honor who you are. Put no other before you. This does not give them honor, but makes an idol of them unto you.

"The third commandment they cite says: You shall not misuse the name of the Lord! And the ancient writings say: Everything you fear in life stems from something within that you are not willing to understand, and what is feared is called evil. But remember, the one who has given you life has created all things, and to call any of it evil is to call your Creator evil. Not everything in life is meant for you and those are the things that cannot be understood by you. The name you have reflects a part of God's great plan. But in order to see what your part is, you must be yourself. Do not accept the direction of groups, for they have been formed out of the fear of being alone.

"The fourth commandment cited says: You shall not murder! And the ancient writings say: You may travel with a person for a time and they agree with you on what is important in life. But one day they change and no longer believe as you. Do not become angry with them and constantly remind them of how they once were, for that is the truest form of murder. It is the killing of their spirit's hope of learning its lessons on this world. Each of you has one body, but there are many other spirits who live within it. But only one spirit at a time may guide the body, the rest must sit and wait their turn. These spirits within each of you are not evil, for they are your brothers and sisters who have come to share their time on Earth with you. The life of the body on this world is difficult and requires great amounts of energy to maintain itself. Were it not for the many other spirits who live within each of you, only a portion of what you have accomplished, could have been done. All have a similar need, but none are identical. Once the lessons needed by one spirit are completed, they move over so the next can experience theirs. And when they do, they see life's important issues differently. But that is only because a new spirit needs to lead the body for a time. Do not become angry with them for doing what is a natural occurrence. For if you examine your own life, you will see you have done the same thing many times as well.

"The fifth commandment they cite says: You shall not commit adultery! And the ancient writings say: It is only possible to love yourself, because it is only possible to know you. Any attempt to love another is to say you know them better than they know themselves, and this is not possible. For the amount of time needed to understand yourself, is equal to your time spent on this Earth. And when you try to love another, you can only see them as who they were yesterday, but not who they are today, for that is an ongoing process only they can understand. Love the part of yourself you understand, then share that love with another. You can only hold another back and in a place that no longer has what they need if you attempt to love them for who you think they are. For to love another in this way, is to be unfaithful to the Almighty who has given you life. Strive to understand better who you are so you may love the one who has given you life more completely.

"The sixth commandment says: You shall not steal! And the ancient writings say: Life's consequences result when you place more value on what another has rather than on what you have. Whatever anyone has in life, is precisely what they need, at the time. For those things have been given with a specific purpose…one only they can know. Do not take what is not yours, for if you do, another cannot learn what they need.

"The seventh commandment they cite says: You shall not give false testimony against your neighbor! And the ancient writings say: What you do, you must do, for you have no other choice. What another does, they must do, for like you, they too have no choice. But to attempt to explain why another does what they do will result in you creating a lie about them. For you can only see them through your own experiences and will explain their actions with untruthful words.

"The eighth commandment cited says: You shall not covet your neighbor's house. You shall not covet your neighbor's wife, or his manservant or maidservant, his ox, or donkey, or anything that belongs to your neighbor! And the ancient writings say: When you are grateful for all you have, you open the doors to receive more. But when you are not grateful for what you have, or envy what another has that you do not, you not only close the doors for more to come to you, but in time, you will lose what you had to begin with.

"Well, that's it, gentlemen," Jade said, as she put the parchment on the table. "That's what was written by Father Paul those many centuries ago."

"Did I miss something?" Stevens asked. "Didn't you say there were eleven commandments? I only heard you read eight, didn't I?"

"Yes, Stevens, I did only read eight. In order to get the next three, we have to take the next step."

"Is that what you were talking about before you began reading, Jade?" Cheeway asked.

"Exactly!" she replied. "It says in the parchment, Father Juan went to search for the other site in the north…another site like the one we found. That's where we will find the remaining three commandments. But it will involve some risk."

"You mean from Father Sanchez and his Brotherhood?"

"Yeah!" Jade returned. "Just think about what I read to you for a moment. None of it lends itself to following what another tells you, does it? But that is what history has been about ever since it began. Following leaders, having them tell you what to do, or how to act. I believe if this information ever gets out, it's going to change the way people think about themselves. And, when they see the fallacy of what they have been living with, they are going to create some major social changes, all over the world. People, like Father Sanchez and his group of cronies, simply won't have a role to play anymore. That's what I believe is scaring them about what we've discovered. And I bet you, if we ever find out the truth, we'll find that it was his order who was responsible for everything that happened to Fathers Paul and Juan."

"So where do we go from here, Jade?" Roberts asked.

"To find this other site, dear brother, the one Father Juan went to the north to discover. What about it, Cheeway, you game?"

"Yeah, Jade, but there's one thing I have to do. I told my brother, Speaking Wind, and Nahe, I would meet them near Coyote, New Mexico. In order to get there on time, I will have to leave in the morning. But when I get back, we could get started. You okay with that?"

"Why must you meet with them now, Cheeway?" Roberts asked.

"Because Speaking Wind must know everything that has taken place. I mean, with Father Sanchez chasing us, none of us know how many more days we will live. And my brother must be told everything that has happened so far. Without him, there will be no other who can tell the world what we have discovered when it's time."

"When it's time? Don't you believe we could talk about it?"

"No, Roberts!" Cheeway stated flatly. "I don't think any of us will be alive by then!"

CHAPTER 14

▼

# THE UNSEEN CAVE OF
# THE ANCIENTS

I knew the Unseen Cave of the Ancients was a hard trail to follow, and on horse-back, I wondered how many times I would end up falling off the horse.

"Don't worry, brother," Nahe said, as if he were reading my mind. "Got one that is real gentle. She likes to help out."

"Thanks, Nahe. I think I'll need all the help I can get. You know it's been over twenty years since I rode?"

"Yup! You were gone from the people and our ways a long time, brother. But like Molly Two Socks said, you're a fast learner. Won't take you long to remember.

"Fathers Juan and Joe! Can you ride well?" Nahe yelled to the back of the truck.

"Well enough, Nahe!" Father Juan replied. "Please, don't worry about us. We will be just fine."

With that said, Nahe turned the truck into his drive. In the distance, I saw his house, the same house he and his grandfather, White Eagle, lived in when we were growing up.

"Brings back a lot of memories, Nahe," I remarked.

"Guess it would when you've been away as long as you have. Gonna let you three out by the corral, then park the truck in the shed. That way, no one will know we're here."

We waited for Nahe by the corral looking at four horses. I was wondering which one I was going to ride when they all walked up and began sniffing me.

"Just figuring you out, Speaking Wind, remember? They choose us, we don't choose them. After all, they aren't as lost in the illusion as we are. The one you need will pick you."

Just as Nahe said that, the white horse with a red stripe running down the front of her face nudged me. Almost knocked me down because I wasn't ready for it.

"Think you've been chosen, brother. She seems to like you and she is also the most gentle of the four."

It seemed as if a bond had quickly established between the horse and me. She found a place near me and stood, waiting for a saddle, blanket, and bridle.

"Spirit Wind!" Nahe returned. "And believe me she can get you anywhere you need to go, fast. But still, she is as gentle as an afternoon breeze…Come on, we don't have time to waste. Don't know when we'll see Father Sanchez, or his helpers again. We need to take advantage of our time. Help me get the saddles, will ya?"

We walked into the tack barn and brought out saddles, blankets, and reins. Although I had no reason to doubt what my brother, Nahe, told me about her, I was uncertain if I could keep up with a hard ride through the rough country. No matter how gentle Spirit Wind would be, I knew there would be a lot of bruises from this ride.

Then, in the distance, we saw dust rising from the road that led to Nahe's ranch.

"Someone's coming, Nahe, can you tell who it is?" Father Juan asked.

Nahe set his saddle down and looked.

"Not like this, but I have something that can tell me," Nahe said, reaching over and pulling out a set of binoculars from his saddlebag.

"Yeah, just as I thought. It's Alvin. And he's not alone."

"Who's with him, Nahe?"

"The black Ford Bronco!" Nahe said, quickly returning the binoculars to the saddlebag. "Get these saddles back in the tack barn. Don't want them to know we're here."

We returned the equipment, then waited by one of the small windows as we observed the dust getting closer to the house.

"Tell the dogs to guard and not let anyone out of their car, Speaking Wind. We'll watch from here."

I stuck my head out the door and yelled at the dogs, "Watch the house dogs and don't let anyone out of their car!"

But instead of responding to my request, the dogs ran to me wanting to be petted.

"I think I'm doing something wrong here, Nahe."

Nahe, Father Juan and Father Joe began laughing out loud as they looked at me. Finally, Nahe stopped laughing and said, "Molly Two Socks was right. There is much you have forgotten since you've been gone."

Then Nahe squatted in front of the dogs and thought his instructions to them. All three immediately recognized what Nahe wanted and took up defensive positions around his house and the tack barn.

"Guess there's a lot I've been missing, Nahe."

"Yup!" Nahe responded. "But nothing like necessity to bring it back quick, is there?"

Alvin pulled in driving my rental car with the black Ford Bronco trailing close behind him. The black Bronco pulled to a stop beside the rental car. Alvin stuck his head out the driver's side as Father Sanchez lowered his window.

"Don't think anyone's here, Father Sanchez. If there were, the dogs would be much friendlier," Alvin observed.

"Don't be a fool, Alvin," Father Sanchez growled. "Those two are good at hiding themselves. They know we are following them and I believe they are here. Get out and look!"

Father Sanchez made a motion and three bodyguards got out of the truck. Alvin followed suit, but more cautiously than the other three. As soon as their feet touched the earth, the three dogs grabbed their legs without making a sound.

"These dogs are part wolf, Father! They won't back away!" Alvin shouted. "They'll tear us apart if we stay out here!"

"Then get back in the car, you coward! I know how to take care of this!" Father Sanchez yelled, pulling out a gun. He pointed it in the air and fired, hoping to scare the dogs away. But it didn't work; the dogs remained where they were, standing between the cars and the house they were asked to guard.

"Don't kill them, Father!" Alvin shouted. "He'll know we were here for sure."

"And how will he know that?" Father Sanchez sniped back.

"Your guns! I gave them to you! They'll leave traces in their flesh that can be traced back to me. Come on, I know another place they might be."

Father Sanchez muttered something to the three men with him then started the car and pulled out of Nahe's drive.

"That was close, Nahe!" I said, as I watched them go down the dirt road.

"They aren't gone, Speaking Wind!"

"But I heard Alvin say he knew another place to look for us. What makes you think they won't?"

"Dog told me, brother. He heard what Father Sanchez said to the three men. Told one of them to wait near the house and see if we returned while they went back to town for a map. He knows we are going to some cave, but he isn't sure which one it is. Don't know how he found out Speaking Wind, unless he knows how to tune into our thoughts.

"You really have forgotten a lot, haven't you?" Nahe said, looking at me as someone who had forgotten how to eat on their own. "From here on, we better not let anything slip out that we don't want him to know about. Remember how to do that?"

"No, Nahe, I don't."

"All right then, here's a crash course in being a Shaman. When you think, or speak of something you don't want someone else to know, hold your right index finger and thumb together like this...where the first line on the finger crosses the first line on the thumb. That keeps your thoughts and words from traveling further than you intend them to. And will keep Father Sanchez from tuning into our plans. Got that?"

"Yeah, Nahe, I got that!"

"Good! Now let's stretch out till the sun goes down."

"Then what happens, Nahe?"

"That's when we get started, brother. Can't chance them seeing us leave the house now—now that we're so close to meeting Cheeway at the Unseen Cave.

"Can't be more than an hour before the sun sets. You know, this time of year, it gets dark real early. I'll give my thanks to the spirits of the land if they hurry it up a little today."

And I knew I would give them my thanks if I lived to see the sun rise tomorrow. I thought the trip up the mountain on horseback was going to be rough, but that was when I thought we would have light to see by. Now, we were going to make our journey at night, and I could see myself full of scrapes and bruises from falling off my horse.

"Okay, Speaking Wind, be quiet and follow me with your saddle. Sun's down now and Cheeway's gonna be waitin'!"

Moving like shadows in the night, the four of us saddled the horses and rode into the hills. I remembered how Nahe spoke to the dogs earlier, showing them what he wanted them to do, rather than speaking to them like I did. And, I wasn't about to take a chance on this horse not understanding what my needs were. I began placing pictures of me staying on her back for the whole trip. I didn't want her to think I was a more accomplished rider than I was. Periodically, Spirit Wind would look back at me and snort. And, they seemed to be perfectly timed with my forming pictures of not wanting to fall off. I knew she understood my request and snorting was her way of letting me know.

We had been riding for a couple of hours and I could no longer feel my body from the waist down. If there had been any sudden move from Spirit Wind, I knew I was done for. I couldn't have held on with my legs and she seemed to know this. Each of her steps was deliberate and timed to keep me balanced on her back. For this, I was grateful beyond any words I knew. So, I reached forward and rubbed her ears to express my thankfulness for her efforts. Without breaking stride, she looked back at me and gave me one last snort.

"Okay, keep your eyes open now. It's just beyond the next turn."

We rounded the next turn of the mountain pass and I saw our destination. It was the Unseen Cave of the Ancient Ones, but I saw no sign of Cheeway.

\*　　　\*　　　\*　　　\*

The Unseen Cave had been given its name because of how well it blended into the side of the mountain. For one who was not aware of its presence, they could stand right in front of it and not know it was there. The colors and patterns of the rock in front of the entrance was so identical to what was behind it, it made it appear as a solid stone wall.

"Heya Hey!" Nahe's voice sounded out through the night air.

"Heya Hey!" came a familiar voice in return.

From what appeared to be someone walking out of the side of the great stone mountain, I saw Cheeway. Seeing him made me forget about the pain I had been in from the long ride, and I jumped off Spirit Wind to greet my brother.

However, when I jumped off the horse, I forgot my legs were numb and fell making a whooshing sound as the air in my lungs rushed out. Nahe, Fathers Juan and Joe, and Cheeway stood there laughing at me, and seeing my spread out position beneath her, Spirit Wind joined in as well.

"It is good to see you again, brother," Cheeway said, laughing as he bent over to help me up. "Glad you got my letter and came. Got a lot to tell you, but we don't have much time."

"It is good to see you again, Cheeway!" Father Juan said. "You remember me, don't you? I am the priest who married you and Mary! Did she come with you this time? I haven't seen either of you for such a long time, I was looking forward to catching up on things with the both of you."

Cheeway did not respond to the priest's question. He simply hung his head. I could feel heaviness from his heart, but I did not know why it was there. Not yet, that is.

"Think we better get the horses in the cave, Cheeway," Nahe said. "Father Sanchez and his three goons might be close. Didn't see a light, Cheeway. Thought you might not be here yet."

"I pulled a tarp over the entrance, Nahe. Found it in one of the rooms further in. Good to know the light doesn't get out though. Come on, let's get the horses inside. Looks like it's going to snow."

"Would really be good if it did," Nahe returned, grabbing the reigns to his horse. "Been asking all the way up here for something to cover our tracks. Hope the snow will be heavy enough to do that."

"Cheeway!" I said, standing almost in front of the cave entrance. "Are you sure we can't be found here? I mean, if they find us, we won't have any place to run."

Cheeway looked at me with a calming smile on his face, then said, "Head your horse there, Speaking Wind, and see what she does."

Without questioning my brother's reasons, I led Spirit Wind to where I thought the opening was. When we came as close as I thought we could, Cheeway told me to let her go and see what she would do.

I draped the reigns over her neck and thought she would continue walking into the cave, but she didn't. Instead, she stopped and remained motionless.

"Did I miss the entrance, Cheeway?" I asked, feeling a little embarrassed.

"No, brother, you're right in front of it, but can't see it without knowing it's there, can you?"

"You okay with this now, Speaking Wind?" Nahe asked, standing next to Cheeway, both about to break into a laugh.

"Yeah, I guess. Just wanted to check, is that all right with you?"

"Speaking Wind!" Cheeway said, standing with both hands on his hips. "Just how long have you been away from the path, my brother?"

"Since we left the lands of the mesa, Cheeway. About twenty years now, I guess. Why do you ask?"

"You've got a lot of catching up to do. Think you can keep up?"

"I know I can, Cheeway. After all, I'm a quick learner. Been told that by a wise old woman."

Cheeway stood there for a moment looking puzzled, then Nahe told him of the encounter we had with Molly Two Socks. When he heard the story, Cheeway looked at Nahe and said, "I think she's right, Nahe. If he weren't a quick learner, all of this would be lost and the doorway could not remain open."

I knew what doorway Cheeway was referring to then felt a surge of energy fill me, the kind one gets when they feel someone near.

"Feel someone coming. Think we better get the horses inside the cave now!"

"Seems like our brother's learning quicker than we thought, Cheeway. What you think?" Nahe said, handing over his reigns to Cheeway.

"Glad to see it, Nahe, really glad. There's a lot resting on him, you know."

"Yeah, I know! Here, take my horse inside and unsaddle him. I'll back track a few hundred yards and cover our trail."

"Nahe!" Cheeway said holding his arm. "I brought Speaking Wind into this because I had to. This is a part of his path, just as it is mine. But you, and the Fathers, don't have to do this. Could bring a lot of trouble if you get involved."

"It's all right, Cheeway," Nahe returned. "Family's gone now, killed by some drunks driving through town about two years ago. Just me and the path now.

"Besides, brothers," Nahe said looking at us. "I'm already involved in this, remember?"

"And we're just as deeply involved, Cheeway!" Father Juan said. "Perhaps just as much as the rest of you!"

"Is this a choice you freely make?" Cheeway asked, holding the reigns to the horses.

"Yes, it is!" Nahe responded, picking up a fallen branch he would use to wipe our tracks up this mountain. "I have chosen this path with my eyes open. Don't forget I was raised with the same teachings you and Speaking Wind were. My grandfather, White Eagle, was brother to Grandfather and Two Bears. All three of us have been prepared for this journey and this doorway you have opened, Cheeway. It seems like I've been preparing for this time all my life. There were times when I thought my path was at a standstill. You know, seeing you complete your doctorate degree at the university then going off to uncover great wonders of peoples' past in far away lands…and seeing Speaking Wind finish his degrees at the university as well, then going to other lands to do his work. Then me, remaining here and becoming Sheriff. Thought I'd fallen off my path, seeing what both of you were doing. But when I look at us now, I can see how important it was that I remained here and learned what I have. Think about it for a moment, brother. Do you think you or Speaking Wind could have made it this far without my help?"

"No, Nahe! No, I don't think we would have made it this far without you," Cheeway returned.

"Nahe!" I said, as I walked to his side. "I have been away from the path many years and have forgotten much. But one thing I still remember is how to look into someone's heart and know them. I not only remember you, my brother, but I have seen within your heart and know it is good. I hold you in a special place and my heart is open to you. It's true that none of us see the reasons for what we do in the present, and it's unfortunate that so many times it takes an event such as this to make us see. But when we do, our eyes are opened to something that has always been with us. And we see standing before us, what we thought we would never attain on our own. For me, Nahe, it is all of you. And I am sure each of you feels the same way about me. Even though I have been away from the path so long I don't seem to remember many things. I tell you, in truth, the teachings are still within me. And they are returning quickly. But now is not the time for such things, for I feel one man looking for us, and he is getting close! We must have left too many markings on our trail, or he is using his spirit to feel where we are."

"You are right, Speaking Wind," Nahe returned, holding out his branch. "I'd better start clearing out our tracks—all of them."

Nahe backtracked our trail as the rest of us brought the horses into the cave to unsaddle them. Fathers Juan and Joe agreed to wait just outside the cave opening and keep a look out for Nahe.

"Been a long time, brother," Cheeway said, smiling at me as we bedded down the horses.

"Too long, my brother, we shouldn't wait so long between visits. How is Mary? Where did you leave her while you came on this adventure?"

Cheeway didn't respond, he only bent his head as he continued unsaddling the horses. I felt there was a great heaviness about him from the question I had asked, and decided to let it rest for awhile.

Once the horses were situated, we walked back to the small fire and waited for Nahe to return. More than a few minutes had passed and I thought it would be appropriate to ask my question of Cheeway again.

"Cheeway?" I asked, sitting across the fire. "Did you not hear my question about Mary?"

"I heard you, my brother. Just didn't want to answer. That's all."

"It's all right, Cheeway, if you don't want to go into it right now."

"Guess I need to get it out in the open. You need to know," Cheeway responded, then suddenly, "Mary's dead, Speaking Wind! They killed her! I know they did!"

"What?" Nahe exclaimed, as he came back into the cave. "You said someone killed Mary? Why?"

"Would you like me to pray for her, Cheeway?" Father Juan asked. "You know, I was very close to her for many years. I knew her whole family."

"If you wish, Father," Cheeway returned, looking at the fire. "But I hope you will feel the same way after you hear what we have discovered."

"I believe I already have an idea what it is, Cheeway," Father Juan returned.

"But why would anyone want to kill Mary?" Nahe asked again. "She wouldn't harm anyone! She even got angry at me for stepping on a butterfly a few years back!"

"To get at me, Nahe. They didn't want me to leave Peru with what I discovered," Cheeway said, looking into the fire and appearing like a beaten old man. "Guess they thought that would stop me, but it didn't!"

He looked up from the fire and into our eyes, "And it won't! People have to know about this! If they don't, the disaster that will follow will be greater than anyone can imagine! I can't let anything, or anyone, stop it from being known."

"What happen to your wife, Cheeway?" Nahe asked, looking with eyes filled by a remembered sorrow of his own. "Can you share this?"

"Yes, my brothers, I feel I must because while they were successful with Mary, they have also made two attempts on my life as well. And if I don't tell you about this, I would do each of you a great dishonor. You see, my brothers, what happened to my life will most likely take place in yours as well. Don't know for sure, but the chances are high. You understand?"

All four of us nodded our heads and listened in silence.

"Wasn't till after I met Nauti and he gave me the map that all this began to unfold."

"Who, Cheeway?" I asked.

"Nauti," Cheeway returned. "A man I met near Machu Picchu, Speaking Wind. I'll go into that in a minute, but for now, let me remain focused on Mary...We had permission and funding, to begin a dig just a few miles to the west of Machu Picchu. I found remains of an ancient seaport there. It shouldn't have been there though, not from what all the existing records of that part of the world have taught us. The location of this seaport is presently eight thousand feet above sea level, but for a seaport to be there and so close to Machu Picchu meant that, at some time in our ancient past, there was a great amount of water there. Can you understand my excitement about this discovery? It goes along with our ancient stories that say the Earth Mother really turned herself upside down after the last earth cleansing. And when she did, lands that were high above the water went below them, and vice versa.

"Nauti had come looking for a job as one of the diggers, but he was really too old. So I told him he could come along as a storyteller, that way, he could have some money to buy food to eat after we finished."

Cheeway looked at us standing next to the fire, "As I said, I will go into this in more detail later, okay?...Nauti gifted me with a piece of strange stone that looked like a map. I knew it was extremely old and that it really was a map showing the location to some old city. But at the time, I didn't pay it much attention. Just put it away and thought I would look at it later. About a week into the dig, Nauti disappeared and no one seemed to know where he went. I felt bad about that, because in a way, he reminded me of Grandfather and Two Bears. I thought he had other business pressing him and left. But I also thought it was strange for him to leave as he did, not saying anything to anyone. But a week later, things began to happen. Not just to me and Mary, but events that affected the entire excavation party.

"Just after Nauti disappeared, a man came to our camp. Said his name was Father Sanchez. He was traveling with three huge men who he called his bodyguards. He asked me if I knew anything about one of the men who had been in the excavation party. An old man who went by the name of Nauti. He said if I could help him find this man, he would be more than happy to donate a little something to my dig. I didn't think much about his request and told him Nauti had been working with us, but had taken off and I didn't know where he went. That's when I knew something was terribly wrong. Father Sanchez looked at me with eyes that must have been holding back a great hate for something I reminded him of. When he looked at me, I could feel the cold emptiness of rage surround me. He told me I was lying to him and anything the old man had given to me was not for me to keep. But I had to give it to him so he could return it to the rightful owner. In truth, I had forgotten all about the old map stone Nauti had gifted me and said nothing about it. When I failed to give anything to Father Sanchez, he scowled at me and said I would pay for my treasonous act. Then he stormed out of the camp with these three giant bodyguards.

"I began the dig with more than thirty men, but each day after Father Sanchez's visit, there were between three to four men that did not return. Soon, there was only Mary and myself at the site. I knew we couldn't do this excavation by ourselves and returned to town to see about hiring more diggers. When I entered town to begin asking for workers, I was met by the police and taken in for questioning. They said I was a prime suspect in the unexplained death of an old man at my dig. They said his name was Nauti. I wasn't allowed to make any phone calls and neither was Mary. It wasn't long before they let Mary go. I didn't know why then, but I found out later.

"She took our truck and was going to the American embassy to help me get out of this mess, but that was not to be either. The police escorted Mary to the outskirts of town. I guess it was to make sure she didn't make any phone calls or visit our friends. When she reached the end of the town, they stopped and waited in the middle of the road ensuring she would not return. From what I was told, Mary had driven a few hundred yards or so when a cement truck ran into her. There were no other drivers on the road, and I was told the police had been blocking all traffic for about a half mile either way of where she was hit. I don't think this was any accident though. They had been blocking traffic about an hour before Mary began her last drive. See how all this is fitting together? When the cement truck hit her, she was crushed inside the car. I was told she didn't die right away though, but remained alive for about a half an hour. Once she died, the police were said to have let traffic through. For whatever their reason, they made sure whoever passed Mary's crushed truck would see it. They told the pass-erbys this was not an accident, but was associated with the dig on the side of the mountain, the dig that was being done, without permission, by the American and his wife.

"They kept me in custody for two days, asking me questions that were not related to the dig, nor to Nauti, or my association with him. On the third day, they told me about Mary's accident and that she was dead. But they would not tell me anything further. They only said they were driving me to the airport and escorting me out of their country. They said I was not welcome in their lands any more and could not return. They took everything from me, even my clothes. Seemed like they were looking for something, but I was sure they didn't find it, otherwise they wouldn't have acted as they did. After hearing about Mary's fate, I didn't want to take anything with me. Not much mattered anymore. All I wanted to do was to claim her body and bring it home. But that wasn't to be either. They said the body was too badly damaged and they had to burn it. They told me this as they handed me an urn filled with ashes. I don't know if I had the remains of Mary, or someone else. Really doesn't matter though, I know I will see her again, real soon."

"So all you were allowed to leave with was the urn of ashes, Cheeway?"

"Yes, Speaking Wind, but there was more in the urn than I thought. When I got back home and opened it—you remember what we do with the ashes of our loved ones? We spread them to the four winds asking for their acceptance by Creator. But when I opened the urn, I not only found Mary's ashes, but also the ancient stone map Nauti had gifted me. With it was a hastily scribbled note from someone who hadn't sign it. It said I should not give up on locating the city, that it held great significance for all mankind. And, it said, I was given the map because of the mark on the back of my neck. Supposedly, this mark was significant and was said to be placed on the one who was meant to discover, what they called, The Ancient City of Prophecy. I had heard of this ancient place, my brothers, and decided to make its discovery my life's quest. Partly for Mary's sake, partly for mine. But mostly, for what it was said to have recorded for all mankind and that was a way out of the impending disasters that are coming to the earth during our generation. Since I have been on this quest, my life has been threatened two more times, but still, I continue. Now that you've heard this part of my story, are you sure you want to be a part of this?"

"Yeah, brother, I'm sure. After all, it seems like all of us have been involved in this some way or another from the beginning. Like everything we've done to now has been in preparation for this," I confirmed.

Nahe took a few moments to think over what Cheeway had said.

"Yeah, Cheeway, I'm sure about it. Count me in."

"Were you able to cover our tracks, Nahe?" I asked.

"Yeah, covered them real good, but didn't have to. Snows comin' down real heavy now. It'll cover anything I missed. Besides, it's startin' to get real dark out there now. Won't be much to see in a few minutes anyway. Imagine by morning, there won't be less than a couple of inches of new snow on the ground. Can't imagine anyone being able to see through that!"

"Very well," Cheeway said. "Take a seat and I will tell you how this all began. It is important each of you know the story from its beginning. That way, no matter what happens, one of us will have the complete story to tell, when it is time for it to be told. Till then, each of you must give your word that this information will remain within you. You can't even tell someone close about it. I can't stress this enough, for if you were to share this information before it is time, there would be more danger added to what Father Sanchez has already brought with him."

The four of us looked at each other thinking over what Cheeway said.

"Puts a heavy load on what you know, brother, doesn't it?" Nahe said, looking at Cheeway.

"Heavier than you realize, my brother. What I am about to tell you has been held in the most secret place ever known. Even the Earth changed herself to keep this secret hidden from everyone. What I am about to tell you was written on black stone walls thousands of years ago, and has been waiting in silence until now. Speaking Wind, I would ask that you keep one ear trained on what I have to say and the other one outside, just in case someone does approach. Can you do this, my brother?"

"Yes, Cheeway, I can do this."

"Startin' to get real good at this aren't you, Speaking Wind?" Nahe observed. "Seems like only a couple of days ago you wouldn't have known what Cheeway meant if he said something like that to you."

"It was only a couple of days ago, Nahe," I returned. "Guess I'm a quick learner after all, huh?"

"Then listen to what I have to share, my brothers," Cheeway said. "This I believe is the completion to my part of the path. And, I believe the rest will remain for you."

# CHAPTER 15

▼

# WATCHERS FROM WITHIN

Cheeway began sharing what he had discovered on his adventure when I felt the presence of someone close. I walked to the cave opening and looked out into the night and the snow that was covering our tracks.

"Quiet!" I said, looking out over the snow covered Earth. "I feel someone coming!"

"How close, Speaking Wind?" Nahe asked.

"Right on top of us, Nahe! Don't move!"

At first, no one even breathed. Then, very slowly, all of us walked outside the cave and looked at the snow-covered horizon. But not one of us could see far due to the falling snow. Under normal conditions, snow on the earth would have made it much easier to see at night, but as heavy as it was falling, our sight was limited to a few hundred feet.

"You two stand by the entrance of the cave. I'll wait here for whoever it is," Nahe said, pulling out his gun and peering between the snowflakes. "Father, you and Father Joe wait inside. Could be trouble and I don't want either of you to be involved in it."

"What if it's Father Sanchez and his three goons, Nahe? They'll outnumber you! They all have guns, remember? Alvin gave them his," Father Juan noted.

"Then I can hold them back for a minute while both of you jump them. Think we can do some damage, don't you?"

"You think Father Sanchez is coming here?" Cheeway asked.

"Yeah, Cheeway!" Nahe returned. "Saw him, his three goons, and Alvin at my house looking for us. Wasn't more than a few hours ago. Guess they had time to figure out which cave we went to. Now, get back and let me do my work. I feel someone getting close."

"Nahe!" Cheeway said holding up his hand. "There's something I have to tell you...both of you."

"Has to wait, brother, I feel danger from whoever's coming," Nahe returned. "Quiet now, before you give our position away."

"But, Nahe, I—"

Cheeway couldn't say anything more before a great dark figure of a man jumped in front of him. Nahe reached up to hit him with his gun, but missed. The dark shadow of a giant grabbed Nahe's gun out of his hand then picked him up, and, with as little effort as I would use picking up a stone from the earth.

"What you doin', Sheriff?" the dark and looming giant said. His voice carried in the wind as if he were speaking with a microphone.

Had it not been for the thought of impending danger about to unleash itself on us, I would have laughed. He was holding Nahe under his arm like a sack of potatoes. Nahe was kicking his feet and swinging his hands in the air and getting nowhere.

But I knew this was no laughing matter and if I didn't do something, we would all be in more danger. So I leaped at the giant, hoping to knock him over. I thought that would make him release Nahe and free us both to over power him. After all, there was only one of them now. Not three like before. But my success was not to be. The dark giant saw me flying toward him and held out his other arm, which I hit with my head. I must have run straight into it, because I didn't remember anything from that moment on. When I came to, all of us were sitting in the cave next to the fire. When I woke up, my first reaction was to attack this giant of a man again, but I was stopped, by Cheeway.

"Hold on, brother! You don't know what you're doin'!" Cheeway yelled, as he pulled me to him. "Already told Nahe about this one and he's fine with it. Look at him!"

I saw Nahe sitting next to the giant. My first reaction was to see if he had been tied or something like that, but he wasn't. He sat free from any constraints, as were both of the priests.

"Cheeway, do you know this is one of the men who travels with Father Sanchez? He's also the one who held a gun to my side when Nahe came to rescue me at Sadie's," I blurted out.

"Speaking Wind," the large giant said. "I held the gun on you so the other two would not have to. They would have pulled the trigger without thinking anything about it. Guess I saved your life this morning, you know!"

"Cheeway, please! Tell me what's going on here. It's been a really long day, you know. I don't need any more surprises."

"Well if you sit down and quit trying to jump all over our brother, I'll tell you what's going on, Speaking Wind," Cheeway returned.

"Brother! You call this man who's been trying to kill you *brother*?" I asked, about to make another jump at him. "He's tried to kill you, Cheeway…twice!"

"I have not tried to kill your brother, Speaking Wind," the giant countered, sounding like a deep and distant roll of thunder. "I have been keeping him safe from harm. I was too late to do anything about Mary, but I have been able to keep Cheeway safe, so far that is."

"Speaking Wind," Cheeway said, as he turned my head so I would look at him. "Listen to me, now. This man has been responsible for me not being killed. Remember the two times my life was threatened? Well, he is responsible for warning me about them and I was able to get away."

"Then why is he hanging around Father Sanchez, Cheeway?" I asked. "If he means you no harm, why does he associate with an evil person?"

"Just sit and listen. Perhaps it would be better if the explanation came from our brother," Cheeway said, looking at Nahe and I with an expression of knowing everything would be fine, once we knew what was going on.

"Yeah, brother!" Nahe returned. "I'd really like to hear this one!"

"Very well then," the giant began. "I am called Xumal. My people are the Patagonians and once lived as free as the wind. We were a free society of people who loved all living things, but we had a great size to us, which was the cause of our downfall. When the white skins first came to the lands known as Mexico, they were truly impressed with our size. In the beginning, that is. They did not seem like a threat to us, since they only came up to our stomachs. We thought of them as children. Even when they sat on their great horses, they still had to look up at us. It seemed we would be able to live in peace with them, until the vengeful men came, those who wore the brown and black robes and looked at our people like they were animals. When the black and brown robes saw our peoples' size, they wanted to have us killed. They made one attempt at doing this, but we were much quicker than they thought and managed to overpower their soldiers. But that didn't stop them. It only made them more determined to dominate us. They saw us as a threat to their way of life, and something they were searching for. So, after many years of badgering us, we decided to let them reside in our villages.

That was the beginning of our greatest mistake. It would have been better if we had all been killed rather than allowing them to use us as they continue to. Over time, they took away our spiritual places and killed our holy men. They even practiced a form of genocide on us. Any child born with a deformity was killed. They would study the parents who brought such a child into the world and told them they were being punished for their sins through their child. And, the only way they could atone for the evil they had done would be to die. Our people believed them after being so long without holy men to tell them otherwise and whenever a child was born that did not come up to the black and brown robes standards, it and the parents were killed. We were told our people were loved by God because we were willing to do this. But we did not see what they were doing until much later, and by then, it was too late. Our race had nearly been wiped out by them and there were only a handful of us left.

"Then, another group of black and brown robes came to our lands. They were much different than the first group; they seemed to have great authority over those who claimed to be the highest judges of all mankind. When they first came to our village, we were surprised to see the reaction of the others. They would show them a silver plate they carried inside their robes and the first black and brown robes would bow and do whatever they were told. Not that we respected these new arrivals, or anything like that. We just hated the first group so much, we would have allied ourselves with anyone who had power over them. And we did. They took complete charge of what remained of our people. They did not allow us to have interaction with other white skins and kept us isolated from everything that was taking place in the lands they called the New World. They would train the men and keep the women and our children in their custody. They told us if we would not do what we were told, they would send word back to our village and our families would be killed. This continues today, my brothers. I have a wife and two small daughters in my village. And, if I were to openly resist Father Sanchez, he would have one of my children killed, and I would be sent a piece of their body—one I would recognize."

"Don't you think that is a little archaic, Xumal?" I asked. "After all, we don't live in the dark ages any more."

"I used to have a son, Speaking Wind. He was with me the first four years of his little life. Do I need to say more about this? It is real, my brothers...very real."

"Xumal," Nahe said. "Why don't you go to the law? I mean, if someone was treating my family like that, I would."

"What law would I go to, Nahe? You? Look at where you had to come before you thought you could get away from us. Is this what you call protection?"

Nahe looked down when Xumal said this. I knew he was right and looked down as well.

"Don't feel so bad, my brothers," Xumal continued. "I wish there was a law I could go to. But there isn't any conventional law you can think of. They are above all laws and everyone who makes or enforces them, too. If they say you are a danger to their Brotherhood, you end up dead…or worse."

"Not much worse than dying, Xumal," Nahe said.

"Yes, there is, my brother. Think of what my people and I have lived with. We are told who can and cannot marry among our own people. The ones who are told not to marry, they have their organs cut out so they cannot reproduce. The married ones are not allowed to enjoy each other's company unless the time is right for them to produce offspring. And when that is completed, they are separated. The women are taken away to tend the needs of others like Father Sanchez, and the men are made to continue their training. We live like a bunch of slaves, my brothers. We are allowed to live as long as we serve their needs."

"You mean the needs of Father Sanchez?"

"Yes, him and others like him who serve the same order. As long as we continue to appear intimidating, can move swiftly, and kill fast, we are allowed to live. But only for them, and not for anything that might be our calling."

"Then what happens when you get old, Xumal? Can't stay young forever, you know," Nahe asked.

"We have no elders, Nahe. No one can remember a time when we did…Does that answer your question?" Xumal returned.

"Yeah, guess so," Nahe returned. "Perhaps, if I was in your position, I would take my own life, Xumal. Don't think I would have the strength to continue a path such as yours."

"There is hope, Nahe, not only for my people, but for all people. That's why I put the note and stone map in Mary's urn. I knew Cheeway would find it and when he did, he would know his path was to uncover the truths of the past located in the Ancient City of Prophecy."

"And this is why you have been protecting Cheeway from Father Sanchez?" I asked.

"Yes, Speaking Wind, that is part of the reason. But there is another, even more important than you presently know," Xumal said, as he looked at us. "Listen to what I say now. It is important each of you understand. Your lives may depend on this information in the future. You have all been marked by Father Sanchez. All members of the Brotherhood know of you. By now, they know what you look like, where you come from, who you work for, who you know, and so on. For the longest time, I believed there were none higher than the order Father Sanchez represents. And this gave root to deep depression for me. I knew if that was true, for me, there was no way out. Not for me, not for my family, and not for my people. We would travel from one country to another killing people Father Sanchez said committed a crime against The Brotherhood. It had nothing to do with breaking any laws. It only had to do with anyone speaking, or discovering, something that could undermine their authority. And, my brothers, their authority is not limited to any one country, or religion. They are involved in all of them. If Father Sanchez needed a million dollars to do something, it was there for him. He only had to walk into any bank, make a phone call or present the managers with one of the many number codes he always carries with him, and they would pay him with cash or check. No questions asked. It seemed like the Brotherhood he represented had all the money in the world. They were not just involved in religion and politics either, they control world food distribution, fuel, power, technology, and organizations. You name it, they control it. I have seen this power they exert over the world, my brothers, and believe me, it is great. Greater than anything you can imagine. When they want something, or someone, they just take it and no one asks why.

"Two years ago, we were to attend a meeting in Rome. Father Sanchez had taken the three of us with him. I guess he wanted to show us off to other members of his Brotherhood. And that was when I met a Mr. Johnson, someone who represented an even more secret order but with the same objectives as those of Father Sanchez's organization. Only Mr. Johnson's organization had authority over the group I work for. Mr. Johnson came to inform Father Sanchez his presence was required by one he was serving at the time. I thought Father Sanchez would brush him off like one of us had we brought such a message. But Mr. Johnson showed him a symbol on a ring he was wearing, and I thought Father Sanchez was going to pass out. He immediately bowed to him and kissed the ring, then rushed off in such a hurry, he forgot all about me. Mr. Johnson then asked to see the inside of my right hand. I showed it to him and there was an expression of acknowledgment from him. He asked to see the inside right palm of my other two companions, but did not see the same thing and dismissed them. He told me to follow him to a secluded place and told me many things about himself, and the brotherhood he represented. He said he represented the highest brotherhood of the world. And, the authority Father Sanchez had over me, was the same authority they had over Father Sanchez. He explained they were much more secretive and were not known of in this world by any others. Outside The Brotherhood that Father Sanchez represents, no one knew they even existed. But he told me they were in control of all things and were the guiding hand that rules Father Sanchez.

"He said what he saw in the palm of my hand was the waking mark, the mark of those, within both orders, who were beginning to understand what they were meant to do. He, myself, and many others within both groups are beginning to awaken and are coming together by recognizing each other by this mark. For this mark is worn by those who would undermine those who have controlled mankind throughout the centuries. We had the responsibility of ensuring The Watchers From The Light would come to no harm. And we were to assist them, by whatever means necessary, to ensure they would uncover what they left behind, thousands of years ago, and bring it back so all the world could learn of it again. But the two groups we were involved in are called The Watchers From The Shadows, and they do not want this information to be released to the public because of what it can do to them. For once truth is known, and people realize the impact they have on all living things, as individuals, The Watchers From The Shadows will lose their power. They will fall away from life as the chaff falls from the wheat.

"He told me the numbers within The Brotherhood are in the thousands. But when our awakening is complete, our numbers would be exactly half of theirs. Our influence would be great, for we were chosen to assist The Watchers From The Light re-emerge safely so they may re-discover the teachings from their past. And, The Watchers From The Light would number the same as The Watchers From The Shadows, but with one distinct disadvantage. They would have to survive, on their own, from birth to the time they would awaken. They would not remember their destiny at an early age, only when they would awaken. And that would be later in their life. But that would be needed if they were to survive. If they were known, before they were ready, they would be killed by those who did not wish them to return.

"Those are three groups you need to know of. They are The Watchers From The Light, The Watchers From The Shadows, and The Watchers From Within. All three of these groups have a great role to play in this world now. And the time for its beginning was not long ago; everything began in the year 1947. The Watchers From The Light originally wrote the messages located in the ancient sites. They also built the Ancient City of Prophecy. They instructed a selected number of people on what this information could do for all mankind, then told them it was to remain hidden until everyone could understand it. But The Watchers From The Shadows, as this new group was called, did not follow their instructions. They got caught up in the power this information gave them. The

Watchers From Within, the group I am a part of, was given power to ensure this information would not become open before its time. And, we were to ensure The Watchers From The Shadows would not do this. When The Watchers From The Light saw The Watchers From The Shadows were using this information for their own personal greed, they spent the time remaining to them, moving the secret sites to new locations, ones that were known only by them. Then they buried the Ancient City of Prophecy so it could not be gotten to by any living person. But the location of the city was put on a stone map and then hidden, not to be revealed until The Watchers From The Light would return again. When The Watchers From The Shadows learned of this, they killed all The Watchers From The Light and what remained of The Watchers From Within. But all they had done was to rid themselves of our bodies. They could not stop our spirits from returning when it was time for the ancient prophecy to unfold. And, since 1947, all of us have returned bearing a mark that is recognizable by those who remember. For my brotherhood, The Watchers From Within, we bear a mark inside our right palm. And The Watchers From The Light bear the red birth map on the back of their necks, just under the hairline. That mark glows bright red when they are receiving information on a spiritual level. And there is much for them to remember. But when they are processing what has been given, the map mark will fade and almost disappear."

"Kinda sounds like the mark of the antichrist, doesn't it?" Nahe said.

"This too, comes from The Brotherhood Father Sanchez represents, my brother. Anyone marked with something unusual was considered to be dangerous to their order. So they began the mark on the back of the neck as symbolic of the mark The Christ spoke of. But he didn't say it would be on the back of the neck. He didn't say this mark would even be physical. It was Father Sanchez's Brotherhood who put this into the minds of people. They knew where the mark would be for The Watchers From The Light, and they wanted to be well protected so when they would kill them, they would have an easy way of explaining to the masses what they were doing was for their benefit. That's why they started this story."

"Is the mark Cheeway and I were born with close to the one you speak of, Xumal?" I asked.

"It is exactly what I am speaking of, Speaking Wind. For that mark tells who the Watchers From The Light are. And each of them carry this mark from birth," Xumal returned.

"Then what about me?" Nahe said. "I just noticed the mark on the back of my neck only recently. It wasn't anything I was born with! How'd you explain that?"

"Easy, Nahe," Xumal returned. "Remember when I told you the mark was more visible when information was being received? And how it would almost disappear when that information was being processed?"

"Yeah, I remember."

"Well, Nahe, the reason your mark reappeared now is this is the time you are receiving great amounts of information, knowledge you will need in order to complete the quest you have returned to perform. I believe you have always had this mark, Nahe, but it was not as active as it is now."

Nahe looked at Xumal in silence, with the same kind of look the rest of us had on our faces.

"Don't look so startled, my brothers," Xumal said. "Each person living on the face of this Earth has something special to do. No one is here for the first time. This is something that has kept many in the dark for generations. We all return with a specific destiny and live to complete a great plan, one that will eventually lead us back to Creator. But there are those who return for a more significant role, and because it is a role that has been left by them from long ago, they carry a mark on them, a mark that allows them to recognize others who have similar roles to perform."

"So your purpose, or role as you call it, is to undermine the authority of Father Sanchez's Brotherhood?" I asked.

"Yes, Speaking Wind, that is correct," Xumal confirmed. "There are many of my kind who are now doing just that! Haven't you noticed how much information has been let loose on the world in the last few years? We have been responsible for that. Soon, it will be too much for anyone to cover up. And when that happens, it marks the beginning of the end for Father Sanchez's Brotherhood, and the one over them. Yours is not the only group of Watchers who is awakening to re-discover their destiny. There are many more than you can imagine. And they too are being assisted by others like me."

"It would seem as though Father Sanchez has much to fear if there are others within his Brotherhood working against him. From what you have said, this must be something very new for him. And for the rest who have live so long believing they have absolute control over everyone," I said.

"Yes it is," Xumal said, as he placed a grin on his face. "It is good to remember that no one is the sole authority over anyone. Not for long, that is. And this is bringing great fear and uncertainty among the two groups I have spoken of. While they do not know who is responsible for their many recent failures, they do know their trouble is coming from within their organizations. And this troubles them greatly. Soon, though, they will begin a purge. I hope I will not have to be a part of it. But my time with you is not long, if I don't return soon, Father Sanchez will grow suspicious. However, when Cheeway met with me yesterday and told me he was going to reveal what he found within the Ancient City of Prophecy, I knew I had to be here. For there are many answers I need that will explain important things to me. And I believe Cheeway knows them, for they were said to be inscribed within the ancient city. If you are ready, my brother, I will hand the talking stick over to you now."

"Yes, I am ready. I am ready to share what has been shown to me, to all of you…my brothers!"

# CHAPTER 16

▼

# ANCIENT REFERENCE
# POINTS ON THE MAP

"Are all of you okay with Xumal's presence here?" Cheeway asked.

"You believe him to be who he says, Cheeway?" I asked.

"Yes, Speaking Wind, I believe Xumal is who he says. And I know his path has touched ours for a specific reason. And I am willing to allow it to unfold so I can see."

"What about you, Nahe?" Cheeway asked, as he put his hand on Nahe's shoulder. "How do you feel about our new companion for this journey?"

At first, Nahe did not say anything. Then, he looked at Xumal and said, "How do we know what you say is truth, Xumal? How can we know you aren't a spy for Father Sanchez and when you discover what you came here to find out, you won't bring him here?"

"You don't know, Nahe," Xumal returned. "Not in the way you have spoken your question to me, that is. You can only see if what I have told you is truth by looking in your heart and listening to what it tells you. But let me say this before you go further with your questions. If I wanted to do what you think, do you believe I would have let Cheeway get this far? Or any of you, for that matter? I had many opportunities of killing all of you, but I didn't. Perhaps you didn't notice how I came to this meeting, Nahe. Look at this."

Xumal pulled his walking blanket off and we saw he wasn't wearing a gun. When he was sure we had seen what he wanted us to, he replaced his blanket and continued.

"Does that help you, Nahe?"

"Kinda, Xumal. Although not entirely."

"Guess only time will tell if I am speaking truth then, won't it?"

"Yeah!" Nahe returned. "Guess that's what were gonna have to wait on."

Cheeway knew this conversation would go no further, not with the premise it had taken to itself. Now, Nahe, Xumal, and I were looking at Cheeway waiting to hear what he would unfold next for us.

"Well then," Cheeway began. "Guess it's time to continue with the events that led to discovering the location of the Ancient City of Prophecy.

"Jade, Roberts, Stevens, and I began to study the map Nauti had given me…"

"Cheeway!" Xumal interrupted. "Don't mean to interrupt you, but did you say this stone map was given to you by someone named Nauti?"

"Yes I did, Xumal. Why do you ask?"

"The name has great meaning to our people, Cheeway! What did he look like?"

Cheeway took a few moments to describe Nauti's physical appearance to Xumal, and as he did, I saw Xumal's face fill with disbelief. At first, I was the only one to notice it, as everyone else was looking into the living flame. But when Cheeway finished his description of Nauti, everyone saw his look and wondered why his expression of surprise was as it was.

"Xumal," Cheeway began. "Were you not told I was given this ancient map by Nauti?"

"Not by that name, Cheeway," Xumal returned. "Father Sanchez only said you were given a map that could locate the Ancient City of Prophecy by some old man. He wasn't sure if it was real or not, but we had to stop you from showing it to anyone. It might cause a panic if people knew such a place might exist. But, he didn't name the old man. He just said he was someone from the village who had been stealing from outsiders."

"And if you knew the name of this old man, Xumal?" Cheeway asked, looking directly at him. "Would it have made a difference?"

"Quite a lot, my brother," Xumal said. "I don't believe we would have been pursuing you, but would have been attempting to locate the old man instead!

"That really throws a great new twist to this whole thing," Xumal said, then sat in a silence only he could hear.

"Xumal, you have given us some curiosity. Can you explain why this name is so significant to you?"

"Yes, Cheeway," Xumal said, as he adjusted himself more comfortably on the earth beneath him. "You see, the name Nauti was worn long ago by one of our ancient people. He was said to possess great medicine for anything that was ailing those who had life within them. He was said to have access to the great stones of knowledge, stones that had been left with our people long ago by the original visitors from the star nation—you know, the last earth we journeyed in. Our spoken history tells of his coming to our people in times of great need. When there were great illnesses among the people, he would come and heal them. He would bring small stones with strange writings on them with him. He said they would speak to him, telling him what was wrong with anyone. And the stones would tell him what to do. He was said to have healed many people each time he would appear, and when he was done, those he healed would only have a small mark on them. But what I have heard is he would open their bodies up with holes and reach inside them. He said the stones were guiding him on how to do this, and when he was done, there wasn't a mark on them. In fact, they were said to feel better than they ever felt before, and there were no scars. I have been told his medicine has been among the people longer than we have had generations living on this Earth. You see, Nauti was one who came to us from Creator and chose to remain and assist us on our long journey. And each time he would appear, he would not have changed. He was an old man when we first saw him, and was the same age when he was last seen. The man you described as Nauti is the same man we speak of in our ancient histories, Cheeway. You described him down to the last piece of clothing our people saw him wear when he last came among us. If this is the same man, Cheeway, no one could kill him. He is a spirit walker, one who no longer needs a physical body to travel in. He is a bringer of light from Creator, but only returns when something great is about to unfold. Did he give you any message, Cheeway? It is important to know, because it could be a clue we all need."

"Well, yes, Xumal, he did," Cheeway returned. "He told me I had been chosen to find the Ancient City of Prophecy, and when I did, it would change everything in this world. The people would not see themselves as they had always done, that they would no longer be blinded by the illusion and would be free to choose their own path to travel."

"That's it, then!" Xumal said, as he looked at us. "This is why he returned as he did. If my two brothers knew this, they would not be willing to follow Father Sanchez! They would know they are sitting with the shadow ones and would not allow any harm to come to you either. Father Sanchez must have known, otherwise he would have allowed us to follow the one he told us about, the one called Nauti. But he said this was not for us to do. He said there were others who were doing this and we were to remain focused on you, Cheeway, and everyone you came into contact with. I must relay this information to them as soon as I can. But still, I would like to know about what you found in the city, Cheeway. For this is something I must return with as well. It will assist in speeding up the numbers of my brotherhood to wake up from their illusion and begin the work we returned to do!"

"Very well then, I will continue," Cheeway said, hosting a look of surprise on his face.

"Before you begin, Cheeway, there is something else I must share with you," Xumal said. "If you see a spirit walker, then before you end your journey with the Earth Mother, you will see them again. They will appear to you just before your time is completed and they come to advise you of a choice you can make. These spirit walkers are those who have learned all their lessons and left with their bodies. For them, there is no need to go through the pains of birth or death ever again. But they choose to return to assist their other brothers and sisters to do what they need done. Those they choose to appear to, are close to doing what the spirit walkers did, leaving with their body. But they usually appear to those who need to accomplish just one more thing before they can ascend. And, before they can accomplish that, they need the assistance of one who has gone before them. Perhaps it is to share the way of spiritual strength, or help them see something they could not see without being reminded. But in either case, since Nauti came to you, Cheeway, it is a confirmation that you, too, will be given the opportunity of leaving with your body when your destiny is completed. I hear it is a beautiful sight to see! I hope I can be there when it happens. I have been told our people used to do this quite frequently, that is, before we allowed ourselves to become trapped in the illusion."

"The three who raised us left in that way, Xumal," Cheeway returned. "This is no new thing for our people either. Perhaps that will assist you in some way as well. Thank you for your insight, Xumal. It is good to know Nauti was not killed and the reasons behind it. But now, I must continue with my story of how the ancient map unfolded for us."

Nahe and I looked first at Xumal, who had relayed his powerful message, then at Cheeway, one we now saw as the next in line to leave this domain with their body, the next in a long line of others we had known who had been blessed with this way of continuing life, as it was meant to be.

For the next couple of hours, Cheeway unfolded all of the events that had taken place on his journey to The Ancient City of Prophecy. He did not leave anything out. Cheeway told us about everything from Mary's death to the translating of the ancient records, and to the old parchment written by Father Juan those many centuries before.

When Cheeway finished, Father Juan looked at him and said, "I know where Father Juan was going, Cheeway! We found a copy of his manuscript in a wall of my church. And, he confirms everything you told us was in the parchment of Father Paul. This is truly one of the greatest finds of all time! For what you have discovered about the commandments has long been a thought of my own. As if there was something missing, something that would make more sense out of why they had been left with us to live by. But everyone I had spoken to about it told me I was wrong. And for many years, I believed them, until now that is…Please take Father Joe with you if you decide to search for the next ancient location, Cheeway. I know how you feel about Father Sanchez, and all he has done to you. But for the sake of balance, please allow my friend to accompany you. Just his presence will serve as a reminder that not all of us are like Father Sanchez."

"I will not be a burden to you, Cheeway," Father Joe interrupted quickly. "Perhaps I will be of more assistance than you know at present. I am young and some of my earlier studies centered around archeology. From everything I've have heard so far, I could be an asset to any further exploration you might make. And, I promise you, I am nothing like Father Sanchez, or those he represents. You must believe me when I tell you, he does not represent the rest of us who have given our lives to follow the teachings of The Christ."

Cheeway sat in silence for a moment. I could tell he was thinking about what he was asked. Then, he looked into the eyes of both priests and told them he would do as they had asked. He said it would be good for him to be reminded of this throughout his journey. But he reminded both priests their lives would also be in danger. For he was sure The Brotherhood already knew of their involvement, and Xumal confirmed what he said.

CHAPTER 17

▼

# THE SEARCH CONTINUES

"So, what's next, my brother?" I asked.

"We must go back to The Ancient City of Prophecy," Cheeway replied. "Jade found a reference to something very important there."

"Why, my brother?" I asked. "Why would you even think of doing such a thing when you know Father Sanchez will kill you if he finds you again?"

"Speaking Wind, my brother, it is not good to turn your back on your own destiny. You know this. I have lived my life following the calling voice of my spirit, and for this, I am at peace with all I have done. You remember what we were taught when we traveled together, that each of us returned to perform a great service for all living things? This is my part, my brother. Would you deny this to me?"

"No, Cheeway, this I would not do. But you and I are the last of our council, my brother. What if I do not have the strength to do my part without you?"

"You will do what you must, Speaking Wind. Always remember that, my brother. If my time on this earth is not to be long, then hold me in your heart with a good face. Not one that is sad, for I will have a seat next to the great council fires of our ancestors, and will be in the company of Grandfather, Two Bears, White Eagle, and Mary."

When Cheeway said this, he grabbed my shoulders and looked deep into my eyes. There were great tears running down my face, and from the sobbing I heard from Nahe, I knew he was doing the same thing.

"I do not leave you, my brothers, I only go before you so I may keep a space for you to sit with all of us. Wish me well on this last part of my journey, Speaking Wind, and remember me as I am now. This is how we have always traveled, let us continue in this way."

"But what can be so important to make you do this thing, Cheeway?" I said, as I choked down tears of sadness. "What more can there be for you to do? You have already discovered the Hallway of Records. Wasn't that the fulfillment of your destiny?"

"My brother, you know as well as I do, our destinies are fulfilled with our last breath of life. Until that time, I am fulfilling the promise I made before I was born. And, my brother, so are you. But as to the second part of your question, what else could I do? I will say this. Jade found a reference to a map room within the Ancient City of Prophecy. It shows the locations of the other site we need to locate. I leave now to plan our return trip, Speaking Wind, and Xumal has given us his assistance in doing so. He will serve as a buffer between Father Sanchez and his organization. He says he can keep them distracted if they get too close and that will give us the time we need."

"You will do this, Xumal? You will protect my brother from Father Sanchez?"

"Yes, Speaking Wind, I will do that and more. I have found others who are like me in the lands where all of you live. You know, other Watchers From Within, and they have informed me they will provide you with whatever protection you need. Just remember to look for this mark on the inside of their right hand, then you will know who they are…Remember, my brother, everything is on its way to someplace. And only that life knows where its next stop will be. But we all return to Creator, eventually. But more than that, Speaking Wind, don't forget what we were taught. Everything we see is alive and because it lives, we are connected to it, as it is connected to us. When we see ourselves sad, hurt, disappointed, and so on, then we call those things to us, and they respond. Then only the sad, disappointing, and hurting things in life come to us. But they do so to remind us how we regard ourselves, nothing more. Nothing in life comes as a punishment…nothing. So until you learn to walk the spiritual path, my brother, life will always present itself to you in this way. Walk in love, my brother, and you will not know fear. Do you remember what Grandfather and Two Bears taught us, Speaking Wind? What they said about the two kinds of people in this world? They said there are those who control with power and intimidation, and while they appear to be great in their time of power, when their time on this earth is over, no one remembers them. Look at the tyrants throughout history, Speaking Wind, how many have been remembered for the greatness they believed was theirs? When they died, so did the illusion of their power and control. Then, there are those who understand the unconditional love within them and allow it to manifest in everything they do and say. And, no matter what they do in life, everyone they touch will remember them long after their life is over. For this is the nature of unconditional love, whatever they do in life will have a lasting effect on everyone who hears what their life was all about. They will not be forgotten, nor will their memory fade with the passing of later generations. This is the path we must follow, my brother. Those who left these ancient mysteries followed this path as well. How else could their memory have remained with us for so many generations?"

"But, Cheeway!" I said. "What if I cannot find my way back? What if I cannot find my spirituality again?"

"That has always been with you, Speaking Wind. I will leave you with a gift of peace, one I have been holding for you for just such a time. My gift of peace is this: Drop the rules, Speaking Wind. For when you do, you will find your spirituality right in front of you, and you will remember your way back."

Cheeway closed his eyes for a moment and I felt what he was doing. He was creating a moment of silence so he might hear what was being said to him from places neither of us could see.

"Cheeway, I…"

"Don't say anything, Speaking Wind, it will only make our parting more difficult. Let us leave each other with the silence of the falling snow. When it is time, I will contact you. Have no doubts about that, my brother. I know there is much more I will give you for safekeeping. For your destiny is to bring our discoveries into the open for others to hear. It's important, if they are to understand why the earth changes are coming. And, if they understand, our efforts will not have been in vain and they can change the impending disasters that are coming to this earth. And, if they can change them in time, life will be given one last chance to continue. I assure you, my brother, there will be more to share with you…much more. I will return. So be ready, my brother…be ready."

"Got the horses, Speaking Wind. We better be going!" Nahe said, holding the reins.

"Just a minute, Nahe, I must…"

"Quiet, all of you!" Xumal whispered, as he held his hand out. "Someone's here. Don't move!"

"Sheriff, that you?!" came a voice from just beyond the tree line.

"That's Alvin," Nahe said. "If he's here, so is Father Sanchez! What you want to do, Xumal? You and Cheeway can't be seen here!"

"Don't worry about Cheeway," Xumal offered. "I can draw them away. You, the Fathers, and Speaking Wind must ride off in different directions when you hear them chase me. Don't worry though, they won't know who I am. I've had a lot of practice with that. Cheeway, as soon as you hear them start after me, run off in the opposite direction. I saw where you left your car. You can get to it quickly enough. The rest of you okay with this? Or do you think I'm responsible for your being found here?"

"No, Xumal," Nahe said. "If Alvin found us here, I know it's only luck. Don't think he could track anything on his own. Anyway, it sounds like he's alone. No sounds of anyone else with him."

"You're wrong, Nahe," Xumal corrected. "Father Sanchez and the other two guards are with him. I can feel them. No more time now. Wait for them to start chasing me, then the rest of you take off. Got that?"

"Yeah, Xumal. Got that real good," I said. "I am glad you are with our council, my brother. Please take good care of Cheeway, will you?"

"I will, Speaking Wind!"

Xumal started off, and with the time we had left, the rest of us prepared to go off in different directions when the fireworks began. We didn't have much time to argue the point, but the plan made sense.

Within a few moments, we heard the sound of horse hooves running after someone. I knew they must have seen Xumal, or at least heard him. That was our clue and we made our great escape.

As I rode Spirit Wind into the night, I heard voices yelling behind me, "There he is, Father Sanchez! Running over the top of that hill!"

There were several shots fired, but due to the falling snow, I couldn't tell what direction they came from. For all I knew, they could have seen any of us leaving the mountain.

I didn't have long to wait to hear another voice yell, "I got one of them, Father Sanchez! Saw him fall behind a clump of trees, just ahead!"

I didn't know who had been shot, I only knew I had to keep riding away from this place, this place that might have marked where I last saw my brother, Cheeway, alive.

# About the Author

Patrick "Speaking Wind" Quirk, a Native American author, lecturer, and publisher, was raised by Grandfather, Two Bears, and White Eagle of the Pueblo People. He knew them as Spirit Callers, but in today's terms we would call them "SHAMAN". He, and his brothers, Cheeway and Nahe, were raised in the mountains of northern New Mexico by Grandfather and Two Bears for almost twenty years of their early life. This is where they were introduced to the ways of the spirit.

However, these teachings were to be put asleep for a time, and were not to be remembered until the time was right. But before the time was right, Grandfather,

Two Bears, and White Eagle left, with their bodies, and several years later, Chee-way, and Nahe, ended their journey with the Earth Mother as well. That left Speaking Wind alone, to sort and process, what he had been given to share.

When Speaking Wind, Cheeway, and Nahe were very young, they were placed in a boarding school for several years. And this became the first of their experiences from having the control of others attempt to bury their spiritual beliefs. During their boarding school experience, they were not allowed to speak their peoples language, or practice their spirituality. And there were placed on them many scars of abuse for breaking these rules.

During the boarding school years, they, as well as others who were either mixed, or full blooded Native Americans, were not taught to read or write. Instead, they were marched to the back of the school and picked up by residents, then taken to their private homes, and farms, where they would work, for no pay. They would be returned to the boarding school, only, when it was time for them to learn of its religion.

However, they asked too many questions from the teachings of Grandfather, Two Bears and White Eagle. Questions the teachers could not answer. So, they were labeled as "Spawns Of Satan" and forced to leave so they would not influence the children who were not following the "devil's evil ways".

When Speaking Wind, Nahe, and Cheeway entered the public school system, they could not read or write. They had not been taught. So not only the teachers, but the students, called them dumb Indians.

That left a mark on them, and gave them the determination to pursue their academic goals. Cheeway completed his doctorate and worked as one of the leading archeologists in the Yucatan Peninsula uncovering many of the ancient writings and civilizations that related to the sacred writings of the Pueblo People.

Nahe pursued a career in law enforcement, then went on to become the Sheriff in a small town in New Mexico.

Speaking Wind attained two undergraduate degrees, two graduate degrees, and completed one half of his doctorate. He taught in the school of business, at the University of Phoenix, then worked as a consultant in Asia, and for almost sixteen years, as a consultant in Europe.

However, for Speaking Wind, all of this was to end in 1993 when he died and was taken to the lands of The Ancient Ones. This is where he was not only reunited with Grandfather, Two Bears, White Eagle, Cheeway and Nahe, but also the "GREAT MESSENGER". This was when the "GREAT MESSENGER" gave Speaking Wind a message to bring back…a message that was to be shared with all who had the eyes to see, the ears to hear, the heart to feel, and the willingness of spirit to understand. It is a message of love, a message of hope, but most of all, it is a message that can replace fear, with understanding, for everyone.

It was at this time, when Speaking Wind was told it was time to begin his work, and return to Turtle Island (The Continental United States) with his son, White Raven. Speaking Wind, and his son, have traveled together since White Raven was six.

For the next five years, Speaking Wind and White Raven toured the United States holding seminars and lectures. In these, Speaking Wind presented Native American spiritual practices and performed healing ceremonies to all those who were ready to receive them. One of the most compelling of the ceremonies Patrick performed were the spirit drummings. During some of these, a dimensional "portal" would open and people looking into the eye of a stranger would be able to see an aspect of their own spirit as they truly were. Many times this image would be something that needed to be worked on.

But it was the drumming at Kinlock, one of the sacred areas in the land now known as Bankhead National Forest, which always resulted in different manifestations. Many times, people heard native flute music playing. And on more than one occasion, several people admitted to actually seeing images of the Old Ones.

Times were very fast paced for Patrick during the 1990's. Years of a grueling seminar schedule and many overnight hours of working on his latest manuscripts finally took their toll. On December 22nd, 1998, Speaking Wind crossed over. Or, as Patrick would say, he allowed his robes to fall away and leave the Earth Mother.

Since his departure, his physical presence has been greatly missed. But his spirit has visited many of us. And while his teachings are carried forward in the form of his books, manuscripts, and recordings, it is his personal impact on a small circle of friends and seminar acquaintances that will remain with us for the rest of our lives.

Washte Speaking Wind.